CONDUCTING LAW A

Through interviews with many of the most noteworthy authors in law and society, *Conducting Law and Society Research* takes students and scholars behind the scenes of empirical scholarship, showing the messy reality of research methods. The challenges and the uncertainties, so often missing from research methods textbooks, are revealed in candid detail. These accessible and revealing conversations about the lived reality of classic projects will be a source of encouragement and inspiration to those embarking on empirical research, ranging across the full array of disciplines that contribute to law and society. For all of the ambiguities and challenges to the social "scientific" study of law, the reflections found in this book – collectively capturing a portrait of the field through the window of research efforts – individually remind readers that "good research" displays not an absence of problems, but the care taken in negotiating them.

Simon Halliday has a Ph.D. in sociolegal studies from Strathclyde University. He is author of *Judicial Review and Compliance with Administrative Law* (2004) and *The Appeal of Internal Review: Law, Administrative Justice, and the (Non-) Emergence of Disputes* (2003). He is coeditor (with Marc Hertogh) of *Judicial Review and Bureaucratic Impact: International and Interdisciplinary Perspectives* (2004) and has published articles in journals, such as the *Journal of Law and Society*, the *British Journal of Criminology*, and *Public Law*. Currently Professor at the Law School of Strathclyde University and Conjoint Professor in the Faculty of Law of the University of New South Wales, he was previously the Nicholas de B. Katzenbach Research Fellow at Balliol College and at the Centre for Socio-Legal Studies, Oxford University.

Patrick Schmidt has a Ph.D. in political science from Johns Hopkins University. He is the author of *Lawyers and Regulation: The Politics of the Administrative Process* (2005) and of articles in various journals, including *Law and History Review*, *Judicature*, *Justice System Journal*, and *Political Research Quarterly*. Currently Associate Professor of Political Science at Macalester College, he was previously Assistant Professor of Political Science at Southern Methodist University, the John Adams Research Fellow at the Centre for Socio-Legal Studies, and Junior Research Fellow at Nuffield College, Oxford.

Halliday and Schmidt coedited *Human Rights Brought Home: Socio-Legal Perspectives on Human Rights in the National Context* (2004).

CAMBRIDGE STUDIES IN LAW AND SOCIETY

Cambridge Studies in Law and Society aims to publish the best scholarly work on legal discourse and practice in its social and institutional contexts, combining theoretical insights and empirical research.

The fields that it covers are: studies of law in action; the sociology of law; the anthropology of law; cultural studies of law, including the role of legal discourses in social formations; law and economics; law and politics; and studies of governance. The books consider all forms of legal discourse across societies, rather than being limited to lawyers' discourses alone.

The series editors come from a range of disciplines: academic law, socio-legal studies, sociology, and anthropology. All have been actively involved in teaching and writing about law in context.

Series Editors

Chris Arup
Monash University, Victoria

Martin Chanock
La Trobe University, Melbourne

Pat O'Malley
University of Sydney

Sally Engle Merry
New York University

Susan Silbey
Massachusetts Institute of Technology

Books in the Series

Diseases of the Will
Mariana Valverde

*The Politics of Truth and Reconciliation in South Africa:
Legitimizing the Post-Apartheid State*
Richard A. Wilson

Modernism and the Grounds of Law
Peter Fitzpatrick

*Unemployment and Government:
Genealogies of the Social*
William Walters

*Autonomy and Ethnicity:
Negotiating Competing Claims in Multi-Ethnic States*
Yash Ghai

(Continued after Index)

CONDUCTING LAW AND SOCIETY RESEARCH

Reflections on Methods and Practices

Simon Halliday

Strathclyde University
University of New South Wales

Patrick Schmidt

Macalester College

CAMBRIDGE
UNIVERSITY PRESS

CAMBRIDGE
UNIVERSITY PRESS

32 Avenue of the Americas, New York NY 10013-2473, USA

Cambridge University Press is part of the University of Cambridge.

It furthers the University's mission by disseminating knowledge in the pursuit of education, learning and research at the highest international levels of excellence.

www.cambridge.org
Information on this title: www.cambridge.org/9780521720427

© Simon Halliday and Patrick Schmidt 2009

First published 2009

A catalogue record for this publication is available from the British Library

Library of Congress Cataloguing in Publication data

Halliday, Simon, Dr.
Conducting law and society research : reflections on methods and practices / Simon Halliday, Patrick Schmidt.
   p. cm.
Includes bibliographical references and index.
ISBN 978-0-521-89591-0 (hardback) – ISBN 978-0-521-72042-7 (pbk.)   1. Legal research.
2. Law – Methodology.   3. Social sciences – Research – Law and legislation.   4. Sociological jurisprudence.   I. Schmidt, Patrick D. (Patrick Delbert), 1971–   II. Title.
K85.H35   2009
340′.115072–dc22   2008053953

ISBN 978-0-521-89591-0 Hardback
ISBN 978-0-521-72042-7 Paperback

CONTENTS

LIST OF CONTRIBUTORS

John Braithwaite is Professor at the Regulatory Institutions Network of the Australian National University and an Australian Research Council Federation Fellow.

John Conley is the William Rand Kenan Jr. Professor of Law at the University of North Carolina.

Yves Dezalay is Directeur de Recherche at the Centre National de la Recherche Scientifique (CNRS), attached to the Centre de Sociologie Européenne (CSE), and based at the Maison des Sciences de l'Homme (MSH), Paris.

Peter Drahos is Professor at the Regulatory Institutions Network of the Australian National University and Professor of Intellectual Property at Queen Mary, University of London.

David M. Engel is SUNY Distinguished Service Professor at the University at Buffalo Law School.

Patricia Ewick is Professor of Sociology at Clark University in Worcester, Massachusetts.

Malcolm M. Feeley is Clare Sanders Clements Dean's Professor of the Jurisprudence and Social Policy Program at the University of California at Berkeley.

William L. F. Felstiner taught law and sociology at UCLA and UCSB, was Director of the American Bar Foundation and the International Institute for the Sociology of Law (Oñati), and is currently President of the Chad Relief Foundation.

Lawrence M. Friedman is the Marion Rice Kirkwood Professor of Law at Stanford University. He is a member of the American Academy of Arts and Sciences.

Bryant G. Garth is Dean of the Southwestern Law School in Los Angeles, California, and Director Emeritus of the American Bar Foundation.

Dame Hazel Genn is Dean of Laws, Professor of Socio-Legal Studies, and Co-Director of the Centre for Empirical Legal Studies in the Faculty of Laws of University College London, where she is also an Honorary Fellow.

Carol J. Greenhouse is Professor and Chair of the Department of Anthropology at Princeton University.

John Hagan is John D. MacArthur Professor of Sociology and Law at Northwestern University and Senior Research Fellow at the American Bar Foundation in Chicago.

Simon Halliday is Professor at the Law School of Strathclyde University, Conjoint Professor of Law at the University of New South Wales, and Associate Fellow at the Centre for Socio-Legal Studies, University of Oxford.

Keith Hawkins is Professor Emeritus of Law and Society at Oxford University, Fellow Emeritus of Oriel College, Oxford, and Visiting Professor at the Centre for the Analysis of Risk and Regulation of the London School of Economics.

John P. Heinz is Senior Research Fellow at the American Bar Foundation and the Owen L. Coon Professor Emeritus at the Northwestern University School of Law.

Robert A. Kagan is Professor of Political Science and Emanuel S. Heller Professor of Law at the University of California, Berkeley.

Herbert Kritzer is Professor of Law at William Mitchell College of Law and formerly was Professor of Political Science at the University of Wisconsin–Madison.

Edward O. Laumann is the George Herbert Mead Distinguished Service Professor of Sociology at the University of Chicago.

Stewart Macaulay is the Malcolm Pitman Sharp Hilldale Professor and Theodore W. Brazeau Professor of Law at the University of Wisconsin–Madison.

Doreen McBarnet is Professor of Socio-Legal Studies at the University of Oxford and Visiting Professor at the Edinburgh University Law School.

Michael McCann is Gordon Hirabayashi Professor for the Advancement of Citizenship and Director of the Law, Societies, and Justice Program of the University of Washington.

Sally Engle Merry is Professor of Anthropology and Director of the Program on Law and Society at New York University.

William O'Barr is Professor in the Department of Cultural Anthropology at Duke University.

Alan Paterson is Professor of Law and Director of the Centre for Professional Legal Studies at Strathclyde University.

Gerald N. Rosenberg is Associate Professor of Political Science and Lecturer in Law at the University of Chicago.

Austin Sarat is William Nelson Cromwell Professor of Jurisprudence and Political Science, Five College Fortieth Anniversary Professor, and Senior Advisor to the Dean of the Faculty at Amherst College.

Patrick Schmidt is Associate Professor of Political Science at Macalester College.

Susan S. Silbey is Leon and Anne Goldberg Professor of Sociology and Anthropology and Head of the Department of Anthropology at the Massachusetts Institute of Technology.

Tom Tyler is University Professor at New York University, Psychology Department and Law School.

ACKNOWLEDGMENTS

The participants in this book repeatedly observe in these interviews that good scholarship depends on the direct and indirect support of others. Although we have long been convinced of this, once again we are reminded of our debt.

Numerous friends and colleagues were willing to read the project proposal or discuss its concept at one stage or another, and they helped us refine our ambition for this book. We mention in particular Sarah Armstrong, Lindsay Farmer, Joel Grossman, Erik Larson, Mikael Madsen, Bronwen Morgan, Anna Russell, David Yalof, and others whose names we inadvertently may have forgotten. We are also grateful to Andrew Hass for conversations about serendipity in the arts and to Brent Plate and Edna Rodriguez-Plate for a unique perspective on sociolegal methodologies.

Three anonymous reviewers join the named colleagues as important influences on this book. The participants in this project, themselves, displayed enough good humor to agree to the interviews; they also provided many helpful comments, much patience during the editing process, and great enthusiasm. Because they are some of the most experienced researchers and teachers in the field, their concurrence about the need for this book gave us additional momentum.

Our colleagues in our respective institutions – the Law School at Strathclyde University and the University of New South Wales and the Department of Political Science at Macalester College – have encouraged us throughout the writing of this book, and our institutions have generously supported this work. Patrick received essential funding through the support of a Wallace Travel Grant from Macalester College. Simon enjoyed a generous grant from the Law School of Strathclyde University to fund travel, accommodation, and transcription costs.

Cambridge University Press, embodied at every stage through our editor, John Berger, has been supportive from Day 2 of this project. We also thank Mary Cadette and Christie Polchowski for the high standard of care and attention to the preparation of the manuscript, and Melanie Sims for her sterling efforts with the index.

We also acknowledge the role played by St. Arnold, the patron saint of brewers. It was in a brew pub that the idea for this book was conceived, and it seems that there has since been a guiding hand ensuring the satisfying refreshment of beer in the four countries in which we worked on this project (U.S.A., U.K., Australia, and Germany).

The personal dimension of one's professional life always emerges in any candid discussion of research, and so it does here too. Patrick professes, against assertions to the contrary, that he truly understands the burden borne by his wife, Lea Anne, and their three children, Ailsa, Aidan, and Simon, during his numerous conference trips and late nights at the computer. As thanks, he offers his promise that one day he will write a book that may actually offer the hope of making the family rich. Until then, they have this book dedicated to them. Simon dedicates this book to his brother Mark, whose own engagement with research methods was something of an inspiration.

CHAPTER 1

INTRODUCTION: BEYOND METHODS –
LAW AND SOCIETY IN ACTION

Patrick Schmidt and Simon Halliday

One may be forgiven for wondering what is to be gained from another book on research methods. Certainly no shortage of research methods texts exists, especially when one includes in the counting the volumes written for the separate disciplinary traditions that comprise Law and Society. Yet for scholars about to conduct empirical work for the first time, or about to attempt a very different approach, more should be said about the social realities of conducting research than is found in most of these texts. A proper grasp of the philosophical underpinnings of various research methods and an adequate understanding of the practical prescriptions about the mechanics of research are clearly essential aspects of one's training. However, the art of cooking is more than the following of recipes. Just as reading recipes in a cookbook does not sufficiently prepare you for your first foray into the kitchen (and certainly does not make you a good cook), most research methods books can only take you so far in preparing you for fieldwork. Orthodox methodological texts have two important limitations in this respect.

First, these texts do not generally convey a sense of what it *feels* like to be out in the field, particularly when things go wrong or become difficult (which is almost always the case). As the interviews contained in this book suggest, research projects are usually longer and their narratives more complex than the researcher would have imagined at the outset. Although this point has to be experienced firsthand to be fully appreciated, the retrospective tales told in this volume work particularly well as a window into the lived reality of research. They demonstrate powerfully that one of the major skill sets required of a fieldworker is not so much the preparation of the project, although this is very important, but the ability to respond to the unexpected, to serendipitous opportunities, and, almost inevitably, to a certain level of disappointment. It is a rare research methods textbook that prepares students for the emotional dimensions of research and academia and helps them set expectations about what constitutes "success" in research and publication.

Second, research methods texts, and the presentation of research findings more generally, often remain quiet about the imperfect path of the research process. Although transparency about research design and data collection is a basic principle of good social science, it takes a brave soul to give a genuine "warts and all" account of the mistakes that are made along the way or of other infelicities in the research process. There is much to inhibit us from such complete candor. Having made mistakes or missed opportunities, scholars learn to paper over those problems with a dispassionate voice and a cool recollection of the methodological steps. The "whole truth" of how research work actually gets done tends to remain unspoken except perhaps to one's students, who hear these tales as reassurance when their own projects are mired in ambiguity and struggle. It is difficult, in research as in any area of life, to share one's insecurities.

Yet, particularly for Law and Society scholars, there is surely both credit to be taken and comfort to be given in being a little more candid. Research methods might usefully be thought of as embodying the "laws" of the research process. Prescriptions about the mechanics of data collection and analysis are, in important ways, the rules and regulations of the social sciences – a self-regulatory system controlled through a mix of community and competition. And just as early sociolegal scholars exposed the gap between law in the books and law in action, so we might, as a scholarly community, consider the gap that inevitably exists between research methods and the realities of research. Although they are normatively important, we should not expect the prescriptions of research methods found in the textbooks to be perfectly mirrored in the research process.

METHODOLOGICAL ANXIETY SYNDROME

Responding to these limitations is more than an intellectual exercise. They have a practical impact on researchers, particularly those new to the enterprise. Many students and scholars experience what we would dub "MAS," or methodological anxiety syndrome. MAS is a pervasive and sometimes debilitating doubt about whether one has the necessary methodological skills to embark on empirical sociolegal work in the first place. It is important to recognize that not all the disciplines that contribute to the Law and Society field engage in the same kind of methodological training. In particular, those coming from law schools may have received no training whatsoever in social science research methods. Yet, sociolegal research has a particular appeal for lawyers who have become frustrated or bored with the limits of doctrinal scholarship, as a number of the interviewees in this book can testify (see, for example, Chapter 5 with Lawrence Friedman, Chapter 8 with David Engel, Chapter 9 with Keith Hawkins, and Chapter 15 with Gerald Rosenberg).[1] It is easy, we suggest, for legal scholars asking sociolegal questions to be intimidated by the apparent mystery of research methods and to be held back from conducting empirical work because of their lack of formal training. Piercing criticism from social scientists of scholarship by lawyers – attacked as insufficiently attentive to the "rules" of empirical research methodology – can all too easily be read as only discouraging exploration or raising barriers to participation in the interdisciplinary dialogue.[2]

However, as a number of the chapters in this book demonstrate, formal training, although invaluable, is not always a prerequisite to the conduct of high-quality sociolegal research (see, for example, Chapter 2 with Stewart Macaulay, Chapter 7 with Alan Paterson, and Chapter 16 with Michael McCann). We do not suggest that training in research methods is unimportant – far from it. There is no immunity from the obligation to be as complete and transparent as possible in describing one's steps in empirical research, and training can provide both the vocabulary and the imagination necessary for conceptualizing and communicating good scholarship. Yet, we suggest that an awareness of methodological issues and the requisite sensitivity to methodological questions can still be gained where formal training has not been available. In the world of computer programing, software developers openly speak of the "naive implementation" of a solution – the first, simplest,

---

[1] For other personal accounts of the draw of sociolegal studies for lawyers, see A. Bradney, "Law as a Parasitic Discipline," *Journal of Law and Society*, 25(1):71–84 (1998); R. Cotterrell, "Subverting Orthodoxy, Making Law Central: A View of Sociolegal Studies," *Journal of Law and Society*, 29(4):632–44 (2002).

[2] L. Epstein and G. King, "The Rules of Inference," *University of Chicago Law Review*, 69(1):1–133 (2002). See also Robert Spitzer, *Saving the Constitution from Lawyers* (New York: Cambridge University Press, 2008), pp. 1–55.

and often "textbook" way to get a piece of software up and running. But they cannot end there, if they are to be successful. Software may even be released to the public in "beta" form, with many problems yet to be identified and new versions to be released. Law and Society research typically proceeds on a similar basis: beginning with a naive design, but informed and evolving through experiences in the field and engagement with the data. However, we have not done so well at naming and accepting the importance of "naive fieldwork" in the research process. In this understanding, then, being methodologically *thoughtful* – possessing the capacity to move from the naive understanding of one's project to the more sophisticated, and to discover the questions, theoretical potential, and epistemological problems latent in one's engagement with the world as one sees it – is ultimately much more important than being methodologically trained. Some of the interviews in this volume should give considerable encouragement in this regard, as examples of how to enter the field even when formal training is lacking while developing one's capacity for empirical research in the process.

MAS, of course, is not restricted to those without formal methods training. It also refers to debilitating doubts about the extent to which one's research projects have met the methodological standards of the field and so may constitute acceptable scholarship. Many scholars, us included, know the feeling of things having "gone wrong" or having realized well after the fact that a step taken was less than ideal, or worse. Such doubts about methods hold some people back from seeking publication in the best journals of the field. The sentiment that "this can't possibly be good enough to publish in the *Law and Society Review*" is a self-fulfilling prophecy when one never submits for publication. Since we began this project, many people have told us of graduate students – in different careers today – who went out into the field, sometimes to foreign countries, to begin their research. Finding "the real world" so different from their theoretical expectations and the approach they had designed for it, they became frustrated and lost in the ambiguity, and they never completed their degrees.

Most forbidding of all, doubt and anxiety generate a collective silence that no one person can break. We suggest that research methods need to be demystified and understood as social practices, just as surely as sociolegal scholars believe that law's claim to autonomy and superiority must be laid bare. The collection of interviews in this volume makes an important step toward that goal.

SERENDIPITY AND BAD FORTUNE

W. H. Auden suggested that "a poet will always have a sneaking regard for luck because he knows the role which it plays in poetic composition."[3] Before embarking on this project we sensed that, just as in the arts, serendipity played a significant role in the production of social science. Of course, others have pointed to serendipity. Consider an example from a recent, excellent collection of methodological essays (see Figure 1).[4] Amid the grand unified theory represented in the figure, incorporating all of the logics of enquiry and analysis, a thin line labeled "serendipity" cuts across and intervenes. It seems out of place, a sharp juxtaposition between the concreteness of the process and the "black box" that happens at some point in good research. But how can this mysterious dimension be explored and communicated to others? Is serendipity more than insight, or even genius that cannot be acquired, only possessed? Serendipitous experiences may be too idiosyncratic and context-dependent to articulate in a systematic way, but that is not to say we shouldn't attempt an investigation into the craft that occurs at this level of specificity.

Of course, amid the chance developments and insightful realizations that help to refine a research project, the research process throws up bad fortune as well as good. Our second instinctive hypothesis was that ambiguity and difficulty were the rule rather than the exception in empirical research. We suspected that behind most research projects – right up to the most insightful sociolegal projects, the ones we teach and turn to for our own inspiration – were stories that would settle the nerves of every aspiring researcher. By reaching out to leading scholars in the field and asking for their reflections on their projects, we appreciated that we were putting people into an academic confessional. We knew we would hear of challenges and how many of these hurdles were overcome (or else these works would not exist as well-read and much-discussed contributions to the field), but we would also draw attention to mistakes and the limitations of these studies. Our approach is not to meet candor with criticism. While there are unquestionably norms and best practices

[3] W. H. Auden, *The Dyer's Hand and Other Essays* (London: Faber and Faber, 1963), p. 47.
[4] Philippe Schmitter, "The Design of Social and Political Research," in *Approaches and Methodologies in the Social Sciences*, Donatella Della Porta and Michael Keating, eds. (Cambridge, U.K.: Cambridge University Press, 2008), p. 294, Figure 14.3.

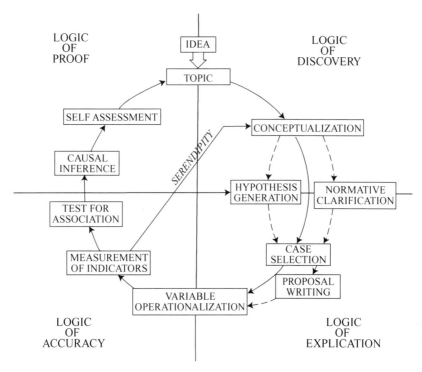

Figure 1: Serendipity in Methodology – One Formulation. *Source:* Schmitter (2008), Figure 14.3.

for research methods, analysis, and interpretation, we maintain a less normative stance, one that views ambiguity and difficulty as *essential* elements of the research process. For research to be at the cutting edge, the researcher needs to be discovering new areas of study, finding new communities or subjects of research, or testing new analytical frames. The ambition to discover something new about the world brings the researcher into engagement with the world. A judge may believe that his or her task is to find the most closely matched precedent to answer the case at hand (however discretionary we know that task to be); a researcher who is not simply replicating existing research does not have that comfort. Every research project is, in some way, a project of "first impression" – a de novo attempt to find the world through a new slice or with a new lens. Uncertainty and doubt are the researcher's faithful companions.

This collection of interviews, if it adequately captures the way research methodology works "in action," does not free anyone of the need to be thoughtful, intentional, and reflective about methods. What it might do, however, is relieve many of the worries that plague students and scholars.

LAW AND SOCIETY IN THE CONFIDENT AGE

Though not a guiding purpose of this volume, in the course of conducting the interviews we came to appreciate the collection as having a secondary value: functioning as an oral history, of sorts, of well-known and well-regarded Law and Society research projects. Law and Society as an academic field and an organization is now firmly established, and the findings of affiliated scholars have found their way into curricula and policy making around the globe. Yet, fortunately, the field is young enough that many of its founders are around to tell their tales. The organizational history of Law and Society has been told in other places.[5] Also, the stories of many research projects, including some in this book, have been retold at conference panels or lectures to students and occasionally have been published as individual pieces. Still, although our primary emphasis has been on understanding how projects took shape and overcame challenges, we have appreciated our position of hearing these stories and believe that others will too. Both for those with long-standing familiarity with the projects in this volume and for those coming to these analyzes anew, there is an intrinsic interest in hearing the research stories that underpin them, one that requires no justification.

Of course, if approached as history, this volume has many limitations. Having focused on the social realities of research, our dialogues with authors leave unexplored – or edited out due to limitations of space – many features a historian might think to ask or include. Perhaps more

[5] See, for example, F. J. Levine, "Goose Bumps and 'The Search for Intelligent Life' in Sociolegal Studies: After Twenty-Five Years," *Law & Society Review*, 24(1): 7–33 (1990); and B. Garth and J. Sterling, "From Legal Realism to Law and Society: Reshaping Law for the Last Stages of the Activist State," *Law & Society Review*, 32:409–71 (1998). For accounts of the development of sociolegal studies in the United Kingdom, see Philip A. Thomas, "Socio-Legal Studies: The Case of Disappearing Fleas and Bustards" in *Socio-Legal Studies*, Thomas, ed. (Aldershot, Dartmouth, 1997); and W. Twining, "Remembering 1972: The Oxford Centre in the Context of Developments in Higher Education and the Discipline of Law," *Journal of Law & Society*, 22:35–49 (1995). See, generally, David S. Clark, ed., *Encyclopedia of Law & Society: American and Global Perspectives* (Los Angeles: Sage, 2007).

significant, the interviewees, although representing a diverse group of scholars and projects, were not sampled with a broader historical record in mind. Having initially toyed with the notion of constructing a collection of the "classic" works in the field, we quickly retreated from that frame for somewhat obvious good reasons. To attempt to capture a group of studies that represent "the classics" would be an almost impossible task and would necessitate a controversial claim, especially in a field as diverse as Law and Society.[6] Furthermore, it would have restricted our focus to the earlier period of the Law and Society movement, which would have undermined our primary goal of creating a useful resource for junior researchers of various intellectual interests and methodological approaches. In our collaborative discussions about the plan of the book, we frequently pointed to more recent works that we thought presented wonderful models of field research but that may not yet have attained the iconic status possessed by older works. We also wanted to focus on projects that have turned attention toward important new domains or have applied exciting new analytical frames. The interviews of Yves Dezalay and Bryant Garth (Chapter 18), John Braithwaite and Peter Drahos (Chapter 21), and John Hagan (Chapter 22), each focusing in their own way on globalization, are cases in point.

Even if not a rigorous history in any meaningful sense, it is difficult not to be impressed by the interplay of forces that have helped to generate many major research projects in the field. Rather than reducing research to an individual enterprise, the interviews in this book repeatedly pay a debt to mentors, such as J. Willard Hurst, or to the concentrations of colleagues found at key institutions in the development of the field, such as the American Bar Foundation, the University of Wisconsin, Yale University, and the Oxford Centre for Socio-Legal Studies. Though merely scratching the surface, by tracing out the common intellectual and institutional roots of these empirical, sociolegal projects, these interviews contribute a deeper appreciation of the emergence of Law and Society as a field confident in its ability to contribute to the understanding of law in action.

---

[6]But see Carroll Seron, ed., *The Law and Society Canon* (Aldershot, U.K.: Ashgate, 2006); and C. Seron and Susan S. Silbey, "Profession, Science and Culture: An Emergent Canon of Law and Society Research," in *The Blackwell Companion to Law and Society*, Austin Sarat, ed. (Oxford: Blackwell, 2004), pp. 30–59.

METHODS AND APPROACH

In our conversations with the scholars in this volume and with interested colleagues, we could not avoid the recursive suggestion that the interviews we were conducting might be put to use in a sociological study of the sociology of law. Our actual ambitions were much more modest, but we nevertheless recognized that it would be supremely ironic if we did not, in a collection such as this, turn the spotlight on ourselves long enough to speak in detail, and with candor, of the methods and approaches we adopted in producing this book.

The idea for the project was floated over beers at The Brewer's Art, an upscale brewpub in Baltimore, where the Law and Society Association annual meeting was held in 2006. We were already friends, having worked as Research Fellows at Oxford University's Centre for Socio-Legal Studies. Having previously enjoyed the experience of co-editing a collection of essays,[7] we set our minds to the conception of another project that would allow us to work together. Our own memories of having completed doctoral research in the Law and Society tradition were sufficiently recent, perhaps even a little raw, that we could see the value of a volume such as this. In particular, in one case a little-known, and now fairly old, volume of reflective essays,[8] and in the other a review essay based on a close examination of an empirical project,[9] had been of such inspiration and comfort to each of us, respectively, that we were confident of the pedagogical payoff of research narratives over and above the methods textbooks. Unusually, perhaps, for projects conceived in a brewpub the night before, we pitched the idea the next morning to John Berger at Cambridge University Press – making it seem like it was a well-formed idea, of course – and his distinct enthusiasm launched our efforts.

One of our first decisions was to choose particular projects rather than authors with an outstanding corpus of work. That meant excluding many luminaries and some of our favorite authors when their individual projects duplicated the approaches and themes already selected for

---

[7] *Human Rights Brought Home: Socio-Legal Perspectives on Human Rights in the National Context* (Oxford: Hart Publishing, 2004).

[8] Robin Luckham, ed., *Law and Social Enquiry: Case Studies of Research* (Uppsala: Scandinavian Institute of African Studies, 1981).

[9] H. M. Kritzer, "'Data, Data, Data, Drowning in Data': Crafting *The Hollow Core*," *Law and Social Inquiry*, 21:761–804 (1996).

inclusion. Our concern for the representativeness of various methodologies, approaches, and subjects meant that many fine examples of empirical scholarship, particularly given the depth of excellent ethnographic fieldwork in Law and Society, could not be included. Our emphasis on empirical research projects naturally led us to reject numerous classic pieces that were based on keen insight into the empirical world but that did not tell the story of a discrete project.[10] Our process of selection led us to produce a diverse list of works across a wide time span. However, the selection was complicated by not knowing what the response to our invitations would be. We proceeded in waves, prepared to extend different invitations depending on the responses. As it happened, the response rate to our invitations was one hundred percent, so we never drew from our contingent list of possibilities.

We chose an interview format for the main chapters, rather than seeking authored essays. We did this for two reasons. First, for entirely practical reasons, we believed that potential contributors from a wider range of approaches (and frequently we had specific scholars in mind) would be more willing to agree to an interview than to authoring an essay. Second, and more substantively, we were keen to capture a more immediate and conversational tone for the pieces. We instinctively felt that this format would make the book more accessible and easier to use for readers, creating pieces that can be paired with the primary texts as a form of commentary and reflection on the works. We were keen to establish a contrast to the more prosaic, and at times drier, style of methods textbooks. We also believed that capturing something of the spoken voice of the authors would enliven the narratives and somehow bring them closer to the reader. It would help convey the essential humanity of research, an underlying aim of the volume as a whole. Last, whereas some useful collections have provided scholars with narratives about the methodological practices used in the field,[11] we knew from more isolated examples and our own experience with interview methods that interviewing would allow us to ask authors to "unpack" the emotional dimensions of their projects or go deeper into various aspects of their experiences. Interviews simply allow one

---

[10] A prime example is Marc Galanter, "Why the 'Haves' Come Out Ahead: Speculations on the Limits of Legal Change," *Law & Society Review*, 9:95–160 (1974).

[11] June Starr and Mark Goodale, eds., *Practicing Ethnography in Law: New Dialogues, Enduring Methods* (New York: Palgrave Macmillan, 2002).

to access more spontaneous and candid answers than an editor giving written comments on a draft of a chapter.

Most of the interviews for the book were conducted at the Law and Society Association Meeting in Berlin the following year, 2007. This was a cost-effective and efficient way of carrying out the work. It was also exhausting. Before Berlin we had "piloted" the interview approach with two contributors from Oxford University whom we knew, Keith Hawkins and Doreen McBarnet. Other interviews, for pragmatic reasons, were conducted after the meeting in Berlin (John Braithwaite and Peter Drahos, John Heinz and Edward Laumann, John Hagan, John Conley and William O'Barr, and Alan Paterson). The interview with John Conley and William O'Barr was conducted by telephone conference call, as was the interview with Patty Ewick, though Susan Silbey had been interviewed in person in Berlin. Although Bill Felstiner had been interviewed in Berlin, Austin Sarat contributed written answers to an edited text of the Felstiner interview.

We prepared a set of universal questions which were asked of all participants and were sent to them in advance of the interviews. These questions covered issues such as the intellectual background of the projects, the setting up of projects, how projects were first intended or designed, the acts of analyzing and writing up fieldwork, the emotional demands of the research, and the authors' reactions to the reception of their work in the scholarly community. Additionally, we asked numerous questions specific to the projects being discussed. Interviews lasted between one and three hours, with an average of approximately ninety minutes, producing transcripts of between approximately ten thousand and thirty thousand words. Our biggest challenge was to edit those transcripts down to chapters of around four thousand to five thousand words. It should go without saying that, without fail, interviews were far richer than this book could accommodate, and so we grew in appreciation of the choices that we were making. Each interview received a two-stage process of editing, with one of us doing an initial cut and the other reviewing the edit against the original, and frequently making considerable changes, both cutting further and saving some material from the cutting-room floor. Some interviews suggested a dominant narrative quite readily, whereas others were more chimeric. We chose not to ensure the uniformity of issues addressed across the chapters, but rather to retain what we felt were the most interesting and useful aspects of each interview. Having said that, and as the concluding chapter by Bert Kritzer highlights, considerable overlap still exists between chapters in terms of the subjects discussed and themes that emerged. It also took us much longer to edit the transcripts than we had originally anticipated – something, of course, that we should have foreseen on the basis of the research narratives we had listened to!

The authors were promised that we would send the edited transcripts for their approval. We invited them to amend the text where they wished, including our introduction to their chapter, and to suggest methodological keywords to be included in their chapters. Every author made some changes to their texts. Most amendments were minimal. It took considerable nerve for some contributors to see their words on the page – what had been said in the comfortable and relaxed atmosphere of Berlin – and to not shrink from our call to allow their doubts, mistakes, and reflections to go forward to press. We thank them for their fortitude.

The one exception to our decision to conduct interviews is the concluding chapter, authored by Bert Kritzer, which pulls together the insights from the interviews in aggregate and reflects on the state of Law and Society research. Bert Kritzer struck us as, perhaps without peer, the scholar most qualified to reflect on the reflections. The editor of *Law & Society Review* from 2003 to 2007, and co-editor (with Peter Cane) of the *Oxford Handbook of Empirical Legal Studies*, for the past three decades he has been one of the leading producers and consumers of empirical Law and Society research. In particular, he has long taken a reflexive interest in the research process and has written much about how empirical research projects have come to pass.

The last matter to be decided in the production of the book was how to title it. One of us is more demanding than the other (in a good way, it is hoped) regarding titles, asking that they be catchy and memorable.[12] In these interviews, we frequently asked authors how their books and articles got their titles, and some of those answers made it through the editing (see, e.g., Feeley, Chapter 4; Engel, Chapter 8; and Rosenberg, Chapter 15). We struggled to title this book, which had so many concepts and themes seemingly at play. One of our colleagues early on gave us the promising suggestion of "Law and Society in Action," a clever twist on an old theme, and we ran with it for months. "Beyond Methods" was also considered, later in the process. Both fell afoul of

---

[12] The other, having once been told by a colleague that he had conjured up the "second-worst-titled book in academia," has long-since abandoned pride in the titling process.

the judgment of our editor at Cambridge, who sensibly advised us that a plain and descriptive title sells more books by giving readers and libraries a better sense of why they need the book. The title and subtitle of this chapter, like gravestones for dead ideas, memorialize our journey through the difficult job of naming one's projects.

ORGANIZATION OF THE BOOK

This book is not designed to be read cover-to-cover, and so in some respects the order of the material may be irrelevant. In our formal proposal to Cambridge University Press, we had suggested organizing the book into sections to reflect the various research techniques used and the traditional subject foci of the Law and Society field. This would have mirrored the approaches taken to research methods textbooks and to various Law and Society readers. Several attempts in this vein left us frustrated that this approach might obscure more than it revealed for a volume such as this. Particularly where single projects have used multiple methods, separating chapters out according to individual techniques would be problematic. Furthermore, in a developing field where research questions and analytical constructs build on and reframe prior work, and where path-breaking work embraces and extends a range of traditional themes, it seems counterproductive to reduce projects to one, or even a dominant, research concern. So serendipity intervened, just as Figure 1 suggests it should – when attempting to place one's data alongside the conceptual framework – and we devised a new, more satisfying order of the chapters. The interviews, accordingly, follow a chronological sequence according to the date of publication of the main research publication being discussed. In the end, the chronological frame helped us see the interviews in a way that confirms an initial hypothesis: uncertainty and ambiguity are not products of a particular age of a field, when it is new, but are ever-present. We hope that these interviews will help lessen the anxieties that attend this condition.

CHAPTER 2

STEWART MACAULAY AND "NON-CONTRACTUAL RELATIONS IN BUSINESS"*

If there is any piece of work discussed in this volume that most unquestionably can be called a "classic," this is it. Necessary to any suggestion of a "canon" of Law and Society is a judgment about what constitutes good or important scholarship. Certainly, one quality of significant sociolegal work is that it illuminates the world as it is in practice, not as lawyers and legal scholars assert it to be. The areas of law most frequently relegated to the dry covers of legal treatises – contracts, bankruptcy, tax, estates, and so on – thus have the best potential to reveal new sides when subjected to the sunlight of critical inquiry. What we learn from such studies can be quite dramatic in terms of the sheer gap between theory and practice, and the discovery of that gap speaks to the power of empirical study of law as a whole.

Stewart Macaulay's landmark article, "Non-Contractual Relations in Business: A Preliminary Study," is one such eye-opening exercise in empirical exploration. Contrary to the assumptions of the legal creed, he found a world in which law was not central – where custom and other noncontractual social practices provide order. Undoubtedly the freshness of his discoveries were aided by the state of the field – indeed, the Law and Society Association was not formed until 1964 – and subsequent research has noted many changes in the use of law by businesses in the late twentieth century. The article nevertheless remains much read and cited. Today, Macaulay's position vis-à-vis methodology and empirical research is not uncommon. Even half a century later, law students and faculty face the challenge of entering the world of empirical research without a strong background in research methodology. Individually, we might ask, what are the elements that make for a successful foray into empirical research? Is it simply the "luck of a good topic" or "the genius of the researcher"? What affirmative measures can and

---

*"Non-Contractual Relations in Business: A Preliminary Study," *American Sociological Review*, 28:1–19 (1963).

should the researcher take to gain every chance of contributing good scholarship – and are these steps the ones that are taught in methodology textbooks? Collectively, too, an opportunity for reflection exists: what has and has not been done to develop the interest and capacity for empirical research?

Methodological Keywords: interviews; preliminary study

Question: What sparked your interest in this project?

Macaulay: It was my father-in-law, Jack Ramsey. He was the retired general manager of Johnson Wax. He asked me about my contracts course. I told him about the casebook we used, *Fuller on Contracts*. Many saw it as the cutting-edge book at that time. This was Lon Fuller – hardly some second-rate hack! But my father-in-law laughed at my description of the contract course. He thought that it rested on a model of business behavior that was totally unrealistic. Here I was, twenty-eight or twenty-nine years old with a very severe case of "impostor syndrome." I'm up in front of a class while wondering to myself, "What do I know?" So having him laugh was not good. But he told me a story about Johnson Wax during the Great Depression. Three firms made the tin cans that Johnson used to package its products. In the middle of the Great Depression, these firms were in trouble because of the great decline in the demand for containers for all consumer products. Instead of getting them bidding against each other, my father-in-law said that Johnson placed the order with the firm that needed it most at any given time. All three survived the Depression, and Johnson's practice was one reason for this. Then World War II came along. The United States went into a command economy run from Washington. Essential items were rationed, and there were shortages of things needed to make consumer products. Think of what the priority for steel to be used to make cans to contain wax must have been! However, Johnson never lacked a can. Those three firms owed it help when Johnson faced difficulty. Doesn't this story sum up relational contracts? The story got me talking with him, and he said, "Well, you think that it's just me? Let me call some people." So he sent me to speak to other business people.

Question: How did that connect with your research interests at the time?

Macaulay: I was interested in legal realism, and it pointed toward the consequences of law. Karl Llewellyn, the great legal realist, always stressed the need for judges to exercise "situation sense." That is, they

15

had to have an informed intuition to find the substantively right result. I had written articles where I tried to be a legal realist, and I had fashioned an analysis of the inconsistent goals that contract law had sought over time.[1]

But the impetus behind my interests was very practical. I was a law professor, and, like many if not most American law professors, I had never practiced law or worked in a business. I had a job to do, but I felt that I didn't know enough. Once I began teaching, I worked my way through two excellent contracts casebooks, and I checked *Corbin on Contracts* as I fashioned notes for my classes. I read carefully the major writing of scholars such as Llewellyn, Patterson, Fuller, Kessler, and Sharp, and I outlined many of their articles. Yet I knew that I could only guess about how any contracts decision or pattern of decisions affected the behavior of business people or lawyers. I worried that I was preparing my law students to be appellate judges rather than lawyers solving problems for business people. I wasn't thinking about matters that later became the concern of the Law and Society Association. At that point, I didn't want to be a legal sociologist; I just wanted to be a good law professor.

Question: Did you seek out, or receive, much input or encouragement from others in the development of the project?

Macaulay: Of course, I was an assistant professor at the University of Wisconsin Law School which was, and is, a very unusual institution. Frank Remington was my colleague at the law school, and he was the chief drafter of the Wisconsin Criminal Code. However, he said that if you really wanted to understand the criminal law, you should ride in the front seat of a squad car on a hot, steamy night in a big city. I thought that if you wanted to understand contracts, you had to "ride along" with business people and their lawyers.

Moreover, Willard Hurst, the great legal historian, was a major influence on many of us at Wisconsin. He had won a grant from the Rockefeller Foundation to develop a new kind of law school; part of it involved training beginning legal scholars to see law as a social institution. Willard, himself, had written one of the first studies of what lawyers had done to foster the economic development of the United States.

---

[1] See, for example, S. Macaulay, "Justice Traynor and the Law of Contracts," *Stanford Law Review*, 13:812–64 (1961).

He was always fascinated by the ways things in the world worked. He would have lawyers over to dinner to pick their brains in the most charming way. He would read the manuscripts of the younger professors and respond with pages of comments and many suggestions of things to read and questions to consider. The University also long had a tradition of interdisciplinary seminars. They were going on when I walked on campus for the first time. When I arrived in Madison in 1957, the law faculty often went to talks by sociologists who were interested in the criminal law and had something to say about it. While no one suggested my specific project, a law-in-action approach certainly was in the air at Wisconsin in the late 1950s and early 1960s.

Hurst called on his contacts, and I traveled to the East Coast to talk with his friends Talcott and Bob – Talcott Parsons and Robert Merton. They were very sympathetic and helpful, and I got two long reading assignments. Of course, I was fortunate that I was too stupid to know who they were. Very few beginning professors got an hour with the leading sociologists in America if not the world. Had I realized what was involved, I probably would have been too worried to have said much. The hour with Merton turned into an afternoon. The contact with Merton was to prove very important later.

Question: Your training was as a lawyer. To what extent were you uncertain about taking on a project using social science methods?

Macaulay: I was very uncertain. Indeed, at the outset I wasn't sure that I would be able to put together anything that I could publish in a journal or a law review. I thought that information about business practices related to contract problems would help me teach, and I might find things to supplement the cases and statutes in the casebook. As I talked to the first business people and lawyers, I also was reading about social science research and looking at examples. One problem was that I didn't know enough to draft a precise questionnaire. I was trying to discover what these people saw as the issues and problems concerning contracts and contract law. I couldn't draw a random sample because I wasn't sure who was in the group that I wanted to study. Did I want to talk to business people who made certain kinds of contracts? Business people who had had contract disputes of a certain type? Business people who had consulted lawyers and gone to court? Lawyers who regularly drafted contracts? Lawyers who had litigated contracts disputes? Or something else?

But I had a tremendous advantage. I had a brilliant wife, Jackie Macaulay. She was then a graduate student in social psychology at the University of Wisconsin. Her interests spilled over into sociology as well. She was both willing and able to shape up her husband. My problem was to ask what could you do when your interest doesn't fit into the canons of "Methods 101." You could just throw up your hands and do nothing. But my idea was and is that you should do the best that you can. You should know your sins and put them front and center in anything you write. You should do what you can to minimize the problems. And if someone else finds a way to do it better, maybe you can take credit for showing them that there was a problem to solve.

Question: Given that this project started as an attempt to make you a more informed and realistic contracts teacher, how did you start the research process? Did you develop any kind of strategy for sampling and choosing your interviewees?

Macaulay: I didn't know who I should be talking with. I used to joke that those in my "sample" were friends of my father-in-law who would talk to me! Of course, this isn't how the books say to do research. That's one of the big downsides when people write about research methods – it is all so neat and pretty. The messiness of much of it just doesn't come through in the books.

I certainly knew that I didn't want all the business people to work for manufacturers of consumer products such as my father-in-law. I knew that I should try to find people from other kinds of business. I knew that I didn't want them all to be from Racine, the city where Johnson Wax was located. And I knew that the friends of my father-in-law might differ from most business people because he was an atypical executive for his time who worked for a family-owned major corporation, and his friends might be more like him than typical people in these roles. Moreover, I needed people who knew something about making and performing contracts and dealing with disputes. I knew that I shouldn't talk just with people who had had disputes or had gone to court because they might be completely atypical of most businesses.

I had to rely on somebody telling me what business practices were like and then suggesting someone else to talk with. I learned that this was called a snowball sample. I kept stumbling over stuff. I began each interview with fairly open-ended questions and then went over a checklist to cover anything that the person hadn't talked about.

The business lawyers I interviewed were great informants. Their perceptions gave me more questions to pose to the business people. I discovered that one's role in business or law affected views about relational approaches and contract rights. Lawyers wanted to nail down deals in written contracts; purchasing agents saw legal approaches as largely a waste of time. This suggested that I try to talk to people who played different roles and see if my impressions about differing views stood up.

I also "invented" my own research method: later in the project I gave talks to corporate lawyers. Lawyers will tell you if you are all wrong or are overgeneralizing. They also offered great anecdotes illustrating some of the points that I had made. They are not shy by nature, and they love setting a law professor right. I got a lot of feedback from this set of informants reacting to my tentative ideas. And these corporate lawyers reacted to each other. At least, several times their comments sent me back to my interview notes looking for issues that I hadn't seen as very important until they showed me what was involved.

Question: How difficult was it to find business people willing to be interviewed?

Macaulay: Getting access was hard. The most productive tactic was to have someone introduce me and say that the business person or lawyer should talk to me. My father-in-law led me to many of his friends. My brother-in-law had another set of friends. A student of mine had been a salesman of machinery used in making paper. He became interested in my project, and so I got into the paper-making-machinery mafia. One of my brother-in-law's friends was a lawyer who worked for an equipment manufacturer. He let me spend a week or so looking through the firm's files concerning various transactions. I found letters, tentative drafts of contract provisions, internal memos, and much more. While I could not quote any of this material or even identify the company, this gave me more understanding of what I had been learning in my interviews. I particularly enjoyed discovering that in a major sale of many machines, the seller had started production and was well under way before the final contract documents were signed.

Getting access to lawyers was even harder. Lawyers are busy, and they always feel pressed for time. I used law school contacts, drawing on our alumni association. And again the snowball effect worked. One lawyer often sent me to another. Once I got in the door, often lawyers would get interested in the project and be extremely helpful. Many of them loved to tell their war stories. Of course, I knew that I had to use them cautiously. A "war story" is interesting, amusing or even shocking because it is atypical. In a very few instances, lawyers agreed to see me but I found myself pushed out of their office after a short time. Most were extraordinarily helpful.

Question: What were you looking for in the interviews and how were you proceeding with them?

Macaulay: First, I was interested in hearing about my father-in-law's assertion about the power of relational norms and sanctions as contrasted to what contract law could offer. Second, I became more and more interested in the battle of the forms – the deal is written on a purchase order and an acknowledgment of order form which have different terms on the back; no one sees this and the deal proceeds with flawed documentation. Third, I was interested in contract litigation. Few business people had been involved in it, but some had heard about the problems faced by others. Of course, I was interested in explanations for practices as well.

I consciously started using people both as subjects and as informants about things. That is, I would interview a person and then I would ask him about stuff that I had found from other people. I kept testing what people told me. I often used lawyers this way. They tended not to like the idea that contract law was irrelevant. They wanted to defend the law as a kind of insurance. The lawyers were concerned that they would be blamed if everything proceeded on trust but then collapsed.

I tried not to be too structured. I had a checklist of things to cover. It wasn't quite as bad as "tell me about contracts," but almost. I was saying, "I teach contracts in law school. How does this figure in your work?" Often they would say "not at all." Then I'd ask whether they actually worked out contract documents. They might say that the lawyers demanded it. This would raise the question, "Why are you wasting all that time going through formalities when you are supposed to be rational business people?" (I would try to say this nicely). I would push a little. "Does it ever matter?" "Have you ever been sued?" "Do you know anyone who has been sued?" Very few did, but every now and then there'd be someone who said: "Oh, the fellows over at Acme got sued and then we all got worried and started reading those things." I wanted them to tell me their stories. I did not want to impose my view on them because I knew that my vision of the business world was pretty shaky.

Question: How did you record your interview data?

Macaulay: I just did what I had done as a law student. You don't learn too many things in law school, but if you are going to succeed, you do learn to take good notes. The trick is to write down enough so that you can rework your notes later. When I was a student, I left my classes in the mornings, went back to the law dorm and then spent the first part of the afternoon creating a set of notes for each class. I could type rapidly and compose at a typewriter. So I took these skills when I did the interviews. I found that tape recorders bothered many whom I was interviewing, and so I took notes. Afterward, I went to a library with a typing area or to a motel. I think that from my notes I was able to come very close to what people had said. I probably couldn't do as well if I tried to do it the next day or so.

Question: You also requested documentation from companies. At what point did you conceive of this approach and how did it relate to your interviewing?

Macaulay: I decided to do it quite early on. Some lawyers and business people had given me copies of some of their forms, and I thought that they looked interesting. Having been told by my interviewees that contract didn't matter, I wanted to see what they had on their forms. Many of them were very detailed. I was asking for purchasing and sales forms in manufacturing industry. I sent a request to all firms in a directory of Wisconsin manufacturers. I got about twelve hundred responses. I tended to get documents from the larger companies because they had standard forms while small firms did not.

At some point, I tried to do a little coding, but I came to think that I was putting in a lot of time and producing little. Yes, there were clauses dealing with *force majeure*, but were they different? I didn't try to do anything industry-by-industry because when I first looked at this, I didn't see any patterns. Many of these clauses seemed to be standard lawyer-drafted things and not tailored to a specific industry. Of course, this often gave me something to use in interviewing people. "Why does this firm do it this way?" People had their explanations, but often it just seemed that they did not know why particular clauses were in their contracts.

Question: You mentioned that your attempts to code the written contracts didn't work as well as you'd hoped. Did you encounter any difficulties when it came to analyzing the interview data?

21

Macaulay: One of the problems of these interviews is that people like to entertain you. So what gets presented as the way things are is really the best story that they've got. There was a particular danger of that when I talked with lawyers who had connections with the law school. They wanted to interest a professor. Some seemed to still feel that they were being graded by me. I tried to be very careful about overgeneralizing from particular stories.

Question: What about theoretical framing? How did you approach the interview data analysis?

Macaulay: I had an implicit model that I was testing. I was asking to what extent, if at all, is the picture being taught in law school accurate? As I mentioned, I had done much reading of the legal realists. But what I found didn't fit the picture that either the formalists or the realists offered. (Sometimes the picture was more or less accurate, but these were exceptional situations rather than the way business usually worked.) Why was this so? Most simply, in most instances the payoff from writing contracts carefully and resolving disputes in court was too low and the costs of going the legal way were too high. Writing contracts carefully is talking about *not* performing. It's a little like prenuptial contracts: "Dear, when we break up and we have our divorce, here's how we'll divide things." When you make a deal, we are talking trust and commitment. This is one reason why printed forms are used. The real deal is between the parties, and there is this lawyer stuff that is just a matter of form. And many have not had their fingers burned. How much fire insurance do you buy if you've never had a fire and don't believe that you will have one? How much do you buy if you think that fire insurance company is not likely to pay off if there is a fire?

During the entire process of the project, I was reading what I could find in law, business, economics, and sociology. I kept assuming that all I had to do was look it up, but I found only a very few things in point. Finally, I read Malinowski's *Crime and Custom in Savage Society*.[2] He called the norms and sanctions of long-term continuing relations "law." He also raised things that I then found lurking in my interview notes. For example, he compared the "native" to the "civilized business man," noting that whenever he could evade his obligations without

[2] Bronislaw Malinowski, *Crime and Custom in Savage Society* (New York: Harcourt Brace, 1926).

the loss of prestige or without the prospective loss of gain, he would do so. I did not cite Malinowski in the ASR [*American Sociological Review*] article but much of that book was very important in helping me frame questions and in pulling together my sprawling interview notes.

Question: Can you tell us about the eventual process of writing all this up into the article that was published?

Macaulay: For a long time, I didn't know whether there was anything there to be written up. I kept wondering if the project was worth doing. I had to convince myself that there was something in it. Partly it was because I was learning as I worked and conducted interviews. The first interview didn't ask exactly the same things as the last ones. Harry Ball was a sociologist who was working on a research project on criminal law at the law school. We talked, and he encouraged me to pull together my ideas. This prompted an invitation to present a paper at the Midwestern Sociological Association meeting in Des Moines, Iowa. I felt like a fish out of water. There I was, a law professor who had taken only one or two introductory courses in social science, having to tap-dance in front of a group of sociologists. However, they seemed interested and even laughed at the jokes. I began to think there might be something to my project.

I drafted a more elaborate version of the paper and submitted it to the *American Journal of Sociology*. It was promptly rejected. I am unclear about the sequence of what happened next. I think that Willard Hurst sent a copy of my paper to Robert Merton. Merton then asked me to present it at a panel he was organizing on "applied sociology" at the American Sociological Association meeting in Washington, D.C. I accepted the invitation, but I still felt like a fish out of water. Now I knew who Robert Merton was, and I wanted to do well on his panel. My wife loved to tell the story of that panel. Pitrim Sorokin was a speaker, and he was one of the grand old men of sociology. The panel was held in a large ballroom, and many attended just to hear Sorokin. He talked well over the allotted time, and when he sat down, Merton called me to speak. About 300 people were there. When Sorokin finished, my wife estimated that about 250 got up to leave. I began speaking to the backs of a crowd filing out and talking. Merton stopped me and said: "Would the intellectual tourists be quiet! We still have work to do." I have no idea how my talk went, but Merton knew that the paper had been rejected by AJS. He asked me for a copy, and I left one with him.

A few weeks later, after I had returned to Madison, I received Merton's many suggestions. He said that I should have a new title, and he offered the one that was used. My wife then went over Merton's suggestions and added her own in an almost sentence-by-sentence edit of the manuscript. I took all of this advice and prepared a new draft which I sent to Merton. He sent it to the *American Sociological Review* with a letter to the editor that said: "You would be a fool not to publish this." It was hardly a blind review, but it helps to have Robert Merton in your corner.

Question: The insights have stood the test of time, but is there anything that in hindsight you would have done differently about the research project?

Macaulay: It would have taken a lot less time to do all the interviews if I had known more about qualitative social science techniques and about business practices related to contracts. I was learning by doing and necessarily when you do this you waste time and make mistakes. There were tries at interviews that didn't produce very much. They were not inconsistent with what I had been learning, and I supposed that they reinforced my trust in the earlier discussions. I could have planned more, and I could have taken a course or done more reading. The problem was that in those days few, if any, social scientists or law professors were interested in doing something like my project. There wasn't a research literature that I found that was right on point. However, I still feel that in new areas you have to ask the elders of the tribe and then check what they tell you. You cannot plunge in with a questionnaire mailed to what you think is a random sample. However, after my interviews and talks to lawyers, I could have defined a population, drawn a sample, and established at least a few points with a good survey. I am not certain that I would have drawn a decent response rate if the questionnaire had been too detailed.

Question: I cannot imagine you feeling at all maligned about how it has been received and read.

Macaulay: Soon after it was published, I did have a sociologist at a party tell me – he had a drink in his hand and maybe he was needling me – "Sociologists die to get into the *American Sociological Review*, and you took their space away." That seemed harsh and, gee, I didn't know what I was doing. I'm sorry!

In 2004, the editor of *ASR* noted the journal's hundredth anniversary by doing citation counts for *ASR* articles dating back to 1936.[3] Eighteen articles had been cited over five hundred times. I was pleased to find that my piece was in eleventh place on that list with 699 citations from its publication to November of 2004. But my article was very much a late bloomer. In the first decade after publication, they found only four citations. In the fourth decade, however, there were 360.

I certainly do not have any notion that I have written the last thing on noncontractual relations in business or the limited role of contract law in the economy. In fact, if my 1963 article is the last word, I think that I'd feel upset because I know that there is more to be said. I have been pleased that there have been a flood of articles drawing on my research in many countries that generally support the arguments that I made. Most of these articles are in business or international trade journals. Sometimes, however, this article is cited for propositions, such as "law does not matter" or "contract law does not matter." Grant Gilmore once wrote that I was the "Lord High Executioner of the Contracts is Dead movement." Literally, my article does not say that. It says only that law doesn't matter as much as many law professors think that it does. Sometimes contract law matters tremendously, and sometimes it doesn't very much at all.[4] We still have not made much progress establishing when and under what circumstances this kind of law matters and to whom.

But I have to say that the shelf life of the article amazes me. I would assume that anything published in 1963 is only of historical interest. I am pleased that the article is still alive. However, if new research nudges it back into history, it would probably be good too – perhaps not for me, but certainly for the field.

[3] See J. A. Jacobs, "ASR's Greatest Hits," *American Sociological Review*, 70:1 (2005).

[4] My next project involved a situation in which a kind of contract law was very important, and the weaker party was not content to rely on relational norms and sanctions. See Macaulay, *Law and the Balance of Power – The Automobile Manufacturers and Their Dealers* (Russell Sage Foundation, 1966). Here I was able to draw on my father's experiences as a General Motors executive.

CHAPTER 3

ROBERT KAGAN AND
*REGULATORY JUSTICE**

Luck, the old saying goes, is "opportunity meets preparedness." Many veteran scholars attest to the importance of luck in research projects and the longer arc of their careers, but the maxim reminds us that the researcher can set up for lucky events by being ready to recognize and seize opportunities when they present themselves. Regulatory Justice, Robert Kagan's dissertation and first book, began in such a moment. The spark of interest, generated by a television news item, and Kagan's rapid response to get into the field, do not match the process laid out in textbooks on research methods. For a start, as he describes it, the questions animating the project would remain latent while he rode the wave of activity in a newly created regulatory agency.

Yet the development of Kagan's project, as much as it may comfort those who cannot see the path forward in a project, is also instructive about the little things one can do to create a project from a kernel of curiosity: formulating an instinct about the gaps in existing scholarship, making use of every available resource and connection, being prepared to take risks, and investing in the project in the form of habits of diligence and care. Although Kagan had some kinds of resources – that is, the preparedness – not possessed by many students of Law and Society, including prior experience as a litigator, the general suggestion may stand: opportunities abound for the enterprising scholar to observe the law in action.

Today Kagan is perhaps best known for his description of "adversarial legalism," the style of public policy making that injects lawyers and litigation into the mechanisms of governance, including bureaucracies. Although his dialogue with legalism in Regulatory Justice *is clearly distinct from his later work on adversarial legalism, one may wonder how the intensive experience of participant observation research, such as Kagan's investment in this one regulatory bureaucracy, can mold a young scholar's views on the*

Regulatory Justice: Implementing a Wage-Price Freeze (New York: Russell Sage Foundation, 1978).

26

legal system. Kagan begins by tracing his path from the practice of law, into academia, and back into participation research.

Methodological Keywords: participant observation, quantitative analysis

Kagan: Well, I think the key to that was that I had been a practicing lawyer, doing a variety of litigation. What I loved about practicing law was the sociology of it. I loved learning the worlds of my clients. I'd learn something about the wire manufacturing business or the oil storage business or something like that. When I went back to school to get a Ph.D., seven years after my law degree, the Russell Sage Foundation had this wonderful program for social scientists to study law and for lawyers to study social science. I got a grant from that program and it gave me the chance to go back to school. Early on in my first year of studying the sociology of law at Yale I realized that one big chunk of the legal world that had been part of my experience – the whole administrative, regulatory state – was not very much on the agenda of sociology of law. People were pretty courts-focused. I thought that the regulatory world might be something I might want to study. I liked how regulation penetrates society in a way that litigation usually doesn't and how you have direct contact with the public, not mediated by lawyers.

The idea of participant observation was on my agenda because of another Russell Sage fellow, Donald Black. Donald Black and Al Reiss (one of my teachers at Yale) had done police observation studies that I liked a lot. Indeed, during my first year Donald Black had a grant to study housing code enforcement in New Haven, Connecticut, and I worked for him and did ride-arounds with housing code inspectors. But I didn't have any clear idea of what to do for my dissertation. When I hit upon the idea of studying the wage-price freeze I had no perspective, I had no idea at all. In August 1971, I was just finishing my exams and was looking for a project. I saw a television news show in which President Nixon announced a nationwide wage-price freeze. It became immediately clear that no one in Washington had any idea how to answer the press's or the businesses' questions about what a "freeze" meant as applied to various issues. It was obvious to me that they had to create a whole new regulatory structure. I guess another part of my background was that Stan Wheeler (my primary teacher and advisor at Yale) had always been interested in legal rules, and here was a chance to watch the creation of a whole system of rules. They would have to elaborate a whole complex code to apply to thousands and thousands of different price and wage transactions. The wage-price freeze, a regulation of the business world, was just at the right intersection – it coincided with my real-world interests and my theoretical interests.

Question: How would you describe the approach that you took to researching that agency?

Kagan: Well, I sort of had to invent it as I went along. This was an unusual kind of a Ph.D. dissertation because I had no perspective. I had no plan. Instead of doing a pilot study and then formulating a project – coming back to the university and getting your question – my pilot study had to become the study itself because the regulatory program was a rapidly changing thing and it wasn't going to last more than three months. So I had to do it *then*. I went to Washington within two or three days. I first went to an oversight body created by the White House called the Cost of Living Council. Through a Yale law professor I had the name of someone and I tried to get in there. But there was a hectic quality to the whole thing. They were just opening up their offices, moving in desks, and trying to figure out what was going on and they just had no time to deal with me. So then I went to the Office of Emergency Preparedness (OEP), which had the job of implementing and enforcing the wage-price freeze. I had heard at the Cost of Living Council that the general counsel of OEP was a man named Elmer Bennett. I had encountered him a couple of years earlier when I was on a litigation matter; indeed, I had worked out of his office doing depositions of price fixers in Washington, D.C. I went to see him and I said I'd like to study this regulatory process. And he said, "Will you work here? I need lawyers." I didn't hesitate too long because it was clearly my "in." We had something to give each other and so I said yes. I just started doing whatever needed to be done.

Question: There's often great difficulty in getting access to high-level agencies. Why do you think he granted you access?

Kagan: Well, I don't think he found the project very threatening. He was a very experienced Washington lawyer. He had been in and out of government and had a certain self-confidence, I suppose. He saw me as an asset with not much risk. In general, I think gaining access is often not quite so difficult as you think it's going to be. I always think of it like dating. First you have to ask, and you need a line. You need a way of saying what you're doing that catches the interest of people in the organization you want to study. You do need to emphasise what you think is important about what your subjects are doing. That appeals to their sense of purpose – or vanity. It takes a little bit of a courtship, and you often have to lose some prospects before you find a subject that will agree to talk to you at length.

Question: Had you approached the Office of Emergency Preparedness with a different sense of the research techniques that you would use?

Kagan: No, I figured that I would just have to adapt to the situation. It was like I was an anthropologist going to some village. You can't be too fixed in advance as to what you're going to do until you find out whether they're warlike or not. I suppose I had thought it was going to be more interview-based but I'm sure it was in the back of my mind to do the participant part. The minute actually working in the agency was mentioned I thought, "This should be good." I just thought that "doing" would be a good way of learning. I make it sound easy but it really wasn't too difficult. You just do it. Of course, at the beginning it was an emotional experience. I plunged into depression when I couldn't get into one agency and then excited as could be when I thought I'd caught a fish. And then plunged into depression again when the agency and the research task seemed to be overwhelming and I didn't know where I would fit in! But in time those emotional ups and downs stabilized. I found my way and saw what my role was as the tasks I and others had to do in OEP became more self-evident in an organization that was growing day by day because it borrowed personnel from other agencies.

Question: How difficult was it, when you were actually in the field and working as an attorney, to shift between observer and participant mentalities?

Kagan: I don't think I found it very hard, although this may be a matter of personality. Whenever I was working on something for OEP I knew what my basic purpose was in being there. I didn't want a career there and so it was always a part of my mind, while I was working on a regulatory issue, that was interrogating, you might say, what I was doing. The going back and forth was not so difficult. Doing the work was compelling. Originally, it entailed responding to written inquiries from businesses, employers, labor unions, et cetera about whether they could increase a price or a rent or a salary, for example, if there was a pre-freeze contract that called for an increase on a date that fell during the freeze. It was real. These were real people asking real questions about whether they could raise their prices if their costs had gone up,

29

and it's going to affect whether someone gets a salary increase. So there was a professional obligation to work hard at that. And that worked in terms of my research goals. The more I did it, the more I could see that working on particular cases brought knowledge because it would bring about new experiences or arguments with other lawyers in the office. The more I was engaged, the more likely I would be drawn into a dispute with another agency lawyer about how a business firm's or an employee's inquiry should be decided under the developing body of regulatory rules. We would go into the office of the deputy general counsel and discuss it. Then I would get to know *him* and what he did and how he interpreted the rules. Often we then would go into the general counsel's office and get his views. Each additional task I would have to do – such as interacting with officials in other offices – would bring more knowledge about the agency's evolving structure, routines, modes of thought and hierarchies, the pressures it faced, its confusions.

Question: It seems that as the three months progressed you were getting increasing responsibility in the OEP. I wonder whether your research would have been as successful if you hadn't been such a good lawyer.

Kagan: I don't even know that I was a good lawyer, but the research would not have been as good had I not steadily gained more responsibility in OEP. I wouldn't have learned as much. The work would have been a little bit more repetitive. Often, particular cases would make it clear that the rule that ostensibly applied to that case would produce a foolish result, or it was a case in which you couldn't find a rule at all because the whole system of rules was still evolving. I got the job of formulating issue papers about such "hard cases" and later to take those issue papers to an executive committee that would formulate additional rules, exceptions, definitions, and so on. That was good because I would meet other people at a high level of the agency, interact with my counterparts in other offices, get sent on particular missions that illuminated how people outside of the agency viewed the freeze regime. I don't remember how I got the job of dealing with hard cases. The General Counsel must have recognized that I could do it and so I think being good at the lawyering probably did help.

Question: Work at the OEP comes across as being busy and hectic. Could you say a little about the process of dealing with your notes and your recollections in terms of translating that into data that could be analyzed?

Kagan: It was pretty simple. I would carry a little notebook and whenever I had a minute outside of a task or a meeting, I would find myself a corner of a men's room, or a hallway, and write notes – often catch lines that would help me remember a recent conversation, a case, a debate, a quotation. Those notes became the basis for my elaborated field notes when I went back at the end of the day to a room I was living in (in my wife's cousin's house in Washington). These little telegraphic notes to myself, often quotes, would bring back the reality of an observation or experience when I would try to reconstruct it on the typewriter in the evening. That "typewriter time" was extremely valuable because that was when I could pause and not only record what happened but interrogate it, ask questions about why things happened: "Why did he say that?" "Why is it so rushed?" "Why did *I* feel that way at the time?" And new questions would then emerge based on that evening thought process. I'd have a little list of questions that I would go back to the agency with and pursue more systematically. I would do a lot of little interviews, sort of opportunistically, in the hallway or on the way to lunch, based on that little list.

What became interesting to me were the unstated norms about how questions of rule application were to be decided – the assumptions that everyone in the agency had. I came to the realization that, to apply rules to cases, bureaucrats rely on what later came to be called an interpretative community. I saw this happening before I'd ever heard this term. So I was discovering this interpretative community, how it operated and how controversies about legal decision making got settled, through a hierarchy involving the more authoritative and less authoritative people within the office. I could then write down such a perception and then ask people explicitly or semiexplicitly about it. I could validate it by being alert to look for it in the succeeding days to see if it was a one-time event or a recurring event.

Question: How long would you spend after the end of a working day, typing field notes and so forth?

Kagan: It was gruelling. It always took an hour and a half to two hours, starting about 9 or 10 at night. I got a little faster at it as I went along because less was completely new. My focus became better. At the beginning I didn't know quite as much about what I was looking for, so everything seemed to be of interest. But gradually, I can't now remember when, I began to develop a typology of legal decision modes, or styles of rule application – many decisions were legalistic. The officials applied a rule literally, without thinking about or caring about the fairness or economic impact of the consequences. But just as often, OEP lawyers and bureaucrats were more sensitive to the consequences; they were moved to make more creative interpretations of the rules. Sometimes they simply made an exception on their own, or they took it to the general counsel and argued that a new rule should be made, to formalize that exception. And finally, some decision makers simply focused on moving through the backlog of cases as fast as possible. They gave noncommittal responses to inquiries or wrote routinized responses that made no sense either in terms of the rules or of policy goals.

So my observations tended to focus, as much as I could, on the reasons for these different patterns. What triggered them? I looked for what made the inquirer's situation or plight more vivid to the bureaucrat – like presenting the facts in more detail, or when a well-connected regulated entity – like the Girl Scouts of America – got to make their case in person. I also started comparing different offices in OEP in how they handled cases. I noticed how the pressure for rapid responses affected decisions.

So my note taking often focused on debates about particular cases that evoked disputes or "appeals" to the general counsel himself or to the Director of OEP, an Army General – I got to see these because I often was asked to work on the hard cases, and I never said no. My field notes came to include a lot of story telling. And I would use the stories to analyze the positions taken by the regulated party and the different officials and lawyers in OEP. Ultimately, I used a lot of these "diagnostic stories" in the dissertation and the book to illustrate different modes of rule application and their organizational and normative causes. I remember really enjoying writing up the case stories. They were a bit dramatic. They involved memorable quotes and characters. And they involved wrenching normative tensions. On one side the agency felt its primary mission was to hold the line on inflation. And officials and lawyers felt the whole enterprise, its legitimacy, depended on applying – and being seen to apply – the rules uniformly. On the other side were the pleas for justice by businesses and employees. Many of them were really being harmed economically by the freeze – businesses that performed important social functions. And that of course was the problem of "legalism" that really is the heart of *Regulatory Justice* – the way in which doing justice by following the rules can result in substantive injustice. I guess for my own psychological reasons, that dilemma has always gripped me.

So more and more, my field notes started to look like real writing, gruelling but more exciting. I probably used the last month of field notes in writing the dissertation a lot more fully than the first weeks – although those initial impressions, like the anthropologist's first impressions of a new community, also had some useful nuggets.

Question: To what extent did the fieldwork make emotional demands on you?

Kagan: Oh, very much, because when you are in the middle of it and you do the agency work, and typing up the notes, and you're just piling up all this data, you don't know whether it has a coherent intellectual story. You have glimpses of it – at least that was my experience. The more you know what you're doing the less emotional it becomes, I suppose. In my case I sort of had a certain faith that it was interesting, but sometimes my heart would plunge. Even when I was in the early stages of writing it up, I felt I didn't have a complete handle and so that was disturbing.

Another emotional thing: I took a few weekends off, and when I was back in New Haven or with family, I felt sort of disconnected. The experience in Washington was so intense, it seemed so important because I was making decisions that affected peoples' fates. But my family and acquaintances didn't get it. They talked about ordinary things. I felt a bit disconnected from them, their pale reality. And that was disturbing. It's an element of "Potomac Fever," I think, the thrill of being close to or exercising power, having big responsibilities. And it was a very useful corrective for me to get away from it, to see it from the outside.

Question: After you had left the field, what was your process for using the data, reflecting on it, and beginning to write up?

Kagan: That is a hard question. The first problem I had was deciding what the questions were because my questions were not clear when I went into the field. When I started fieldwork I think my primary thought was that I would like to understand the building of a body of rules. A body of law had to be created. How does that happen, what are the internal cognitive dynamics of it, and what are the political factors that shape it? The first part of my book is about that. But fieldwork drew me into the process of deciding cases. It became clear to me that the study was about what people do when they say that they're applying rules to cases or when they have difficulty doing that. So I really had to formulate that question. But ultimately the first part of the book, the building of the regulatory system, was a less clear question. The second part was a clearer question. So I ended up struggling more with doing the first part of the dissertation. I had to start reading and there was a dialogue between reading and organizing the notes. I talked a lot to my advisor, Stan Wheeler, who was good at helping me get at what were the questions that really drove me. He would sit and listen to the detail and help me come up with the questions. And once the questions became clearer then my mental categories from the literature, particularly about devising the structuring of regulatory agencies, became clearer.

Then I went through the typed notes and coded. I allocated my specific stories and observations to different questions and subquestions, chapters and subchapters, in my emerging outline. I wrote a long discursive outline. I also hit upon the idea of going back to Washington and studying the files, doing a more systematic sample of cases. That was interesting. The arguments that people would make to the freeze agencies in their letters were, "Oh you can't do this, that's not fair!" The language of fairness was in every letter. But it also seemed to me that people meant different things by "fair." Or they would use the word "unjust" but people meant different things by it. I also had been alert to how officials in the agency used "justice" in arguments with each other when they thought they could win an argument by making a justice claim. So I became interested in reading about justice and I started reading a little bit of philosophy. That gave me some idea about one thing I could look for more systematically in the files, to classify the nature of claims people made. But I also had some hypotheses to test, based on my notes. I went back to Washington and used a systematic sample of cases to test some hypotheses about differences between face-to-face and written arguments, or the difference between elaborately constructed arguments and brief, less sophisticated arguments, and how those differences affected the amount of attention a case got, and the outcome.

Question: How long did it take for you to see your thesis emerging?

Kagan: It took a while. After the first three-month wage-price freeze, I had worked for the Price Commission (the successor agency to OEP) for two or three months – through March 1972 or so. By September, Stan Wheeler had encouraged me to give a talk to the Yale law faculty. Even then, I felt like I didn't know what I was doing at all. I could tell interesting stories but it was clear to me I didn't have a strong set of conclusions or punch lines. In fact when I went on the job market that fall I had an interview at Berkeley's Political Science Department. I think if someone came to our department now and gave the job talk I gave then, I don't think I would hire me! It was still too discursive. I didn't know how to put all the different pieces together. So I think it probably took another year before all the writing started to cohere. I did get the job at Berkeley, but I didn't go there the next fall – September 1973 – postponing my move for a year, mostly for family reasons. For the 1973–1974 academic year, I got a job with Stan Wheeler and Lawrence Friedman working on the history of state supreme courts, devising a coding scheme and overseeing the coding of thousands of cases. I could work on that while writing the last draft of my dissertation. I had a lot of paper by the fall of 1973 but it was not until the day that I got in the car and drove off to California in August 1974 that I got the final version typed up – there was no word processing then, and absolutely no typing mistakes were allowed – and sent it in. So, writing did take a while because I wasn't clear on what I was looking for in the beginning. That's the trade-off of doing that kind of fieldwork-based study. The benefit was that by plunging in and keeping alert to what I found interesting I was able to get at something that was ultimately interesting; but at the writing stage it was harder to pull the themes from all the noise and richness in the data, and to see the main theoretical story through the welter of conflicting observations.

Question: In what ways was writing the book different from writing the Ph.D. dissertation?

Kagan: Oh, it was much easier. I wasn't too unhappy with the Ph.D. dissertation. I was clear about how much change I wanted to make for the book. And I had also taught constitutional law for a year and some-how I feel that that helped me write better about the jurisprudential aspects of the sociology of legal decision making.

Question: To what extent was it a help or a hindrance to be writing the book a few years after you had finished?

Kagan: I think it was a help. I've often told this to graduate students who have just breathlessly, finally, reached the end of their Ph.D. dissertation and gone off to a job. I tell them not to look at it for a year, just to get through the year of teaching. They will find what it is in their dissertation that they most want to tell people about. Or they'll see more clearly where it fits into the literature or the misunderstandings that they think are out there that they can correct. And that will help crystallize the book.

Question: What would you say were the most challenging aspects of the project?

Kagan: I think the key intellectual demand was to be able to reflect and write up my notes at the end of each day after working at the agency. What made it hard, aside from being exhausted, was that I was isolated from academic colleagues. If I had been coming home to a roommate who was a sociologist of law, or I had a faculty member in an office around the corner who I could meet with every few days and talk to, I would be getting that outside perspective. I didn't have that and it made it more difficult. And so I think the key for effective field research is to stay in touch often with fellow students and faculty. Write memos, send your advisors little memos about what you think you're finding, because maintaining an objective and detached perspective is the most challenging part of it.

Question: You approached the work of the Office of Emergency Preparedness as a lawyer but many people approach the study of regulatory agencies as sociologists or political scientists without a law degree. Are there lessons about how you would formulate that project without having a legal background?

Kagan: I think my legal background was my ticket through the door, but it wasn't necessary to do the research. A lot of people who worked in the freeze agencies and answered public inquiries weren't lawyers. They learned how to do it. The world is full of bureaucrats who have no legal training but who work with legal rules all the time. They learn the culture of rule application or rule interpretation in their agency. So I don't think it's a barrier not to have a law degree. It gave me more self-confidence and it certainly got me in the door. A law degree gives people more *confidence* in approaching legal materials at the beginning, that's all.

Question: One of the most interesting features of the book is the hypothetical dialogue in Chapter 10, where you imagine an exchange between a client and the agency. How did you go about writing that? How confident were you that your answers were truly speaking for the agency?

Kagan: That was not in the dissertation. I had a lot of confidence about what the people in the agency thought and how they justified what they did. I thought it would be interesting to *challenge* that, intellectually, normatively. That was my ultimate step outside the agency. The dialogue is basically not empirical. It's a reflection on the tension between legal predictability and legal flexibility, law and equity, national policy goals and the costs imposed on particular individuals. The dialogue addresses the "rule-utilitarian" problem – where you're maximising utility by applying a rule even if it's not ideal or fair or desirable for each particular situation. In a sense, that was my dialogue with legalism, wasn't it?

Question: When reading *Regulatory Justice* a reader might read into it a glimpse of your subsequent agenda on adversarial legalism, in part because you were interrogating yourself about legalism. You sometimes found yourself emotionally drawn to the rules, at other times to the situations of the clients. Did you feel that you were formulating your own views on the American legal system, around legalism, and your agenda for the future?

Kagan: I think while working at OEP, helping to decide cases and then questioning myself at night, I became conscious of the powerful effect that accepted understandings and rules have on people and how that can be blinding. I think that became part of my understanding of the legal world. But I wasn't totally preoccupied with that because I also saw the opposite. I saw people sometimes disregarding the rules. I saw rules being reformulated. I saw legal decision makers being paralysed by indecision, when they didn't have enough time or information. So I saw legalism as a variable phenomenon. While I was working on *Regulatory Justice* I didn't plan the next book. When I started working subsequently on regulatory enforcement I think I saw legalism as one possibility, but I was also interested in what made regulation effective. I think it was only in the course of doing the field research on regulatory inspections and compliance that Gene Bardach and I ended up highlighting "legalism" as a core aspect of "the problem of regulatory unreasonableness" – which is the subtitle of our *Going by the Book*. The idea of "adversarial legalism" is really rather different – it's an effort to encapsulate what makes the American legal system distinctive, as compared with the legal systems of other democracies. It uses "legalism" in a different sense – not to describe the rigid application of rules to individual cases, but to describe a whole way of structuring legal institutions and the use of

37

litigation in policy implementation. I barely refer to *Regulatory Justice* in *Adversarial Legalism*. But I have started using *Regulatory Justice* more recently in my teaching and writing, as I seem to be coming back to the problem of justice at the front lines of large bureaucratic decision systems.

CHAPTER 4

MALCOLM FEELEY AND *THE PROCESS IS THE PUNISHMENT**

Court systems can be an imposing maze. They are institutions meant to communicate the weight of public authority, but they contain all the frailties of the humans who inhabit them. Courts speak of the enduring principles of law and justice, yet they hide deep corners of discretion. Some version of "court" is found everywhere students of law look, but the global ubiquity of courts belies the need to understand the local, contingent, and contextual. For Law and Society scholars, "the court" – not just the room, but the organization that supports it – has been an essential unit of analysis. To understand its significance has required getting inside the maze to chart its work, its people, its norms, and its impact. How can a scholar comprehend how the court works "in action"?

One of the most enduring attempts to understand a court organization, Malcolm Feeley's in-depth look at a New Haven, Connecticut, court, began down the road in New York City. The groundwork was being laid for a three-city comparative study with two collaborators, the aim of which was to examine Boston, New York City, and Philadelphia. It was an exciting time – in the shadow of Watergate and political trials in the big cities. Indeed, too exciting: prosecutors and judges were hostile and sceptical to researchers, who might as well have been one of the new breed of journalists seeking to expose corruption. Trying to get access to prosecutors' files to construct a portrait of their work – even a quantitative one presenting aggregate data – went nowhere.

In the meantime, by way of a postdoctoral fellowship, Feeley went to Yale, which was rich with mentors in the social scientific study of law and connections to a much more intimate court system – the one right down the street. Still, Feeley begins by talking about the great problem of gaining access.

Methodological Keywords: qualitative research, quantitative research, participant observation, interviews

**The Process Is the Punishment: Handling Cases in a Lower Criminal Court* (New York: Russell Sage Foundation, 1979 and 1992).

Feeley: The idea of a three-city study didn't disappear, it just dribbled away. Once I got to New Haven I reoriented myself. It is small city and you can wrap your hands around it, meet the key people right away. Also, the courthouse was just a few blocks away from the campus. Apart from heavyweights in the law school who were willing to help me, a young lawyer – Jonathan Silbert – who had just been hired on one of the programs at Yale, and who was also a criminal defence lawyer, took an interest in my project. He walked me around and introduced me to the judges, prosecutors, and public defenders, and convinced them I didn't have horns. That helped a lot. (I've stayed in touch with Jon; he is now a judge in that same court.)

Still, I couldn't get the access I needed to the court's ostensibly public records. Some of the judges and clerks thought that a researcher was an investigative reporter – someone keen on coming in and finding dirt. There was plenty to be embarrassed about, no-show jobs and the like, but I kept telling them I was not interested in the extraordinary, just the boring, routine ordinary. Even then, I beat my head against a brick wall. I was very careful not to do what I had inadvertently done in New York: I never quite asked a question where I'd get a definite "no." In New York I had gone in and just been straight with them and they said "no." Once I had this answer, I learned, it was virtually impossible to get a "no" turned to a "yes." So I never quite framed my inquiry so directly. I just asked, "How would you go about it?" and "What would be needed to learn about this?" – so that I never got a "no."

However, during this time I was invited to regularly attend meetings of the New Haven pretrial diversion program advisory board. This meant that I was sitting around with prosecutors rather than being stiff-armed by their secretaries. I figured, once I was in the door I'd get something. And I did. Pretrial diversion is a program that you can go to and prosecution is suspended during that period. If you successfully complete the program, the prosecutor will usually drop the charges. It's a way to avoid a conviction and/or a record, and a sentence. Theoretically it's an attractive alternative. However, the New Haven program was not running anywhere near full force – only to about fifty to sixty percent capacity. At the meetings, the director was constantly complaining that the prosecutor was imposing too many criteria, so that too few people were eligible. The prosecutor said, "I'm not going to let in really serious, violent people charged with serious violent offences," but went on to claim that he was very generous and that there were plenty of arrestees who were eligible for the program. I saw my opportunity. I said, "You guys can argue about this all day long, but it's a simple question to answer. All you need to do is take a random sample of the arrests that come in, look at the characteristics of the people that are arrested and see what proportion are eligible and what proportion are not." Their response: "Gee, that's a good idea." The program ended up paying me over the summer to provide this information, and incidentally to allow me to collect the sort of data I'd been anxious to collect for a long time.

Since then, I've urged students, however theoretical and nonpractical their own concerns are, to nevertheless get their hands dirty and work with agencies and courts. Among other things, it's a way to gain access; it's a way to sit down and talk with the personnel over coffee, to be colleagues with them rather than strangers who come in to look over their shoulders, and to ask a few questions. Even if you never do any research, there's real value in taking jobs with public agencies – summer jobs or whatever it is. You'll be a fly on the wall and learn a lot.

Question: You mentioned here and in the book that the project began as a quantitative study, but in the end that became a very limited portion of the book. How did you change your enquiry in the course of the research?

Feeley: To do a quantitative analysis that comes up with a variety of factors that accounts for variation in outcomes, one has to have "clean" outcomes. I quickly discovered, when coding my data, that there are a vast number of cases that don't have clean outcomes. A person is arrested and the first question is, what accounts for the case being dropped or not dropped? Is it social class? Sex? Age? Seriousness of the offence? Or is it because the police officer did a bad job making the case? The fact of the matter is there are lots of cases that are dropped because officials learn that there are seven warrants out for this guy. So they may drop the particular charge and press on the others. Or they may consolidate the charges. As a consequence, it is difficult to read too much into the outcome "case dropped." The same thing can happen with sentencing. A defendant might receive a seemingly lenient sentence, and one might look to the socioeconomic status of the defendant for an explanation. But in fact it might be that there was a plea deal and lenient sentence in New Haven in order to facilitate a resolution of a much more serious charge and much stiffer sentence in Bridgeport. There are so many variations and permutations and possibilities that it's bewildering. It was very hard simply to code a case as it progressed through the system. At some point along the line I realized the quantitative analysis was good for providing a map to a process that had all sorts of feedback loops, but that it wasn't so good for a multivariate analysis of outcomes.

As I struggled to code the cases, I started thinking of a descriptive analysis to supplement the quantitative analysis that I'd originally planned to do. I was aided in this process by colleagues at Yale. One of them, another postdoc with me, was Jack Katz, who is now the dean of American ethnographers. We talked through things. He was a good person to bounce things off, and he kept pointing out interesting things I had said. He sharpened my vision and in the process I shifted my emphasis somewhat. There were others – Stan Wheeler and Bob Kagan in particular. I was fortunate to be there at that time, with so many smart people. We lunched together and talked all the time.

Question: Had you drawn up a clearly defined plan of how long you'd be in the field observing the courts?

Feeley: When I went to New Haven, I had my research design. I had a detailed code sheet and was planning to get access to court files to collect my data. I had planned to do only a little observation. I was going to have one chapter accounting for variation in whose case goes forward and whose is dropped. Almost all of the discussion of criminal courts focuses on plea bargaining, and I thought it missed a lot since figures regularly show that about half of all cases are dropped outright. This evidence was in front of the researchers, but no one had explored it in any systematic way. That is, about half to sixty percent of all arrests are dropped outright, with no plea bargain even. I was reacting to Abraham Blumberg's immensely influential article (and later his book) about the practice of law as a confidence game, where he talks about plea bargaining. Blumberg's own data challenge his argument in a central way since they reveal that half of all cases are dropped outright, but he didn't comment on this at all. I wanted to look at this outcome. That was one of my big things and indeed that's where the title comes from. Dropping the cases is a significant decision in the process. Often it's not because the evidence is weak but because the arrest and initial sanctioning has served the social purpose – what people think is reasonable for the particular incident, such as stopping a fight or curbing some unruliness. So, I had a plan to explore each of the major outcomes – drop cases or go forward; adjudication of guilt and plea bargaining; and sentencing (short vs. long) – and try to account for them in a multivariate analysis that considered a host of legal and extralegal factors. Once I found that the seemingly separate stages were in fact not so separate in such a large portion of all my cases, I modified my plan. I didn't abandon it, and indeed the book has some interesting multivariate analysis in it. But I did realize that I had to explore the convoluted process that shapes so many of the outcomes in the cases. This led me to modify if not abandon my initial plan and it led me to spend much more time in the field than I had ever imagined I would.

Question: Among the choices you made in structuring the project, given the split court system in New Haven, was simply to study the lower court, though you had set off to look at both parts of the system.

Feeley: That was largely a practical and pragmatic decision. At the time the two courts were in separate buildings and each had a dynamic all of its own, although the lower court handled arraignments for virtually all criminal cases, everything from mass murderer to trespass. It would then send the felony cases over to superior court. I just got fascinated with this one little court as a system because it seemed to be pretty much self-contained; it was the system designed to dispose of cases internally. It made sense to look at it as a unit. In fact, I finally did get access to the superior court and collected data on a random sample of cases, but I never did analyze it. I still have the tape somewhere in one of my closets, I'm sure, but I had my hands full looking at this court. Had I ever done the other superior court, I would have done that as a unit by itself. In it I would have pointed out that the superior court judges wouldn't eat lunch with the district court judges. It just made sense to look at the lower court all by itself. Incidentally, about the time I was done with my data collection, the two courts were merged into a single court. The merger had been foisted on them by the legislators and while they then were in the same courthouse, it was different floors and the judges still didn't eat with each other.

Question: How did you structure your day, and actually do your field-work, to observe the wide variety of people in this somewhat closed system?

Feeley: I was really fortunate, in that I knew I was going to be in New Haven for an extended period of time and I could just bounce back and forth from court to my office. During that one summer of data collection in the records I was down there all the time, and at the same time I started sitting in to observe proceedings. In short order, I became a fixture there. Particularly when there were hearings rather than trials and I would be the only person sitting in the gallery. Often the judge called me up and asked me what I was doing taking notes, being a little irritated and then relieved that I wasn't a reporter for the *New York Times* or the *New Haven Register*. Then often, grabbing me by the shoulders, they would say, "Come on with me, I've got to show you something." These guys had great, great suspicions of Yale, Yale-trained lawyers, and Yale students. I don't know that I did anything to develop trust but I kept coming back again and again, asking questions, and maybe it was because there wasn't any stuff appearing in the newspapers that they got a sense that I was not out to do a number on them. So, they came to trust me and confide in me.

One of the things that really comes through in this book, or at least I wanted to come through, is that these officials bring moral meaning to their work. These guys thought they were doing good and lots of times they *were* doing good. But even if in my judgment they weren't doing good quite the way I would like it, they usually thought they were doing the right thing. Everyone I met brought moral meaning to their work. So many participant observation studies convey a cynical attitude without real evidence to justify that cynicism. It's hardly surprising that if someone works for thirty years in a particular job, particularly a professional job or jobs of choice, they seek to bring moral meaning to their work. And so, once you took these guys seriously, they would talk your ear off and I had no reason to believe that they were lying. I think they appreciated my questions. My questions weren't such that they required closed answers, and I was around long enough to listen to them elaborate. I'd come back and talk to them again the next day and the next day. I just started out by taking notes and then pretty soon they knew who I was, and then they'd come up voluntarily to say, "there's something really interesting going up on the second floor" or something. That's what eventually led me to be able to go in and sit in on the plea bargaining sessions, in what was at one point called Mancini's Bargain Basement, after Judge Mancini, the presiding judge at the time. They would get all these cases that had been lingering and then they'd try to work through them. The prosecutors lined up, sitting on one side of this big judge's chambers, the defence attorneys on the other, going through the cases saying "Can we get rid of this?" and "What's going on here?" and disposing of a lot of cases this way.

Question: Did that put you in a position of having the confidence of judges and defence counsel and prosecutors and court personnel, where you had to be careful because you heard all sides of court politics?

Feeley: In these cases it never presented a big problem. There were never cases where there were elaborate defences planned, where deep confidences could be jeopardized. That said, I can't remember a prosecutor sitting down and talking to me at great length in the cafeteria or someplace with a defence attorney near to us. The three of us *did* sit down to discuss various things, such as the role of bail bondsmen, and then they'd start arguing. I loved to get people arguing with one another, in order to see what was going on.

Question: You did at some point sit them down for more formal interviews. What was your strategy for the appropriate time to do that and what were you seeking to get from a more formal interview that you couldn't get from these very informal contacts?

Feeley: Often I would get people to explain things to me when I was around, more informally when I was hanging around I'd be watching the process and then I'd ask, "Why did you do that?" or "Why did the judge do that?" Other times I just wanted to sit down and ask more systematically about what they were thinking, what were their strategies, and how they were organized.

Although I learned to distrust the abstract statements people made. Let me give you an example. I would ask judges about their philosophy of sentencing. I read everything that I could find on criminal courts and I had a whole list of propositions that I wanted to test out, and some of them had to do with judges. Some argued that judges had different sentencing styles that were related to their personalities. I wanted to ask judges about their sentencing styles and philosophies, but quickly became suspicious of abstract question and abstract answers. I remember asking a number of judges, with more or less the same results, "How do you go about sentencing?" "Well," they'd say, "I look at the record, I read the probation officer's pre-sentence report, and I listen to the defence attorney and prosecutor," whose views have often been reflected in the pretrial sentence report. At times they would go on and on in this vein, giving me long, elaborate descriptions of what they did. After a while, I learned to say, "OK, now tell me how you sentence in the ninety percent of the cases where there is no pre-sentence report." These reports are only written for the more serious cases. The more

45

serious cases were few and far between, but were more interesting so the judges would generalize and treat them as the rule rather than the rare exception. This was a good lesson that taught me to ask about concrete cases and situations.

At times I listen to my colleagues talking about their teaching and I realize they're talking about their one of their favourite lectures or the one really terrific student in the class, and not the ordinary and routine. Psychologists tell us all the time that our map of what we do is colored by the more problematic things that make it rather than the boring, ordinary routine. At any rate, as I hung around the courthouse, I became suspicious about the abstract things people would say. That's why I liked to hang around the court and to asked people to comment on things they were doing or had just done – explain particular actions.

Question: After you committed to understanding the process qualitatively, how did you assess your progress and how did you know when it was coming to a conclusion?

Feeley: I mixed notes of observation and notes of question-and-answer because I'd be doing both within the same hour period. I'd sit and watch for a while and then during a break talk to somebody who had been in the courtroom. I had the advantage of just looking through my notes, finding something a little problematic, then going back to watch that same sort of process more, and then ask more questions. I just didn't dive into the field, do all my research and collect all my data and all my notes, have my data to analyze, and write them up. It was an interactive process that I found extraordinarily useful. I had the luxury of an extended postdoc and a site that was close by. I guess I knew to stop when I kept hearing the same thing over and over again and wasn't learning anything new.

You know, there were still probably areas where I could have learned something new. I have a preface in the paperback where I note something that I wish I had thought about more systematically when I was doing my research. Years later, I realized I had not spent enough time thinking about and talking to the police. I treated the court decisions as decisions of that internal work group, as it were, and I'm convinced that I missed something important – subtle signals given by the arresting officers as to what to do with their cases. I suspect that in a lot of cases the prosecutor, judge, or defence attorney – or all of them – were taking their cues from a variety of informal ways in which police officers were saying "this is a really bad guy, go after him," or that "the problem was solved with the arrest, so I don't care what you do with this case." Now, I did see such communications occasionally in the more salient issues when the police officers made a big deal about them – say when there was a genuine assault on an officer or a serious effort to resist arrest. But I didn't look at the flipside, that is, how often the police said, "Look, the problem was really solved with the arrest because I pulled the two guys apart that were fighting, and so who cares what happens to the case." I don't know what I missed because I never did see it, but certainly that was a set of questions that I should have probed and didn't. It was only a number of years later that I realized that I had missed it. Mark Lazerson and I wrote a pretty good article on police–prosecutor relations, but it was long on theory and short on data.

Question: With the luxury of being able to interpret and write while still collecting data, how did the book take shape? Books don't always get written in the way that we read them.

Feeley: You know, I started out as an orthodox positivist and I still think I am a positivist. This book is certainly not antiquantitative. As I pointed out, the reason I didn't follow through with my quantitative analysis and make such a big deal of it was simply because it was too messy. (I remember one review of the book took this as a tirade against quantitative analysis. I think the reviewer got it wrong.) Going in with an orthodox study, there was going to be one chapter on the decision to drop charges, another on the decision to adjudicate guilt – that is, a study of plea bargaining – and then a chapter on sentences. It took me some time slowly to work away from this framework as I confronted these data. I kept expecting to organize my chapters this way, and then supplement the quantitative study with qualitative, participant observation material. Participant observation is addictive; I kept going back. And somewhere along the line I slowly started to reconceive the organization of the book. It took a long time, since the three core chapters had been conceived at the outset and it did not dawn on me that I could get rid of them and reorganize the book. But the addictive feature of observation slowly led me to rethink my organization. Since, I've done work in archives and this work is also addictive. I'm drawn back again and again to such drawers of stuff that have not been read for decades in search of treasure. I keep thinking, "There's going to be something there if I just go through more boxes or more files." At any rate, it was the massive amount of notes from observations and discussions with the court officials that finally led me to realize that, if I was to draw on it, I had to reconceive the structure of my book. I started working through the analysis and I don't know if the quantitative analysis shrunk so much as the analysis of the process just kept expanding.

I had some epiphanies, you know, light bulbs going off over my head. One of them was when I realized that a lot of my analysis revolved around the pretrial costs. I started totting these costs up – the cost of the bail bonds, the time served, all the pretrial costs that come with the title. This came slowly, but I realized I had something really nifty when I was able to reorganize the book around the problem of petty offences and high process costs. The title only emerged after the manuscript was all done, however. I was going to call it *Substantive Justice and the Adjudicative Ideal*. But in a talk with Stanton Wheeler (a sociologist on the Yale Law School faculty and the mentor to us Russell Sage Foundation postdocs there), I kept struggling to explain what I wanted to do in one of my last chapters. At one point, I said, "I'm trying to say that no one is so concerned about the sentence because what's going on here is that the process is the punishment." He immediately said, "That's your title."

Question: Were you concerned that the identities of the various court personnel, lawyers, and judges would be identifiable to people in the New Haven courts, even though it's anonymous?

Feeley: That's interesting. My study took place just about the time that debate about human subjects was beginning in earnest in Washington. But there were then no rules that I knew of. I never premised any of my discussions with a promise of confidentiality. However, every now and again someone would ask for anonymity, and I did promise it. As I said, there were no Institutional Review Boards back then. I figured that I was studying a public institution, that anybody can go there, and that I was asking sophisticated people about their work and they knew when to ask for confidentiality. Still there just are not lots of names in the book anyway. How come? It wasn't due to concern with confidentiality. The basic reason that I didn't provide the names of many people I quote is that I didn't want to clutter up the manuscript with a long cast of characters who only entered occasionally. I still think that I was looking at general processes that are going to be found in any American court, and the underlying social logic. I didn't want to particularise it.

Question: Did you have any ambitions of seeing any change on the ground as a result of publication?

Feeley: Well, I had very low expectations about publications. I think people write and then send things out into a black hole; you know, it doesn't connect with anything, it just disappears. You're pleased even when someone complains since it shows that at least someone has read it. I tend to write for academics. I do have, at the end of the book, a little policy analysis where I compare New Haven with Sweden and its penal orders. Indeed, sometime later I went off to Sweden to look into the administration of penal orders. Some of my friends on the law faculty at Yale at the time complained I didn't emphasize enough all the unconstitutional practices that I describe, but I said, "I'm not coming in as a reformer, and I'm not imposing a standard on what I find." I said that if they wanted to pick up these concerns and run with them that was fine, but that this wasn't my objective. In fact, I thought that to emphasize them would distort the book.

CHAPTER 5

LAWRENCE FRIEDMAN AND
*THE ROOTS OF JUSTICE**

Legal history tends to have a distinctive identity within Law and Society – perhaps because of the different methodological training of historians compared to social scientists, or because of what Lawrence Friedman calls the "presentist" assumptions of scholars focused on the social and political concerns of today. Any perceived difference between the aims of legal historians from others in the field, however, should not obscure the sense that history fills the same vital role as comparative research: providing a "control group" that illuminates the enduring from the deviations and the universal from the extremes.

The Roots of Justice *certainly accomplishes that aim, allowing contemporary scholars of criminal justice to see in the courts of yesteryear – in Alameda County, California – the same "confusion," "circus," and "kaleidoscope" (p. 324) that we may recognize today. In particular, Friedman and his co-author, Robert Percival, achieve this view by recovering from the dusty archives a level of statistical detail that invites social scientists into concrete comparison. The meeting point for the old and the new is the set of larger questions and themes of the Law and Society tradition, which never lie far from the surface of the book.*

Such connections between legal history and the Law and Society tradition were embodied in the influential person of J. Willard Hurst (1910–1997), long-time professor of law at the University of Wisconsin. Hurst was an early proponent of interdisciplinarity among legal scholars and of seeing history as a way of understanding law as the "dependent variable" in a social context. Friedman, himself one of the preeminent legal historians, begins by speaking, as so many senior scholars do, about the importance of a model or mentor to a young scholar.

Methodological Keywords: archival research

* The Roots of Justice: Crime and Punishment in Alameda County, California, 1870–1910 (Chapel Hill: University of North Carolina Press, 1981).

Friedman: I was much influenced by Willard Hurst at the University of Wisconsin. He founded the study of legal history, really. I was always very interested in the social sciences and in the study of law from a non-formalistic point of view. I don't know whether it's personality, genetic flaw, or what, but I had hated law school and I particularly hated the fact that it was so thoughtlessly normative, that statements were made about this or that being the "better result" without any empirical grounding. The whole method of teaching and the vast bulk of the research struck me as essentially arrogant but mindless – a terrible combination! By contrast, Hurst was grounded in fact, in actual observation. He realised that theory had to be the handmaiden of research.

I was very attracted to Hurst's approach for two reasons. First, it struck me that he had a more promising and fruitful approach toward the study of law by grounding it in the social context. Second, the history part attracted me for reasons that were quite personal. I had made a few feeble attempts at doing contemporary research involving interviews. But the projects never got anywhere. I realised that I detested interviewing people. I fumbled and stumbled, and I was embarrassed and humiliated when people didn't want to see me, and so on. I thought, "Forget that! You can't interview the dead. How about archival research?" So I switched to history. Among other things, I decided to do a longitudinal study, between 1870 and 1970, of two courts. One was in Alameda County, home of Oakland and Berkeley, and the other, in San Benito County, a beautiful rural county to the south of San Francisco.

Oakland was an urban center, San Benito a rural area. I would drive down to Hollister, in San Benito, with a research assistant and we would look in the files there. And we would also go over to Alameda and look in the files there. We were just taking a sample of the cases and asking who won, who lost, what the cases were about, and so forth. My hypothesis was that they would be very different. But it turned out that the closer you got to the present, the less different they were and I thought that was awfully surprising. But one day, when having lunch in Hollister, I ordered a bagel. Now, I'm not going to compare that to the apple that fell on Newton, but I thought to myself, "A bagel in Hollister? When did the bagel come to Hollister?" And then suddenly I realized. Of course! It took an hour to drive there. You can be in San Jose, with a population of a million, in less than an hour from there. It wasn't really a rural county! They had television. Today they'd have the Internet. And so they also get bagels. There's no reason, nowadays, to expect dramatic differences between the two counties. So that was an "Aha!" moment for me. The point is that, when you do archival research, the ideas come afterwards, most of them anyway.

The truly amazing thing is that that study, published in 1975, was only the second-ever longitudinal study of trial court records. There had been one really odd work in the 1930s by someone who was stimulated by Hurst. It was a study of Chippewa County, Wisconsin – totally obscure and basically a study without any ideas in it, just, "Here's the data." Apart from this study, in all the thousands and thousands of pages of legal research, nobody had ever done a longitudinal court study.

Question: How did you move on to *The Roots of Justice* project?

Friedman: Having done that study of Alameda and San Benito Counties, which focused on civil cases, I decided to do something more elaborate. I decided to look at criminal cases and I had a stroke of fantastic luck. I discovered a first-year law student named Robert V. Percival, who is my co-author on *The Roots of Justice*. Aside from being a wonderful person, he was unbelievably good in every regard as a researcher. He was fantastic and that was a very happy collaboration; he really deserves a lot of the credit for the book.

The basic idea behind it was utter simplicity. The problem with 99% of so-called legal research is its absence of simplicity. Somebody thinks they're going to solve the problem of "What is justice?" or some other highfalutin' idea. Of course they fail and in the process they write a hundred pages of hot air. All the things I've tried to do have been much more modest and I think I succeed sometimes because I don't bite off more than I can chew or that a human being can chew. In *The Roots of Justice* what we wanted to do was to construct a picture of the criminal justice system in one place at one particular point in time. The place we chose was Alameda County. Why? Because we were in the Bay Area. Why not the far more interesting county of San Francisco? Because its records were destroyed utterly in 1906 by the earthquake and fire. They don't exist and, although it is right across the bay, Oakland suffered far less from the great earthquake. In fact, lots of refugees fled across the bay to Oakland. The records in Oakland were intact. They were just sitting in a basement.

Question: To what extent was your historical enquiry founded on hypotheses?

Friedman: When you do archival research, unlike the hard sciences, you don't need as much of an apparatus of theory in a hypothesis. You can compare it to archaeology. Archaeologists know that underneath this mound there's something there. Maybe they think this might be where some particular ancient kings have their tombs, but they're not sure and they don't sit down and formulate elaborate hypotheses. They just say, "Well, we've got to dig there and see what we find." I think a lot of archival research has to be the same. You are very sophisticated archaeologists. You don't go in there totally mindless but you have to say, "Well, let's see what's there. We might be surprised."

Basically, *The Roots of Justice* was a pure digging up of a buried city. That was nothing amounting to a formal, scientific hypothesis. We had the general Law and Society framework, and certain ideas and expectations. We were curious to see how the system would treat the Chinese, for example. There were ideas that I had already formed, pretty obvious ideas – for example, that at the different levels, the police court, the superior court, things would be handled very differently, that there would be a different kind of process, a different attitude and that the more serious the case the more it would conform to notions of due process. I wasn't prepared, for example, to find plea bargaining, which we did find. That was a surprise. What makes historical research exciting is precisely the element of surprise. You have to be ready to be surprised. I guess that sounds naive but I think a certain amount of naivity is very useful from time to time.

Question: To what extent did you frame *The Roots of Justice* project in the light of contemporary intellectual concerns within the Law and Society movement?

Friedman: Obviously the questions you ask are determined by contemporary issues. But if you start out saying I'm going to find race and gender prejudice, well of course you are going to find that. And if that's what you're looking for I think you might be making a mistake. Although it's impossible to do it 100%, you have to approach the past in its own terms. You have to be prepared to be surprised. I can imagine the postmodernists sneering and giggling at this point, but you really have to try to have an open mind. You can never produce a perfect vacuum. If you were to clean a room you could never clean it completely, but everyone knows the difference between the clean room and the dirty room. There is such a thing as a fact. So-and-so was born in such-and-such a year on such-and-such a date. Now that's a fact. It's not a social construction. Society may have constructed the whole concept of birthday in the sense of something you celebrate or its importance but there's an underlying reality. The overarching Law and Society notion is that the legal system is embedded in society and determined by society and that colors my approach. We could have gone into these files and said, "What does this tell us about legal doctrine?" But that didn't interest us in the slightest. Of course we had to be aware of it because there are rules of procedure that courts follow or don't follow and that is interesting to find out. But we weren't interested so much in the doctrine as in how a criminal justice system operated at that period in that kind of society. So it was a total Law and Society project.

Question: How did you begin the archival work?

Friedman: We just went down into that basement and started looking at records. I can picture the room. It was a big, dirty room. (I always tell my students, don't go into legal history if you have allergies!) It had drawers and drawers and files and files of records including not just the court records – the actual files – but also old pieces of furniture with rusty drawers. If you pulled them open you sometimes found interesting things. We found a drawer full of ancient bail bonds, for example. Also, a lot of the papers filed by the district attorney's office of Alameda County were usually signed by the deputy. One of the deputies was a young man named Earl Warren.

Although we sampled cases, before we did so we spent a period of time just reading – not a formal pilot study, as such, but a time of browsing and getting the feeling of what the records are like. What did they look like? What's in them? What are the things that we're going to be able to get and what are the things we won't? So to that extent we didn't plunge right in. I would open files at random and read them to get ideas. The figures, the statistics are blind without some understanding of the stories. And stories without the statistics are just stories. You need both.

Question: Certainly, *The Roots of Justice* has some fascinating anecdotes which help to bring the text to life. Did you keep an eye open for that when you were going through the records?

Friedman: Of course, I did. Maybe it even distorts things a little. I look for the most vivid or weird, interesting thing unless it really distorts the whole picture. I wanted the reader to be interested. So these anecdotes are a very important part of my way of working. I look for them also because the point one is making is best illustrated by concrete examples.

Question: How do you determine what is the right balance between quantitative and qualitative historical data?

Friedman: It's very hard to give a definitive or even useful answer to that question. You have to have both because the numbers are meaningless unless you flesh them out with some statement about how they relate to actual people and actual events. And the actual people and events are themselves meaningless without the numbers because you don't know if you're dealing with something that's unique or whether it's typical. So to me this kind of research demands mixing the two. Neither stands on its own very well. But the exact proportion is very difficult to tell and may vary from place to place, from topic to topic, and so on. In the case of a divorce study, for example, the balance would tilt toward the quantitative. That's because divorce files are lies and stereotyped – the stories they tell can't be taken at face value. So the quantitative measures – information like there are more women seeking divorce than men and so forth – tend to outweigh, on the whole, the qualitative stuff. If, however, you're dealing with murder trials it's the opposite because each one is so different that you have to pay very careful attention to the particular case, to the story, to the context. In some ways, the chapter that was the most fun to do in *The Roots of Justice* was the one on the big murder cases. That's a fascinating subject but very hard to deal with. You can't really deal with it quantitatively. You have to ask the questions: Why was this a headline case? What made this something that caught the public imagination? What is it about this particular court room drama that made it front page news in the *Oakland Tribune?* These big trials tell us something very important about society. But then when you're studying drunkenness arrests, the figures are very important, the aggregates.

Question: To assemble that complete, balanced portrait, how far did you reach beyond the court records, and to what extent did you make conscious decisions about what to leave out?

Friedman: The court records were our primary source. But we had other sources. The one that was particularly useful was housed in the Oakland Public Library. The library had actual police records of everyone arrested in Oakland between 1872 and 1910 – where they were arrested and why they were arrested.

In addition to the case files and the records for the police activity, we also read the newspapers. Those were valuable both at the top and the bottom. They would have stories about what happened in the police courts for which we had no records. They would sometimes tell amusing stories, for example, about some drunk who was brought into court, and so forth. And the newspapers, of course, also carried trial reports. The court files were very valuable but they were not transcripts of trials, just legal records. The only testimony they had in them would be the testimony preserved because of appeal or because of what happened at the earlier stage which resulted in the person being held for trial. The newspapers were also the source for things like hangings and the very rare appeal cases.

On the one hand, we made a conscious decision not to leave out any aspect of the criminal justice system of this county from top to bottom. On the other, we left almost everything out in the sense that we sampled, though not the appeal cases or executions because there were relatively few of them. There's always a question of how many cases you need in a sample in order to tell a coherent story or to have statistics that add up to something. But what you leave out is the bulk of the data. We also left out the formal legal literature of the period. We didn't look at any treatises or anything of that sort. That was left out because we didn't think it had any relevance.

Question: Even when sampling and drawing a line someplace, you had a mountain of data. How did you handle and organize it?

Friedman: Of course, today with a laptop it would be a lot easier to record the data. At that time we were using big sheets of paper. We would have a list of things and then would take it back to the office and analyze it by hand. I don't know whether the quality of research has gotten better, but the way of handling it has gotten a lot easier with laptops and digital cameras.

Somehow you look at the data, you see what you have, and somehow a plan forms in your mind about how to write it up and you just do it. There was a great political scientist who once said that you gather your data, you look at it and you say, "Speak to me!" And somehow, it speaks to you and says, "This is how we should organize it." Somehow an organization suggests itself. At some point we decided it was logical to talk first about the police courts, the arrests of the drunks, then about the trials of serious crime, then about appeals and about the big cases, and then a summing up.

Question: There may be tendency to think of historians as working alone. Doing legal history collaboratively, with Robert Percival, how were the responsibilities of the project shared?

Friedman: I had more responsibility for the writing and Robert Percival had more responsibility for data gathering. But he was totally invaluable throughout– a wonderful collaborator, and helpful on all aspects of the project.

I've done a lot of collaborative work with students. In general, when working with students, I have what in the movie industry they call the "final cut." I'm very, very concerned with the writing. If I work with a student I write much of it and what I don't write I turn into "Friedmanese." I didn't like law school and I particularly didn't like legal writing. I found it heavy, jargon-ridden, and boring. I made up my mind that I was not going to bore people. They might not like what I write but I wasn't going to bore them and I wasn't going to mystify them. I've always strived, I think with some success, for total clarity.

Question: What were the most challenging aspects of the project?

Friedman: Driving to Oakland and back during rush hour! What's challenging about this kind of research is just the amount of work. We had a mountain of data. There aren't any shortcuts. If you want to study a sample of criminal cases in a county over a certain period, you just have to do the work. And you have to do a lot of work before you can start writing anything or saying anything. This can be a big disincentive to younger scholars in legal education who are expected to produce something fairly quickly.

Here is a paradox about criminal justice. There is a gigantic legal literature and there is also a gigantic historical literature, but almost none of it is like our book. Very few actually get into the files. Of course it's not hard to understand why. Dreaming up a theory of the Fourteenth Amendment to the Constitution requires a lot of brains, but you don't have to get up off your butt and go somewhere and dig.

Question: With the benefit of hindsight, is there anything that you would do differently or change?

Friedman: Not really. I'm quite pleased with the book, and I think it turned out the way we wanted it to. I'm not saying it's perfect. Anything I would do differently? I haven't thought about that. I don't tend to look back on old projects, and think of what might have been.

One of my colleagues once said that the most theoretically interesting thing about the book is that there's no theory in it. But I think there's a lot of theory in it. It's just not blatant. We didn't talk about Foucault, Habermas, and the like, God help us. Life is too short for that. I think we accomplished something. By putting all our sources together, we drew a picture of a whole criminal justice system in action in a particular period in a particular place. For its period I think it's unique because no one has done anything since. There are comparable studies, a few for other periods and places. But for the time being this will have to do for late-nineteenth-century criminal justice.

Willard Hurst had once told me that I ought to do a history of property law in the US. He said it was a very neglected field. Nothing has been more important in American history than the land, the disposition of the land, the land tenure systems, ownership of land, methods of dealing with land. He was 100 percent right, and yet I didn't do it. Why? Since *The Roots of Justice* I've written about family law, a book called *Private Lives*, and I just published a book called *Guarding Life's Dark Secrets*, which deals with such things as blackmail and the regulation of sexual behavior.[1] Alas, it's more fun to work on these subjects than dealing with mortgages.

[1] *Private Lives: Families, Individuals, and the Law* (Cambridge, MA: Harvard University Press, 2005); *Guarding Life's Dark Secrets: Legal and Social Controls over Reputation, Propriety, and Privacy* (Stanford, CA: Stanford University Press, 2007).

CHAPTER 6

JOHN HEINZ AND EDWARD LAUMANN AND *CHICAGO LAWYERS**

The landmark study of the Chicago bar by Heinz and Laumann may project the appearance of having been a deliberate, rigorous, "scientific" project – one that follows a logical scheme and presents data accordingly. Students of the field may take away that perception, in particular, for how the book marshals and presents a raft of quantitative data. Unquestionably, Chicago Lawyers, *together with a follow-up study conducted two decades later – published as* Urban Lawyers *(2005, with Robert Nelson and Rebecca Sandefur) – is an achievement in the sociology of law, possessing both rigor and sophistication in copious amounts.*

But what figures and tables obscure, and what Heinz and Laumann are quick to reveal, is the process by which meaningful quantitative analysis is generated. "Quantification" is not a method itself, but an analytical result of a process that requires intuition and reflection. Thus, their collaboration and use of others in their work can be seen as a vital support structure for the analytical as well as the managerial side of a large project, and the qualitative research they describe plays a key role in support of the survey-based data collection employed in these projects. Even with the benefits of time, institutional support, highly qualified teams, and a multiplicity of perspectives, the blinkers of the moment constrain and shape the research process. The limits manifest themselves here, with a twenty-year follow-up in the wings, as a form of path dependence – recognizing mistakes but living with them for purposes of comparability. The work may project an aura, but it requires a form of humility.

The interview begins with Heinz and Laumann describing how they became a partnership through an invitation that they were reluctant to accept.

Methodological Keywords: surveys, network analysis, multidimensional scaling

---

**Chicago Lawyers: The Social Structure of the Bar* (New York: Russell Sage Foundation, 1982; rev. ed., Evanston, IL: Northwestern University Press, 1994).

Heinz: We were introduced by the executive director of the American Bar Foundation. I was about nine years into my career as a professor at Northwestern Law School at that point. I had gone to graduate school in political science briefly, as a student of Robert Salisbury at Washington University, and then I went to Yale Law School, where I was Harold Lasswell's research assistant. At Northwestern, I was Director of the Program in Law and Social Sciences, one of the original Russell Sage Foundation–funded law and social science programs.

Laumann: During my Ph.D. at Harvard I had worked with Talcott Parsons, which made me interested in the professions, and then for my early work I conducted two major surveys, one on class structure in New England and then one on ethnic and religious differences among white men in Detroit. On sabbatical in Germany in 1970, I began a study of the structure of elite community leaders in Cologne. So a lot of the elements of *Chicago Lawyers* had been pretested, if you will, when I came to Chicago in 1973.

One evening my wife dragged me to an architectural slide show about Chicago at some apartment. I was not particularly interested in going but I was standing there nursing a drink when this guy blew in the door. He did a double take because he wasn't expecting to be hosting a party. He grabbed a drink and came up to me. He said he was Spencer Kimball, at the University of Chicago Law School. He invited me to come to a meeting for the reform of the bar headed by Alex Elson, a lawyer in town. They wanted to do a self-study of the bar to inform their reform of the Chicago Bar Association. I had a lot on my plate and wasn't looking for anything more, but he invited me to just come for a free dinner. I met Jack at this dinner.

Heinz: The Committee on Development of the Law within the Chicago Bar Association was a fairly elite and intellectual committee, with a political agenda to some extent because it was the Vietnam War period. Some of the committee members wanted a more progressive agenda and so they were looking for a study of the Association that would have some critical edge to it. I was the director of the Law and Social Sciences program at Northwestern in the early 1970s. They wanted us to identify someone to do the project. We sat down and went through the directory and tried to figure out people to do it.

Laumann: We just looked at each other and said, "Well, maybe we ought to do it."

Heinz: Which was probably what Kimball had in mind in the first place! But we had to talk ourselves into it because we weren't all that interested in the Chicago Bar Association nitty-gritty part. My background was in political elites and in the legal profession, and I was certainly influenced by Ed's previous work, *The Bonds of Pluralism* and *Networks of Collective Action*. Once we figured out that we might make it into a study of the profession, it became a lot more interesting.

Laumann: I was really motivated because of the interest in elite networks. So a lot of the methodological innovation that I think is reflected in this is in the focus on inequality, ethnicity, and professional networks. Those were things that the Bar was not much interested in. They had a strict hands-off policy – and they never made a peep about what we should ask – but the most tedious chapter in *Chicago Lawyers* is on the Bar Association because we had to pay our dues.

Heinz: They were happy to provide advice but they didn't dictate anything. If you look at the questionnaire in the back of the original edition, you'll see a lot of questions in the interview about the Chicago Bar Association, how the association worked, whether they liked the food, and all that kind of stuff. That was all in there because of this agenda of this committee and to some extent we had to pay them off for the access, but the project evolved out of that into a much more ambitious and much more theoretical agenda.

Question: How did your collaboration figure into the development of the project?

Heinz: We worked very closely together in those days. I remember, down in Hyde Park, we'd go on those long walks to restaurants in some remote location and have lots and lots of big, long conversations about how to shape the project. So it grew out of a lot of conversation between the two of us. Even so, I think the conceptualisation process probably didn't go on as long as ideally it should have, and part of the reason for that was because the Chicago Bar Association committee had been the impetus for this. In a sense we got started on it before we had thought it all the way through, and it's kind of remarkable that it turned out as well as it did.

Laumann: First of all, we had to build a relationship, and we became intellectually very close and friends as well. That was an important thing, that eventually we could just rely on each other to have the same instincts about how to analyze something. At the start, we basically were catching up with each side's disciplinary understandings. That just doesn't happen instantly. I would say that the design of the survey instrument was probably naive with respect to what we ultimately developed theoretically. We didn't know about hemispheres. A lot of the interpretation was conceptual work that was done as we went along. In fact it's my prejudice that empirically grounded work should inform and create theory rather than deductively sort of starting from some a priori position. You have some general ideas that you imagine are going to work in a certain way, and then you get kicked in the face that it doesn't even look like that.

Question: What kicked you in the face the most?

Heinz: Empirically, what fields of law actually exist in practice in the real world? Constitutional law, for example, is not a field: it's a subject that's taught in law school. If you go out there and look for lawyers who practice constitutional law, you may find a half a dozen who are U.S. Supreme Court advocate specialists, but it doesn't exist as a field of practice. And does zoning work exist as a field apart from other real estate transaction work or is it just a part of a more general real estate practice, so that people who do real estate also get involved in zoning issues? Well, it turns out there are some zoning specialists, but you don't know that before you go in. Eminent domain, the same thing: it turns out that it is a distinct speciality for a few people but the question is the extent to which these types of work, like eminent domain and zoning, become enmeshed in a larger cluster of different types of work to create something like "real estate." That's something that was not at all well explored before we went into it. That was probably the biggest design defect in the original study. We weren't smart enough to foresee it.

The best example of that, which we said a bit about in chapter 2 of *Urban Lawyers,* is that because we had not anticipated the two-hemispheres hypothesis we used tax, real estate, and litigation as fields. We were so naive that we didn't realize that these are not fields. Those exist in the world as corporate tax, personal tax, or small business tax; commercial real estate versus individual personal real estate trans-actions; and personal litigation versus corporate litigation. We had thought of the three things as fields because I was a law professor: tax, property, and civil procedure/litigation are courses in law school. But in the real world those things split by client type. Because we didn't have the conception of the two hemispheres in our head at the time we started, we misdefined those fields in the survey and we had to scramble when we did *Urban Lawyers* to try to make up for that, to provide comparative data.

Laumann: And it caused us a lot of anguish and worrying, trying to keep comparability and still be able to incorporate the new. You could take a conceptual theory of law and ask, "What are the domains of it?" and certainly deduce from it some kind of logic from the common law or statutorily created categories, a highly idealized structure. Rather, we ended up with a client-centered field of practice, in a sense practically, to be able to ask questions that lawyers could reliably answer and evaluate, to get the prestige evaluation of the fields or to get law professors to evaluate various features of it. Those were things that we discovered after we had done the fieldwork and we began to say, "Well, how are we going to theorise this now?" or "How does prestige get driven here?" The whole process that led to the dimensional scaling of the fields of practice was in some ways empirically driven but very theoretically at the same time in a highly interactive mode. It was very much data coming back at us, obviously having some patterns, and then us asking ourselves the questions. I think one of our major conceptual innovations was the field of law itself as an analytic object.

Question: How did you divide or share the roles in the project, with all of the management and data analysis involved?

Laumann: We were both actively involved in all phases, even to coding and things of that kind, although Jack had a lot more hands-on – the phone calls and the chasing down of interviews and all that. There were people who did that sort of thing under Jack's very close supervision and he was more actively involved, but in a sense I was represented by my students, who tended to work in these kind of roles. We were blessed by – and I think we can't underestimate it – a series of really outstanding research assistants. We hired Terry Halliday to manage the survey, the interviewers, and do quality control on the interviews. In the studies that I did in Germany and then in the U.S., we interviewed a lot of elites and we trained our own team because using professional interviewers from some hired guns was, in my view at that time, and still would be, extremely counterindicated because the interviewer had to know and understand what he was going after. So we trained our own – all graduate students.

Heinz: Ed and I were very much hands-on. Ed had more experience with how to mount and manage survey research than I did, and I was the day-to-day management part of it. I actually took a year off in 1974–1975 from Northwestern Law School and spent the whole year at the Bar Foundation running the project. I'd never managed a big thing like that before. It's a lot of just keeping track of detail bits and pieces and making sure they don't get lost. You're managing a fairly big staff of people, a number of different employees, with all kinds of quality issues, like whether the interviewers had asked the questions right and whether they had recorded what the person actually said. And scheduling the interviews, making sure the interviewers showed up, and when the lawyer gets called to court at the last minute and the interview has to be rescheduled. Then you've got to collect all the data, interviews averaging more than an hour in length with hundreds of variables, and coding all that, and managing the data set. We did have a very strong group of graduate students on the statistical part of it, the methodological part of it. We were very fortunate and there were at least three dissertations that were published as books that were spin-offs, done by graduate students who worked on the project.

Question: One problem with surveys is the need to perfect them, so far as possible, before you send them out into the field. Another is that they only give you answers to the questions you ask. How did you supplement your quantitative data with other approaches?

Heinz: Some of the people out there in the world knew things that would have been very helpful for us to know when we were designing the research, but we didn't always learn those things until we went out and did the fieldwork. It was very helpful that we had the American Bar Foundation connections and were in contact with the profession. They were full of suggestions. In addition to the ABF, we had two different kinds of more formal advisory committees when we were designing *Chicago Lawyers* – one a committee of practitioners, and the other a committee of scholars.

Laumann: We did a lot of long exploratory interviews at the beginning of *Chicago Lawyers*, some of it arranged through the members of the Chicago Bar Association committee, some of it arranged through contacts from Northwestern Law School or through the American Bar Foundation.

Part of the challenge was trying to come up with conceptualisations of how lawyers think, because one of the tensions I had as a sociologist was that I was always prepared to say, "In general how do you do X?" because we tend to want to know the general and not each case and the mentality of it. The interviews that I had were eye-opening. The lawyers didn't think probabilistically. They talk about exceptional cases, and they want every case to fit. There was a real learning of a sort of intuitive sensibility about how lawyers think. How could we characterize the issues in meaningful ways? We were interested in how much autonomy they had in conceptualizing and managing the kind of work they did, and it's very hard to come up with how to ask that question.

Later on in the process, Jack and I would be talking about something about which we didn't really have a good feeling, such as whether there were going to be some new rules over class actions or whether they were going to relax the barriers against conflicts of interest. So we organized three or four encounters with really excellent informants. One was a judge who had been involved in that issue, and once we went to an ABA-sponsored conference. There was a lot of ethnography that was routinely deployed. We probably should have used more of that.

Heinz: One of the most exploratory parts of the research was in the identification of the set of notables – who they were, and their biographies. A hell of a lot of work went into figuring out how to create the set of notables in order to get the range of variation that we wanted, and getting the biographical information about all of these people – which was much less available in 1975 than it is now because you didn't have the Internet and the lawyer newspapers and directories that you have now. We had to do a lot of digging to come up with the right set of notables.

Laumann: That was a very high-risk venture because we just didn't know whether that was going to work. A lot of lawyers don't know more than a few notables.

Heinz: We had to do a lot of interviewing of lawyers to say, "Tell us who are the most prominent labor lawyers in town," "Who are the most prominent environmental lawyers in town," and so on. Because the practice of law is so segmented, they only know their own area. Then you'd start asking, "Which ones of these are Episcopalians," and people would say, "Hell, I don't know." That took a lot of interviewing, a lot of digging, a lot of soaking and poking. There were a lot of conversations with lawyers about putting that list together, making sure that we had the data right on the characteristics of these people.

Question: This work is done with pseudonyms, but with the biographic details of the notables, it would seem transparent who they are. Given your connections to the Chicago legal community, how worried were you about how this was going to play and how you write about this?

Laumann: We haven't had any problems or complaints, but we did worry about it. I worried about the ethical stuff but we went out of our way so a casual reader couldn't figure out who the players were.

Heinz: We made a distinction between giving identifying characteristics to people who were interviewed and giving identifying characteristics to people who were not interviewed. The technique that we used in *Chicago Lawyers* was the latter. These notables were target people who were not themselves interviewed. As it turned out, actually, one or two of them did come up in the random sample, but in order to do what we did in the book we did not have to interview them. We got all of the information about them from publicly identifiable sources and we didn't owe any obligation of confidentiality to them because we hadn't interviewed them.

Now the serious ethical question, if there is one, is whether there is an invasion of privacy, whether there's an expectation of privacy that one will not take publicly available information and put it together in such a way as to disclose structural characteristics, like ethnic separation. That's arguable, I think. Our view was that these people were sufficiently prominent within the professional community that they didn't really have much expectation of privacy with respect to this sort of thing. Most of the reaction from the notables is that they were flattered, and at least one of them bought about ten copies of the book!

Question: It's a rare opportunity to have the chance to do a full-scale project again, as you tackled the Chicago Bar in 1975 and then again in 1995. When did the idea of a second wave project occur to you? What did you learn or what did you take from doing it again?

Laumann: It was a very-low-visibility question for a long time. One of the big questions of course from the beginning was whether to try to do a panel study. We could have tried to go back, and we still had the names when we started the second study. I personally wasn't as interested in that because that would be highly biased given the enormous growth of the bar. We were looking at a totally new situation in some ways and it was really to capture a snapshot from a baseline that struck me as far more interesting, than to study people twenty years older.

If we were thinking about the optimal design, it was not clear that "the lawyer" was even the best unit for focus. Again, we didn't know at the time when we did *Chicago Lawyers* that there would be such a huge change in the scale of the bar – not just the growth in numbers but the movement away from solo practice into very large firm practice and so on. If you really wanted to characterize the embedding of lawyers in organized settings then the unit of analysis should have been sampling by type of organization or skill of organization, and that would have destroyed the comparability of the second project to the prior one. That interest in comparability, I think ultimately, was the correct choice but it was sacrificing this insight into the new bar. In 1975 it didn't occur to us to ask about competitive bidding, for example. It wasn't even legal then; it was unethical, and then it becomes a really defining characteristic twenty years later. We don't have any comparable data. Happily, it's fine because it would have been zero but we can only infer that because we didn't ask.

Heinz: We were interested in the change in the profession rather than the changes in these people and their careers over time. The question of whether to make the individual lawyer the unit of analysis was a question from the beginning. We knew in a general way that these changes were happening but we didn't know the extent of it. But once we'd done that in 1975 we were pretty well committed in 1995.

Our interests changed over time in part based upon what was going on in the profession. There was much less interest in 1975 in career mobility. There is some stuff in the book, such as mortality tables, but by 1995 there was all this talk about how lawyers are moving constantly – at least, Ed and I thought they were, so we paid a lot more attention to career mobility. It turns out they're not and the results show some counterintuitive things. As another example, because we used a true random sample, we only end up with a handful of women in 1975. If we had oversampled in 1975 we would have had a much stronger basis for comparison of women over time. We were right at the point of when the women were coming into law school. The questions changed to some extent depending upon what was happening behaviorally.

Laumann: In 1975 I don't think it occurred to us there was going to be anything like the transformation in such a short compass of time, although we were standing in the beginning of it.

Question: When did you begin looking at the data? When you were about to undertake the analysis, where did you start?

Heinz: We didn't do much analysis before we had the whole data set in hand. We would look a little bit at preliminary numbers on some things but not much, just to see if we had enough. Once the data were all in hand, then we divided it up into pieces for the purposes of analysis. The first article we did was on the organized bar. The committee at the Chicago Bar Association was eager to find out the answers about that and so we tabulated those data and carved that piece out, with pretty minimal data analysis, mostly simple distributions.

Laumann: That was paying the piper. We had a fairly large team, so there was a lot of parallel processing, particular individuals managing a particular topic, a chapter at a time. I think it's worth saying that computerization of software packages was much better than it had been ten years before but it was by no means out of the woods. Nowadays kids have these programs on their desktops and they can run them any way from Sunday, but at the time those were very time-consuming and lengthy processes.

Question: Probably the most cited concept from *Chicago Lawyers* is the notion of two hemispheres. When did you see that thesis emerging or how was that coming about?

Heinz: After we started analyzing the data we started seeing a lot of things falling out by client type. We did an analysis of the organization of work specialisation and we saw that it fitted very clearly by client type – this hierarchical clustering of fields and clustered by client type. The two hemispheres came a little after this, but pretty much at the same time we said, "This is really the big divide." That said, it's my view that the two-hemisphere thesis, although it's clearly the most famous part of our work, has been overdrawn and overemphasized by people who have used our work. In a sense, they've oversimplified it. We're fairly careful in *Chicago Lawyers* to say that this is a division but it is not the whole story and it isn't perfectly separated, by any means. These are not watertight categories and to some extent it bothers me that that has been used incautiously.

Question: What criticisms were you most expecting to hear?

Heinz: Number one, it's bloodless: it's by the numbers and it doesn't give us the feel, texture, or emotion of the profession. Number two, it's inaccessible and too difficult. Our other book, on Washington lawyers, was not so much criticised as just unread for that reason.[1] There was one review by a Washington journalist who said it was a book that only a graduate student could love, and there's some truth to that. We've had high-powered teams – with Bob Salisbury, Bob Nelson, Rebecca Sandefur, and others – from a variety of different disciplines and methodological perspectives. There are not very many readers who have background in all the different methods, so there's some part of these books that's going to be unfamiliar to almost any reader, and I think that has limited the audience. I think in many ways the Washington lawyers book is the most important book that we have done. It's certainly the most ambitious but it's a difficult book and difficult partly because it's demanding methodologically. Those would be the two biggest criticisms that I think of.

Laumann: In a sense, with "the hemisphere," another way to spin that is that it was appealing precisely because it was a take-home point that even a dullard could understand.

Heinz: We shouldn't underestimate the extent to which that has an effect. It's sort of a catchy thing to call it "the hemispheres" and it sticks in the mind.

Question: As may be expected with projects of this scale, the timeline from origins to final publication is nearly a decade for each book. What did you have in mind for a schedule or strategy for these projects?

Heinz: There were a lot of articles that were published during those ten-year periods. That was a conscious strategy. You don't want to hold the data for ten years before you start releasing them. You want to get the data out, not only to inform people but also so you start getting feedback on it. It was very important to us that we start publishing at least some pieces of it. It takes a lot of time to digest it, to figure out what analyses are needed, and it's a process of enquiry where one question leads you to another. Not until you get the answer to that first question

---

[1] John P. Heinz, Edward O. Laumann, Robert L. Nelson, and Robert H. Salisbury, *The Hollow Core: Private Interests in National Policy Making* (Cambridge, MA: Harvard University Press, 1993).

can you properly formulate the second one, so you really do have to proceed incrementally. The difficult part then becomes to decide what comes first. Should I take some piece that could be carved off – like the organized bar[2] – or should I try to take some piece that I think is fundamental, that underlies everything else, and try to do that first so I can build everything else on that structure? We tended to do more of the former than the latter because I, at least, was never confident enough that we knew what the foundation was. In *Chicago Lawyers* the organization of work and the fields of law certainly turned out to be that, but I don't think we knew that going in, and we didn't do it first.

Laumann: To really underscore the point, and I don't know that I've ever seen this put quite as bluntly as I would like to put it, survey work of this kind is never and should never be deductive in the sense that we have a whole set of questions which we're going to design a survey instrument to measure, and we will then tell you what the data tells us, end of story. There needs to be a much more capacious understanding in which there's a lot of things you're asking about which you at the time didn't have a clue or at least only a dim sense of its potential utility. There is a way of constructing surveys in which you need to have these intuitions, these exploratory interviews with lots of people who have grabbed different pieces of the elephant and described parts of it to you, parts that you don't quite know how they go together.

And you embrace it. In fact, that's where the textbook methodological prescriptions I think are just full of it because they would have you sacrifice everything on the altar of statistical rigour. Finding a little suggestive element in the data that doesn't quite meet statistical significance and killing it because it doesn't have these priors that you've established for it is a recipe for disaster in my view. I think the excitement that *Chicago Lawyers* in particular generated was the fact that we kept stumbling on to things that Jack and I never in our wildest moments could have told you in 1974 we were looking for, things that didn't and wouldn't have occurred to us. It was learned from the data, the number of times we just sat going through printouts of distributions. It takes a lot of time to do, but that kind of hands-on familiarity with the data is critical.

[2] J. P. Heinz, E. O. Laumann, C. L. Cappell, T. C. Halliday, and M. H. Schaalman, "Diversity, Representation, and Leadership in an Urban Bar: A First Report on a Survey of the Chicago Bar," *American Bar Foundation Research Journal*, 1(3):717–85 (1976).

Heinz: There's a lot of staring at the numbers and saying, "What are these numbers telling us?" There's not a statistical analysis that you can do that tells you what the patterns are. You have to discover the patterns, which means you have to look at it and see what you think is there, and then maybe you can test for it. We got the U-shaped diagram (see Figure 3.1 of *Chicago Lawyers*) and said, why is it this shape? You have to look at it before you see that litigation fields are at the top and office practice fields are at the bottom. Oh, and what's left-to-right? Ah, yes: running from personal clients on one side to corporate on the other. Nobody tells you that. The analysis shows you the spread but you have to figure out what it is you're seeing, what you're looking at.

Laumann: And then the surprise is that you get a correlation of .9 with the prestige order!

Question: To a significant extent *Chicago Lawyers* was digging in new soil, and yet these projects had a monumental scale that make them authoritative and also difficult to replicate in other areas. Have these projects matched your ambitions for the kinds of discussions you were able to both generate and resolve?

Heinz: We never set out to write the last word on the field, and I think in some ways that would be a very foolish goal. What you do is you hope to stimulate stuff, to write something that other people can build on, and that will be sufficiently interesting that it will stimulate other people to think of new questions and do additional work. From that standpoint I think we've been more successful than I would have hoped. In the concluding chapter of *Urban Lawyers* we posed some questions about the future. One of the things that we really haven't addressed in our work – and to some extent other people are addressing it – are some real questions about changes in the ideology of the legal profession, blurring the line between law and business.

Laumann: So there's a lot of work left to be done.

CHAPTER 7

ALAN PATERSON AND *THE LAW LORDS**

For researchers conducting interviews, many different kinds of research subjects exist. The common distinction between "elite" interviewees and their opposites – "mass publics," perhaps – captures some of the difference. Relatively elite subjects, such as corporate lawyers or court officials, often possess inside knowledge that you hope to acquire or have a privileged vantage point. Often coming from a limited pool of people who share their perspective, each interviewee is valuable and must be approached with care. Yet many elite individuals nevertheless can be relative unknowns beyond the narrow confines of their field. Many Law and Society projects involve elites of this variety – see, for example, McBarnet (Chapter 14) or Dezalay and Garth (Chapter 18). The extreme end of the "elite" continuum may well be its own category, however: those who by their socioeconomic standing or unique political position are extraordinarily difficult to access, challenging to interview, or particularly sensitive subjects. Interviewing presidents, ministers, and justices – and getting useful data – is a challenge unlike any other.

Alan Paterson's doctoral dissertation, later published as The Law Lords, brought this student of jurisprudence face-to-face with fourteen of the judges who sat in the highest appellate body in the United Kingdom and forty-five leading barristers and judges from the lower courts. At a time of great deference to the judiciary, and in light of the traditional reserve of the senior judiciary, it was a remarkable achievement. It would be over a decade before H. W. Perry, Jr., broke similar ground in the United States by interviewing sitting Justices of the U.S. Supreme Court.[1] Many factors affect one's ability to get access to elite subjects: who you are, who you know, the social setting of the day, and the concessions you are willing to make. Only some of these are in the scholar's control. Many researchers

---

The Law Lords (London: MacMillan Press, 1982).

[1] Published later as *Deciding to Decide: Agenda Setting in the United States Supreme Court* (Cambridge, MA: Harvard University Press, 1991).

may dismiss an elite interviewing strategy without attempting it; others will attempt it but fail. In this interview, Paterson, one who tried and famously succeeded, reflects on the factors that made it happen.

Methodological Keywords: interviews, elite interviews

Question: What kind of intellectual journey brought you to conceive the project?

Paterson: Essentially it was just curiosity. I think good researchers have to be curious. You need it to sustain you through the dark days of the grind. I was a fairly young law graduate from Edinburgh University. I had done an undergraduate honors degree, much of which was straight black-letter law. I was interested in doing some further study, but about what made the law work – not so much the law in books but the law in action, all these old phrases. For some reason my interest alighted on the judiciary: how do judges make up their minds? How do judges make decisions? I'm not quite sure why judges were my interest. It may have been because I had studied jurisprudence in my law degree. Part of my curiosity was that the judiciary in the House of Lords at that time had only just begun to articulate their creative role as lawmakers. Lord Denning, who had a quite overt interest in developing the law along lines that he was interested in, was very much out on a limb. He tried to persuade his colleagues in the Court of Appeal that they could depart from their earlier precedents, as the House of Lords could after 1966, but the majority of the Lord Justices would say, "There's a collective view that the Court of Appeal is bound by its own previous decisions and no individual judges can change that." What they left unsaid about the doctrine of precedent was what its status was. Was it a rule of law or practice? Was it a constitutional norm or merely a well-ingrained habit? There wasn't a great deal of judicial discourse at the time as to exactly what precedent was (as opposed to how it operated). There was plenty of material on the minutiae of which court binds another court but not how this doctrine evolved – the human process, indeed the political process by which it evolved.

Anyway, I applied to study at Oxford and I was accepted to do a DPhil.[2] My proposal was that I would look into judicial decision making and how the common law develops through what Hart called "hard cases,"[3] particularly at the House of Lords level. At Oxford,

[2] "DPhil" is the abbreviation used at Oxford University for a Ph.D.
[3] See H. L. A. Hart, *The Concept of Law* (Oxford: Clarendon Press, 1961).

Ronald Dworkin had just replaced H. L. A. Hart as the Professor of Jurisprudence and so one could attend graduate seminars every week in which Hart, Dworkin, Joseph Raz, John Finnis, Neil MacCormick, and Richard Wasserstrom – six of the leading jurisprudes in the world at the time – would all be in the same room. It was fascinating. Certainly it encouraged me to have chapters in the thesis on the jurisprudential issues raised by "hard cases" and that could be researched without the need for interviews. Yet looking back now, I'm intrigued by how much jurisprudential analysis there was in the research. If I was doing it again today I probably wouldn't even enter that territory.

Question: You started your Ph.D. at a time when Law and Society was at its infancy in the U.K., and before the Centre for Socio-Legal Studies at Oxford had been founded. Especially where so much of the intellectual current focused on jurisprudence, to what extent were you having to plough your own furrow?

Paterson: Well, to begin with I had relatively little contact with anybody outside my supervisors, D. N. MacCormick of Balliol College (Professor Sir Neil MacCormick of Edinburgh University as he subsequently became) and Philip S. C. Lewis from All Souls College. None of the other postgrads at my college was doing law, certainly not anything sociolegal. So, although I had plenty of friends who were postgraduates in other academic fields, intellectually I was not in a group of like-minded souls. My formative influences didn't come from close colleagues in the discipline, because there just weren't any. My supervisors were very helpful to me, but they were both very distinguished and I wasn't really in their league. I was on my own a lot, except when I was rowing or punting, of course. Doing a Ph.D. can be a very lonely experience. You sink or swim. Maybe that's why I enjoyed the summer school in Madison, Wisconsin, so much. Relatively late on in my doctoral studies I went to a six-week graduate summer program put on by a kind of precursor to the Law and Society Association. It involved scholars like Marc Galanter and Stewart Macaulay. They were talking about aspects of the legal system from a sociolegal point of view. I thrived in the camaraderie and stimulus of graduate students from all types of social science background looking at sociolegal questions in a way that I had not encountered in Oxford up until then. It was probably the most formative experience of my career, let alone of the doctoral period.

Question: Did that experience influence the direction of your research?

Paterson: Yes, it certainly affected how I wrote up the thesis and analysed the interviews. I think it gave me a lot of confidence. The formative bit was the interdisciplinarity aspect to it – seeing the sociolegal world in such rich focus, and being with others, talking to them, and the novelty of looking at the law and the legal system in this way. That summer there was a course on dispute resolution by one of the anthropologists who'd been in the Berkeley Village Project, talking about alternative dispute resolution in Ghana. It was all about multiple layers of dispute resolution and legal pluralism at a time when little of that had crossed the Atlantic except in the conclaves of anthropologists. I got a better set of tools and a better appreciation of how theory and methodology worked together. I had only done a course in statistics at Oxford and, to be quite honest, I didn't actually use it in the research.

Question: At what stage, then, did you decide to try to interview the Law Lords about their decision-making processes?

Paterson: It was quite late on in my third year at Oxford. I did my interviews in my third and fourth years at Oxford. Earlier on I had formed the view that getting interviews with the judges, especially the Law Lords, was never going to happen, and that I would simply reply on their printed judgements and the odd extrajudicial lectures or essays, even though I knew that would yield fewer insights into the actual process by which decisions were reached in the Appellate Committee. There had been a few attempts by others to interview judges in the United Kingdom which had failed, and I had spoken with several of them. Nobody at that stage had done a systematic interview-based study of our judiciary. The world has changed from forty years ago in terms of respect for people and institutions. In those days the judiciary were almost seen as being from another world, especially the Law Lords. You see, back then the Law Lords didn't talk to the media, or at least the media didn't try to speak to them. So there was no guarantee that I was going to be able to interview anybody. I thought I might be able to interview some barristers, which I was keen to do, and maybe some retired judges, but not existing judges. My supervisor knew one or two of the Law Lords, but really couldn't estimate if I would be able to persuade many to be seen by me.

Question: So how did you change your mind?

Paterson: Well, it was kind of: "Let's try it." If you try it and it fails then what have you lost? But if you form the view that they'll just say no, well that becomes a self-fulfilling prophesy. Moreover, around that time I also had the good fortune to be appointed as the very first research associate in the newly formed Centre for Socio-Legal Studies at Oxford and that provided me with the infrastructure necessary to organize and transcribe a large number of interviews. Being located in a sociolegal environment for the first time in Oxford also probably helped.

Question: How did you go about seeking access?

Paterson: Through my supervisor's contacts. Although the judges didn't have as close contacts with academia as they do now, some of them had links with Oxford colleges. I had read about elite interviewing from the textbooks and had decided the way I was most likely to be successful was the snowball technique. You get one and if the experience has been OK at the end of the interview you say, "Would you be willing to mention me to a colleague and, if so, which one do you know particularly well that you could provide an introduction to?" So I produced a letter which said I was a Ph.D. student interested in judicial decision making. I sent it to a judge that my contacts knew particularly well, asking whether I could interview him. And by this process of snowballing, of getting one, then another, then another, and so on, I gradually acquired more and more interviews.

Question: That sounds deceptively simple, particularly given that you succeeded where other more experienced scholars had failed.

Paterson: It's an interesting point because I don't think it has so much to do with personal merit. I was in the right place at the right time. I stumbled over something that worked and that was good fortune. I knew that others had been unsuccessful. But I had the curiosity coupled with the brass-necked naivity to give it a go and then the tenacity to keep on going. I felt very privileged.

I think it was much to do with the fact I was at Oxford and some of the Law Lords had connections with Oxford and knew several law fellows reasonably well. Professor Rupert Cross's brother, for example, was a Law Lord. So there were links and it was the ability to use those links which then would snowball. Because I was Scottish I was not quite alien but I think people from another jurisdiction get a licence to ask questions which somebody from your own jurisdiction might not get.

And I was not seen as remotely threatening or worrying because I was young. I wasn't even an academic. I was a postgrad. I was coming with a recommendation from Oxford fellows or from another Law Lord. This was also in the days before Griffiths had blown the lid off things with *The Politics of the Judiciary*.[4] Would I have been able to do it so easily after Griffiths? I'm not sure that I would. They would have been more sensitized to the dangers.

The other reason, maybe, why I had success where others didn't is that I didn't have to seek permission from anyone other than the Law Lords themselves. Now that is what others had done in order to interview judges in lower courts. But the Law Lords were, in a way, unique in the sense that at that time they did not have a head. The only person who might have regarded himself as their head was the Lord Chancellor, but most of the Law Lords didn't seem to see him in that light. In the end I did not to write to the Lord Chancellor at the initial stages. Out of the blue, having no contacts to him, and nobody in Oxford having a particular link to him, that would have been a very high-risk strategy. Moreover, the Law Lords didn't always see eye-to-eye with Lord Chancellors. The Law Lords saw themselves effectively as at the top of the tree and therefore able to make their own decisions about whether they could be interviewed. I did go to the Lord Chancellor at the end of the whole thing and said, "This is who I have interviewed. Would you be willing to be interviewed?" As it turned out he wasn't, but was willing to answer a written questionnaire.

Question: Did you give any undertakings about confidentiality?

Paterson: Yes, the undertakings were that what was said in the interview would be shown to them and they would have the ability to adjust it. Secondly, that the whole of it, interviews and the doctorate, would be confidential in the sense that it would not be shown to the outside world. The agreement was that the doctorate would be open to the examiners and my supervisor but to no one else for twenty-five or thirty years. I made that undertaking with the first judge and stuck to it with the rest. That came out of discussions with my supervisor about maximizing what I could put in the doctorate. Oxford University had a provision then that if the data for your DPhil was obtained confidentially then the DPhil could be kept under wraps, provided it had been externally examined in the proper way.

[4] J. A. G. Griffiths, *The Politics of the Judiciary* (London: Fontana Press, 1978).

The deal was also that I wouldn't publish from the doctorate unless the judges agreed to the bits from them that I proposed to use. So when I was writing the book some years later I went back to each one and said, "I want to use this and this and this." I got each and every quote approved. If they didn't approve it I asked whether they were prepared for me to attribute it to a Law Lord but not to identify them. There were one or two that made some amendments but the great bulk of what's in the doctorate is now in the book. Relatively little was excluded. So if anyone had hoped that there would be real gems in the doctorate which are not in the book I suspect they're going to be rather disappointed.

Question: How did you weigh the benefit of obtaining the data against the undertaking not to disseminate the analysis?

Paterson: Well, I was relatively confident that I would be able to disseminate it eventually. All that would happen was I would have to get it agreed and I wasn't unhappy with that. Also, at the time I wasn't committed to an academic career. I had done the DPhil because I was curious. My main interest was trying to learn how judges make decisions. I wasn't so interested in what other people were going to make of this. In other words, it wouldn't be a complete waste of time because I had learned something. It's back to this isolation thing. I wasn't seeing myself as part of a community of scholars and so I wasn't wondering, "How will this go down with peer reviewers?" or "What influence will this have?"

Question: Your approach proved successful in the end, but were there any hitches in the process?

Paterson: Well, there are at least two downsides to using the snowballing approach. One is that the person you're interviewing, for whatever reason, may turn out to be not thought highly of by the person that you ask them to introduce you to. You wouldn't know it until you got the rebuff. I certainly had one case that looked like that. I was referred on by one Law Lord to another and the second Law Lord probably either didn't get on with or didn't rate the Law Lord who recommended me. That led to an impasse, though fortunately not to a general one, since for most of the Law Lords the novelty of the approach seems to have outweighed any concerns.

The second thing is that the snowball technique is very slow. You get your first, and then you get further introductions and you have to write to them. Then you get some more, and so on. It took me over a year to complete all my interviews.

Question: In the world of elite interviewing these were particularly elite subjects – the most senior judges in the U.K., probably even in the Commonwealth at that time. Did your recognition of their status – and you, the student, approaching them – affect your strategy or approach for conducting the interviews?

Paterson: No. I think naivity played a big role. I might be more nervous if I did it now. I certainly was very respectful. I went with a suit and a tie. I gave them their due because they were very impressive people. It was impossible not to be impressed by them. I had also tried to learn a little bit about them. I read *Who's Who*. And I was familiar with a lot of the key decisions they had participated in. I took the decision to tape-record if I possibly could. They were always given the choice to have it turned off. In the approaching letter I stressed that it was much easier if I could tape-record – so that I could apply my full mind to them rather than having to take copious notes, and them having to wait while I wrote it all down. Of course, what I didn't know then was how expensive and time-consuming it is to transcribe, although the Oxford Centre was very helpful in that regard.

Question: One of the main tasks of an interviewer is to put the interview subject at ease, to make them feel comfortable. How did you do that with the Law Lords?

Paterson: You mustn't waste a Law Lord's time. Even I was aware of that. You had to give them an estimate of how long you would be and stick to it unless they were saying, "No, no, I'm enjoying this." At least once I was going over time and the comment was, "How much longer is this going to go on?" Now, he wasn't being unkind, it was just that using my estimate he had organized to go out to lunch. So that probably didn't endear me to him.

And, of course, you start with some general questions that they are able to talk about. Having said that, one of the questions that hit the jackpot from a researcher's point of view was a very early question. It was, "When you joined the House of Lords, coming from the Court of Appeal, what was it that surprised you about the way it operated?" That question led one of the most cerebral of Law Lords to reply, "Discovering the extent to which you have to play a role in influencing your colleagues to reach a decision." He then went on to articulate in

79

an insightful way the nature and extent of group decision making in the Lords. All that came from a very general and innocuous question.

Question: You promised to let the judges check the transcripts and had guaranteed confidentiality. Were there any other techniques that you consciously used to try and encourage candid answers?

Paterson: No, not that I can recall. I learned by a roundabout route that one Law Lord had given a less than candid answer to a particular question. Well, it doesn't surprise me. I was a whippersnapper Ph.D. student coming to ask intimate questions about how they made decisions. Some of them were likely to opt for unrevealing generalities rather than revealing specifics, where they felt the questioning was straying over the line. I was sufficiently naive that I wouldn't necessarily recognize when that was happening. Some of them clearly did give me anodyne answers where they could have said more. In the ideal world, if they had been more candid would I have learned a great deal more? Possibly, I don't know. I have since interviewed one Law Lord. I didn't notice a significant shift between the quality of information I got from that Law Lord and the ones I had interviewed 25 or so years before. But the fact of the matter is that I got enough interesting comments in the interviews to make it worthwhile.

Question: What kind of direction did you find in the academic literatures when you were beginning the analysis?

Paterson: Well, there was nothing in the U.K. literature that I was aware of on judicial decision making as group decision making. Political scientists in the U.K. have really never seen the legal system and the judiciary as central to the study of political power, which I found curious in the extreme, then and now. So I had to go to American political science on the judiciary. The ideas in the book about the interactions between the judges came largely from the political science literature in America. The interviews revealed what the political science literature in America had suggested might be the case, namely the importance of studying small group interaction as a way of learning how appellate judges reach decisions. Curiously, I drew on social theory to emphasize the importance of judicial interactions with other social actors, such as the counsel in the case. Indeed, my interviews revealed what I hadn't expected – the extent to which the barristers play a role in the group decision making.

Question: What about your theoretical framework – role analysis?

Paterson: That's a bit of a dead end now. Would I write it up differently if I was doing it again? Role analysis looked then, and probably looks even more so now, a fairly procrustean or deterministic approach, even in the conflict theory guise that I used. But I don't know that I regret the role analysis overarching theory. I was interested in the role of judges and role analysis was about interaction between social actors, norms and expectations, and shared understandings. I think part of what I had to say which was novel, at least to the wider world, was that shared understandings exist between barristers and the judiciary about how things are done, how things are argued, what kind of argument carries weight, and which does not.

Clearly the way I'd written the book I intended it to have an academic audience and to have an impact on the academic world, because it revealed aspects of how the legal world worked that in my mind hadn't been published in the U.K. before. Yet because it was written in the somewhat arcane framework of role analysis, I think it deterred some of the professional readers. Having said that, it's my impression that the readers who enjoyed it the most have been the professional readers, the barristers and the judges, and the journalists and commentators rather than the academics. One senior judge told me this year that he thought it was one of the most impressive books he'd ever read as a practitioner because of the insights it gave him into the judicial decision-making process. The top barristers knew some of the stuff I was writing about because of their conversations with the Law Lords at lunches and dinners in the Inns of Court, but I was putting it together in a more systematic way.

Question: What are your feelings about how the book's been received and used by academic audiences?

Paterson: It had a small influence on some of the jurisprudential scholars at the time, not only for what it had to say about hard cases, which was fairly unsophisticated, but in its discussion about interactive decision making and legal culture. I think that introduced insights that some of the legal philosophers thought were interesting. Certainly the reviews of the book suggested that it cast light on what had up to then been rather uncharted waters for intelligent lay commentators.

It also demonstrated the art of the possible. It should have encouraged others to think, "Well, I'll go and talk to the judges. If Paterson can do it, I can do it." But there wasn't much evidence that it did have that effect because it was quite a long time afterwards before anyone started to talk to the Law Lords again in a systematic fashion.

Question: Perhaps exceedingly, your topic was one that could reach beyond academia to a general audience. Did you think about writing it up that way?

Paterson: Yes, I was aware that the book could have been written in a way that was much more accessible to the public. *The Brethren* had been written by Bob Woodward in 1979 about the U.S. Supreme Court.[5] He had talked to a huge number of clerks and got a lot of interesting information about how decisions were made. He wrote that up and published it in a racy way and it hit the bestsellers list. Whether I would have generated that kind of interest I'm not sure. The book appealed to my publishers because they billed it "How Britain's top judges see their role" on the book cover. But they didn't put a huge amount of pressure on me. I could have written the book in a *Brethren*-type way and it might have sold a lot more copies but I'm not sure it would have done my career as a young academic much good. I was also conscious that I had got the judges' agreement to be interviewed as part of a scholarly activity, rather than a journalistic one. So there was an element of fair play about it, not to mention keeping one's word over issues felt by the Law Lords to be sensitive or confidential. I was very privileged and incredibly lucky to talk to so many of the Law Lords and I was wary about not doing anything that would shut off access for other researchers. *The Brethren* at the time did get quite a lot of flak. Some of the Supreme Court weren't terribly happy with its publication. I am sure if I had written my book in a similar style it would have caused a lot of bad feeling. So I don't regret it.

Question: With the benefit of hindsight, is there anything you would do differently?

Paterson: There are always things that one could improve on, but only one springs to mind. When *The Law Lords* came out the BBC rang me up and said it wanted to profile the book on their prime time radio show, "Start the Week." But I was in America and I said, "I'm not coming back to do that." Now that probably cost me hundreds of sales. What a mistake! I think I missed a trick there.

[5] Bob Woodward and Scott Armstrong, *The Brethren: Inside the Supreme Court* (New York: Simon and Schuster, 1979).

CHAPTER 8

DAVID ENGEL AND "THE OVEN BIRD'S SONG"*

Understanding litigiousness involves many perspectives on how societies generate, shape, and process disputes. Whereas some may begin the study of disputing with the law and the formal institutions charged with implementing it, or what happens "in court," a long tradition of Law and Society scholarship has emphasized the importance of seeing how cultural practices give life and meaning to the law. Though some of this scholarship has come from anthropology, much of it has been produced by scholars from other disciplinary backgrounds who have been attracted to ethnographic methods and the promise of understanding legality through the eyes of "regular" people – not lawyers or judges but the ordinary people who experience "law."

Like other scholars in this collection, such as Carol Greenhouse (Chapter 10), Sally Engle Merry (Chapter 12), and the team of Patty Ewick and Susan Silbey (Chapter 19), David Engel sought to explore legal consciousness as it existed in the narratives and lives of such people. As he describes it, the route of this intellectual approach stems from a personal journey, one that helped open his eyes to his own country. Unlike some ethnographic studies, however, he conducted his research without full-time immersion in the community he was studying. This interview explores some of the substitutions and strategies Engel made to seek his desired depth of understanding, and some of the challenges that inhere to the approach. Both in the substance of the article and in the research process itself, we find the temporal dimension – for the latter, the time that Engel spent in the field and in mulling over the data. The product of that gestation was a memorable article with a memorable title.

Methodological Keywords: ethnographic interviews, community observers, docket study, participant observation

*"The Oven Bird's Song: Insiders, Outsiders, and Personal Injuries in an American Community," *Law & Society Review*, 18:551–82 (1984).

Question: Could you say something about the intellectual history of the project behind "The Oven Bird's Song"?

Engel: I had been in the Peace Corps in Thailand for three years. I came back to law school and felt a bit like a fish out of water in my own culture and in the strange setting of legal academia. I was dissatisfied with the narrowness of legal scholarship and teaching, so I took a joint degree in South East Asian studies and read quite a bit of anthropology and history. After graduating from law school I went back to Thailand and spent two more years doing research on Thai courts and legal culture. I found my own feet as a researcher somewhere in the intersection of ethnography and legal studies. The only non-Thai scholars who, to me, really seemed to capture what was going on in contemporary Thai society were the anthropologists, so I gravitated toward the methods of legal ethnography in a book I wrote about a Thai court and community.

In 1976 I came back to the United States and got a position at the American Bar Foundation. I began to think about what sort of research I would like to do. Although it wasn't clear to me at the time, it seems quite clear to me now that the study of Sander County, which led to the "Oven Bird's Song" article, was kind of a replication of the work I had done in Thailand. It was an attempt to look at law in my own cultural setting and to view it from a distanced perspective that I might not have had if I hadn't been in Thailand previously. My Thai research had raised a set of questions about how local trial courts related to the cultural setting in which they operated. So the challenge was to find a place in American society where I could conduct a study like that.

My experience in devising the project reflected a particular period in Law and Society research. I wasn't the only one who had returned to the United States from having lived in a quite different society. So there was a shared interest in trying to research the undiscovered regions of our own society. It was part of the political ethos of the time too. There was some tension over what was "Middle America" and who were the "silent majority" – all of those politically fraught terms that Richard Nixon had used to justify his socially conservative agenda. At that time the paradigm that spoke most powerfully to people who wanted to do comparative sociolegal research was dispute processing. So I went into the study with that very much in my mind – I initially thought that I would use dispute processing as a way of understanding what was going on in the community. I anticipated that researching disputes in the community and disputes in the court would produce a sort of map of a small-scale community in the United States – where the disputes came from, where they went, how they were handled, and so forth. But my ideas about the value of the dispute paradigm changed considerably in the course of my work.

Question: As you were developing the project, were you getting any feedback from colleagues or co-workers?

Engel: I was very lucky to have been at the American Bar Foundation. It was a great environment for me. I spent quite a bit of time working on the design of this study. When I reached a point where I had stalled or where I needed more input, I created an ad hoc advisory group. I just asked three or four colleagues if they would spend an afternoon talking with me about the work that I was doing and they were very happy to do that. I did it on a couple of occasions and those meetings really helped me to formulate a research design that I think worked well. The fieldwork didn't depart very much from the original design. It went pretty much according to plan.

Question: How did you go about finding a setting for the research? What kind of criteria guided the search?

Engel: At that time there hadn't been many sociolegal studies of an entire community in North America or Europe. In order to keep things manageable, I wanted to make sure that the court's jurisdiction covered the same social entity that I was trying to understand – that it corresponded to some sort of coherent cultural unit. But practicalities were also important. I looked for a setting that was sufficiently small in scale, somewhere that didn't have two or three urban centers. Also I was living just north of Chicago at the time and I wanted to be able to drive to and from the site in a day. So that limited my choice of locales. I looked around for small counties within reach of the city and I found Sander County.

Question: In your work in Sander County, as well as looking at records, you were engaged with quite a wide variety of people. Can you say a little bit about the process of gaining access?

Engel: There were three parts to the study and each part posed its own access issues. The court study depended on the permission of the clerk. Part of my education as a researcher was learning that, even though records are in theory open and accessible to any researcher, the clerk of the court can effectively say "no." They can't deny access to any of the files but they can deny you access to a chair or a work table or a willingness to retrieve a number of files each day for you to read. That was what had happened with my first choice. Sander County was actually my second choice of a setting. So that was the first problem of access – to find a court official who was willing to facilitate the study.

Then, after reading a number of cases, I tried to contact the parties to set up interviews. That was quite difficult, probably the most difficult part of the study. Many of the defendants, in particular, had made it a practice to be not easily reachable. Some of them simply didn't pick up their phones. So I found myself going from door to door. I found people's addresses, rang their doorbells, persuaded them I wasn't selling insurance or encyclopedias or trying to collect debts. That turned out to be really interesting because it made me think more about what it was that a researcher tries to extract from people, in some ways not too different from what a door-to-door salesperson does. It helped me to understand the people involved in litigation, the lives that they led and why being difficult to reach was important to them. But I also found that, once they allowed me into their house and talked with me, it was quite gratifying for them because the process of litigation had usually left them without a sense of closure. The cases often ended without their knowledge. They had expected a full trial where the judge would pronounce a verdict and instead things just sort of dissipated into nothingness. So they welcomed the chance to talk about it and try to think their way through what had happened.

The third phase of the study involved what I called "community observers." That was quite fun. It was an attempt to think about who would be situated in such a way that they would have an understanding of, and a perspective on, what went on in the community. The community observers ranged from beauticians and barbers to ministers and funeral parlor operators; from lawyers, police officers, and government officials to insurance adjusters and tavern keepers; from well-known and long-established residents such as farmers to some of the newcomers who were factory workers and union officials. Most of these people were quite happy to talk to me, and there wasn't much of a problem of access. Beauticians were among the best informants, actually, as were the tavern keepers. The funeral parlor operator also was quite insightful.

Question: Why beauticians?

Engel: They talk to everybody. There weren't that many in the county so probably most of the women who lived in the county came to them. While there, they shared information. So beauticians just knew a lot. People also told me it was important to understand the bowling leagues, but I don't think I ever interviewed any people from those organizations.

Question: How did you determine who was a community observer? Did you have a sense of that before you went into the field?

Engel: I had many entry points that I thought would be obviously good choices. The ministers and the beauticians were among them. And then I used a snowball technique. One contact would lead to another. After every interview I asked them who they knew in the community who was particularly insightful or who would have access to experiences that might be different from the ones they had. I made sure they weren't always identifying their friends. Sometimes they mentioned people that they had been at loggerheads with for many years. That was how I got to some of the old-time farmers, in fact. Some of the people who viewed themselves as more progressive elements in the community pointed me to some of the older farmers who still had very conservative values or were still involved in traditional ways.

Question: What did you say to your informants when you asked to interview them? How would you describe what you were doing?

Engel: I told them I was doing a study of the county and trying to understand how different groups in the county handled their affairs, and what they did about disputes when they developed. To make the connection between the court study and the community observer study I used four skeletonized cases that I had taken from the dockets. They involved different areas of law and I had simplified them. They were just short paragraphs really. I described these cases to the community observers and asked them if they had ever seen similar issues or had had experiences like that. It gave me a sense of how those same problems that had been litigated were handled outside the court.

Question: Did you have an easier rapport with some informants than others, in ways that might affect your perspective?

Engel: Some interviews were more productive than others. I would probably have a more coherent philosophy now about how to conduct interviews, but at that point I was learning as I was going along. I certainly tried to put people at their ease. I made it clear that I was there to be educated by them and to listen respectfully. I followed an interview outline, starting with the most open-ended questions and gradually becoming more specific. But there's an important point here. As a researcher, your own degree of comfort or discomfort during an interview is not an indication of how valuable that interview is. Sometimes the most uncomfortable interviews turn out to be the most revealing, especially when we try to understand the reason for our discomfort. I remember I was interviewing an evangelical Christian minister, and in the middle of the interview he asked me if I was ready to get down on my knees and let Jesus into my heart. I found that intensely uncomfortable but the interview turned out to be one of the most informative and useful. So rapport is helpful but it can be overrated.

Question: That must have been quite an unexpected and unsettling moment. How did you respond?

Engel: It was a great moment, actually, because it really challenged my sense of insulation and distance as a researcher. From my point of view he was a subject of my study. But from his point of view, I was a potential convert and a new member of his congregation. So now I relish my discomfort because it really made me understand his intentions and his view of the world. All souls who walked through his door, whether or not they viewed themselves as having some sort of immunity, were people that he needed to minister to. I'm not sure exactly what I said. I probably stumbled around for a little. I did not get down on my knees and let Jesus into my heart! I think when he asked me if I was ready to do it I just told him that I was not. He took it in stride. I think from his point of view it was a case of "well, if not today, then maybe later."

Question: How did you record your interview data?

Engel: I tape-recorded all the interviews and after each interview I would drive to some secluded place and take notes for about an hour. I think that's very important to do. I've found that if you sit down immediately after the interview, even if it has been tape-recorded, you can almost transcribe the entire conversation by memory. But your memory decays very quickly, so it's important to take notes immediately on what the interviewees looked like, how they were dressed, what their body language was like, what the room was like, and also anything that made a strong impression. Even if you don't understand why, if you make a note of it then maybe later you can figure out the reason.

Question: You mention in the article that in addition to conducting interviews and examining court records you immersed yourself in the community. Could you say something about how you did that?

Engel: I didn't do it to the extent that an anthropologist would where he or she might live in a community for years. I just spent full days there, probably three days per week on average, over a two-year period. I talked to people. I attended a few community functions. I went to a Rotary luncheon, and so on. It was a modest attempt to hang out in the community. But the research centered more on the interviews.

Question: How did you decide when you had completed enough field-work to finish?

Engel: You reach the saturation point. When people begin to tell you stories that you've already heard, when you feel the learning curve has almost completely flattened, I think that's the point where you can feel confident about leaving. I tell my students that there are two really difficult decisions involved in fieldwork. The first is to get yourself into the field to get started, and the second is to get yourself out. Both come with some degree of anxiety. Getting in is anxious because you don't want to make a false step. You want to be sure you're beginning at the right place and doing it in a way that's going to lead to success. Leaving the field is anxious because you're afraid that there may be something there that you haven't yet discovered. But you can't do it for the rest of your life. You need some point where the research ends and the analysis takes over.

Question: Your fieldwork was quite long and involved. You had a range of encounters and experiences. I'm curious about the extent to which there was an emotional dimension to the project for you.

Engel: I had been out of the country for so long, and had been so deeply immersed in a different culture, that I had a real fascination with what my own culture was and what it had become. I remember turning on the TV when I first came back from upcountry Thailand and just watching people with a sense of strangeness. So this research was really a voyage of rediscovery in some ways. There was a kind of fascination. Regaining contact with people in "Middle America" was emotionally satisfying. I felt perhaps more curious and open to people in different walks of life and to my own society because I felt that my position in that society was more indeterminate than it had been before I left the country.

Question: How did you organize and manage the data for analysis?

Engel: I didn't have a good system. There were no software programs at that time and I'm not sure I would have trusted them if they had been available. There were some quantitative data from the court records and that was easier to manage because there were routines for doing that. The interview materials and my notes on them all had to be transcribed. I had to check the transcriptions for accuracy and that was a way to review what I had found and to try to make sense of it. So there was a whole secondary process of note taking and analysis that occurred at that stage. I organized them mostly around the themes of the four cases that I presented to the community observers.

Question: At what stage in the project did you see your thesis emerging?

Engel: The "Oven Bird's Song" article was not one that I had anticipated as a product of the research when starting it. In thinking about it afterwards there was a shift in my own understanding of how I wanted to frame my scholarship. This was at a time when interpretive techniques had become more important for sociolegal researchers. Clifford Geertz's *The Interpretation of Cultures* had just recently been published.[1] The notion of "thick description" was really very powerful, although it was later overused. It had a galvanizing effect on my own thought. Instead of just mapping discrete binary conflicts that crop up and go places in society, it seemed much more important to explore questions of meaning – not only what people did but how they explained and thought about what they did.

So in this article I felt I was shifting to a different level of analysis from the one I had started with. The article really changed over time. I think more than anything I've written this article developed in layers. The first draft would be almost unrecognizable now because I added layer after layer as I understood my own materials better and better. This little article took a long time to write, probably over two years. I eventually ended up with a conclusion that was much more about the role of memory and the sense of time and history that caused people to interpret their experiences in a way that didn't conform to the realities of how injury cases were actually handled in their society.

[1] New York: Basic Books, 1973.

There was great concern in Sander County over a problem that, objectively speaking, wasn't even there. Ultimately I realized that the challenge of the article was to explain this anxiety about law in the context of social and cultural change.

All of this became much more apparent to me as I was going over the data. Fieldwork and analysis were quite different stages in the process. We design our fieldwork to be as complete and coherent and intellectually well founded as possible. Yet it always leads to something that's different from what you expected. As a colleague likes to say, if we end up intellectually exactly where we started, there's probably something wrong with our research.

Question: What are your feelings about how the article has been received and used in subsequent literature?

Engel: I am gratified that it has received some attention among Law and Society scholars and has been useful to some legal scholars who do not do sociolegal research themselves. Some of them have explored the distinction I observed between two forms of individualism based on rights and on self-sufficiency. My own feeling is that ethnographic research deserves a place in the legal academy, and it is a shame that so few legal scholars attempt it. On the whole, I think that legal academia is not interested in qualitative empirical research. So that part of it is a bit frustrating: the way legal academics continue to think about research and do research. With respect to my article, though, I've been pleased that it was read and assigned to students even in law school courses.

I think there have been some misconceptions about the article. It is sometimes understood to say that the legal culture of a small town is different from that of a big city, as if Sander County was meant to be a contrast to Cook County. I really didn't intend that at all. There's actually a point in the article where I write that the concerns about social change and about newcomers versus old-timers can take different forms in different social settings. I think in urban settings you might find the same sort of lament for an imagined ideal society. You may find those ideas expressed in different ways outside a small rural community like Sander County, but they may amount to the same thing.

Question: "The Oven Bird's Song" is only one of the published outputs from this research project. After this piece you went on to publish with Carol Greenhouse and Barbara Yngvesson. How did that collaboration come about?

Engel: It was through the Law and Society Association meetings. Some of us began to discover each other. We found ourselves on the same panels. In particular, Carol Greenhouse and Barbara Yngvesson and I realized that our three studies were quite similar though we hadn't intended that to be the case. In fact we didn't even know each other when we conducted our fieldwork. But we ended up writing a book together, comparing courts and communities in three different regions of the country. So it was a fortunate moment for us in the history of the Law and Society field. I was lucky to connect with these two gifted scholars and to form a lasting friendship. I had thought that the end result of my research would be a book which presented the global view of my project. Instead, it became the joint publication with Barbara and Carol. I would never have anticipated that that would happen but it was a really satisfying way for the three of us to explore issues of locality and universalism in our work.

Question: In retrospect, is there anything you might have done differently in this project?

Engel: When I started the project I didn't realize the temporal dimension would be so important. Knowing what I know now, I would have structured the interviews more around that: asking people to narrate their life stories beginning with early childhood memories and going forward. If I had built in more of a temporal perspective within each interview I think that might have told me even more about the changes that the community was undergoing. The disputing paradigm is sort of ahistorical. That's one of its weaknesses. It is temporally shallow because it tends to focus on relatively brief but memorable eruptions as opposed to the evolution of relationships, norms, and practices in the community over generations. So going back now, I would have tried to construct interviews that would have tapped into that in greater depth.

Question: The title of your article, taken from the Robert Frost poem, really sticks in people's minds. Can you tell us how you came to that?

Engel: I had always loved the poem and, as I said earlier, the article went through different layers of understanding. The final layer was the one where I understood that these interviews conveyed a kind of post-lapsarian view of the world. The poem expresses exactly that, talking about "that other fall we name the fall." The oven bird's song came from the sense of a diminished world. So for me the light bulb went on when I realized that the discourse of opposition to law and of concern about personal injury litigation was itself comparable to the song that the bird was singing: a lament for the past and a question of "what to make of a diminished thing."

CHAPTER 9

KEITH HAWKINS AND *ENVIRONMENT AND ENFORCEMENT**

Although Law and Society has matured as a field, many scholars remain driven by curiosity to undertake "exploratory" projects, seeking to open up the world of practices in varied settings for legal interaction. Environment and Enforcement *was written on particular new ground, at a time when "regulation" – now, Keith Hawkins notes, something of "an orthodoxy" in sociolegal studies – was just starting to receive scholars' attention, particularly in Britain. In such a wide-open context, the qualities of an exploratory project are taken to the extreme, where one may lack both theoretical touchstones and specific fieldwork models to build on.*

Participant observation can be particularly well suited to revealing the unknown. When Keith Hawkins was presented with the opportunity to undertake the empirical study of environmental enforcement, he had already been converted to qualitative fieldwork for the kinds of knowledge it produced. His background in criminology in an oddly helpful way set up Hawkins to undertake the "anthropological" frame of mind: to assume the veneer of the ignorant but interested and innocent outsider. Unlike Robert Kagans project on Regulatory Justice (see Chapter 3), Hawkins was not a "participant" in the literal sense but rather an observer who would spend months observing the routines of regulatory encounters.

Lacking a clear expectation for what one might find in the field is not the same as being unguided by a clear objective. Hawkins's first reflections – about how he arrived at his project after a decade of interest in other legal topics – drives home the recognition of important, general questions at the heart of Law and Society research.

Methodological Keywords: participant observation, interviews, documentary analysis

---

* *Environment and Enforcement: Regulation and the Social Definition of Pollution* (Oxford: Clarendon Press; New York: Oxford University Press, 1984).

Hawkins: I started out doing a law degree in the early 1960s. I didn't find it very interesting intellectually. Instead of getting involved in questions about what the law was on X, Y, or Z, I found myself asking questions about what factors outside the law might influence the judges' decisions. What interests was the judge trying to advance or protect in making a decision in a particular way? I decided after two or three years of law that I was much more interested in law as a social phenomenon and that that was something I wanted to pursue. The only way that you could follow that sort of academic interest in 1964 was to study criminology. So I applied for the graduate course at the Institute of Criminology at Cambridge University. I found that a very rewarding experience intellectually and decided that I wanted to do research. I became increasingly interested in questions to do with the relationship between legal rules and other social, economic, and organizational rules that people live by and decide by.

To cut a long story short, I ended up being allocated to a project on parole being funded by the U.K. Government's Home Office, with Leon Radzinowicz as my supervisor. I started doing some preliminary reading and became very interested in the question of how parole boards actually selected prisoners as suitable for release. It didn't seem to have been researched before. That began my career interest in the exercise of legal discretion and decision making by legal officials. I was later elected to a research fellowship at my college which allowed me the luxury of more time to develop these interests and eventually to finish the dissertation. It took me six years and turned out to be twice as long as the average dissertation!

In 1972 the newly founded Centre for Socio-Legal Studies at Oxford University advertised for a "research lawyer." I wasn't sure whether after my nine years in criminology at Cambridge I could justifiably describe myself as a research lawyer, but I got the job and became the first member of the research staff. The Center later began a program on environmental regulation with Anthony Ogus, Paul Burrows, and Genevra Richardson. They came to the conclusion that they really needed an empirical input so I designed an empirical enquiry for that program.

Question: To what extent did your prior work in criminology present you with hypotheses to test in relation to environmental regulation?

Hawkins: I tend not to work with hypotheses in a formal sense. I much prefer to work with a set of organizing ideas which I can then articulate in terms of a guiding research question. The question I was concerned with was about the nature of compliance. So far as I was aware, no one had looked at the question of compliance. Coming out of positivist criminology at the Cambridge Institute in the mid-1960s, everyone was concerned with law breaking: why do people break rules? I became much more interested in the question: under what conditions do people comply with rules? It became a particularly acute interest in an area like water pollution because, when I began some preliminary visits with inspectors just to get a feel for the kinds of work that they did, I noticed that in pretty well every site I visited, from small farms to huge factories, there were the physical signs of compliance. That in itself was interesting when you considered the legal sanction for noncompliance – a very small fine in the Magistrates Court. If the sum was so derisory, why would people comply with the law? That became the organizing question.

Question: Why did you choose a qualitative approach to the research?

Hawkins: During my Ph.D. I had gone off to the United States for a year with a fellowship at Columbia Law School. This allowed me to study the work of American parole boards firsthand, there being no parole system in the United Kingdom at that time. I found myself in Columbia Law School with essentially no research guidance at all, having to cut my teeth on a project which required me to understand how members of parole boards selectively exercise their discretion to release certain prisoners but not others. In the course of doing that work, I discovered the joys and the value of ethnographic research. I stumbled on it. I don't know how many times I must have painfully reinvented the wheel. I hadn't read any interactionist sociology. I hadn't read any labelling theorists or any of that stuff at all. I happened upon it myself, slowly and painfully.

I managed to get the cooperation of the New York State Board of Parole and the California Board of Parole (the Adult Authority). I also did a little bit of supplementary research in Connecticut and the state of Washington. I started out needing to learn again about parole boards and what they did. There was no literature that I could get my hands on that gave any indication at all about how they did their work, what a parole board hearing was like, and so on. It struck me that the first thing I needed to do was to go around with the commissioners of parole and visit the various prisons and sit with them and watch them in action. So I sampled commissioners of parole and I sampled prisons.

I visited maximum security institutions and minimum security institutions and everything in between. I tried to sit with as many different parole board members as I could. I was allowed to look at the case files as they interviewed the prisoners. I sat at the back of the room during hearings and was allowed to scribble notes on what I saw and heard, what I thought was going on. I began to learn quite a lot from all of this.

But of course, given that the Cambridge Institute at the time was a good, positivist criminology institute, there was always this sense that one had to generate some numbers somewhere along the line. So I designed a very detailed decision schedule for parole board members which listed what seemed to me to be the decision criteria, based on my observations. Then I gave them a seven-point Likert scale to indicate whether it was strongly influential, slightly influential, or no influence, and/or whether it was not taken into account at all – all very painfully conventional, I have to say. I managed to get all eleven commissioners of the New York State Board of Parole to fill out an equal number of schedules on randomly selected inmates, stratified in terms of them appearing for their first hearing once they were eligible for parole. I ended up with 660 of these things.

When I got back to Cambridge I was very fortunate to benefit from the late Dick Sparks and his newfound enthusiasm for doing data analysis on the creaky old giant machines they had in the Cambridge University computing lab. These were, of course, very early days in computing and data analysis. I got my data assembled in 660 data cards and I did two-by-two tables and I analyzed everything conceivable that one could possibly want to analyze about the things that the commissioners said they had taken into account in reaching decisions. All of that appeared in my Ph.D. dissertation.

But I have to say that I learned very much more from the qualitative data than I ever did from all of the number crunching and quantitative data. So I developed a certain bias against quantitative analysis as a means of handling my kinds of research questions. I don't want to be critical about quantitative methodology. It can do things that qualitative methodology clearly cannot do. But for the sorts of things that I've been interested in, I've always found qualitative data very much more insightful and useful. I had learned enough about studies of policing after my Ph.D. to realize that, for me, most of the really interesting work had been qualitatively conducted – work by, for example, Jerry Skolnick, Al Reiss, Donald Black, and Peter Manning. So for

Environment and Enforcement I decided to design a project that was essentially a kind of police officer-on-the-street study transferred to the regulatory inspector on the riverbank.

Question: Even within a qualitative approach there are choices about particular techniques or combinations of techniques to use. Why did you choose participant observation as your primary technique?

Hawkins: I have used participant observation wherever it's possible and of course it's much easier when you're monitoring continuing activity. If there is activity to observe then you've got something to get to grips with, and you also have some raw material which you can discuss and debate with your research subject. You can explore with your research subject: "Why did you do that? Why did you say this? What were you trying to get at when you did this or said that?" I frequently would do that, especially when I was driving around with the inspectors in their cars. Driving with them to a regulated site is a good way of finding out about the site – what the inspectors are going to do, who the key personalities are, what the nature of the problems are, and what strategy they propose to adopt.

Question: How did you structure the participant observational work?

Hawkins: I've tended to do participant observation in two stages. The first stage comprises preliminary data collection to produce a descriptive analysis of how the work being studied is done. I, for one, had no idea how inspectors worked. There was nothing in the literature that gave any sense of how they did their job. I was very conscious of the fact that the subject had not been explored very much in this country, and certainly not at all ethnographically. So in this preliminary stage I tried to formulate some general ideas which captured what I thought was happening. Then a second phase was focused more on developing ideas which had come to the fore, or on filling gaps that may have become apparent. That's been a pattern I've tried to follow throughout as much as I could.

In *Environment and Enforcement* the gap between phases lasted a few months. I had plenty of time to go back to Oxford and go through my notes really very thoroughly. That was one of the benefits of working in the Center, particularly in the 1970s and 1980s. We weren't under pressure to produce things quickly. We were able to spend time thinking and reading, spending more time in the field than would have been the case had we had a finite research grant.

Question: You also used interviewing as a technique in this project. When would you do this?

Hawkins: I've always tried to supplement any participant observation work I've done with interviews. I've followed up by trying to get people to develop ideas that have occurred to me, or ideas that I've exchanged with them in the past, to articulate things they have said or done. It's a way of getting more comprehensive, organized data.

Also, when you work in organizations, particularly on something as elusive and ephemeral as decision making, you have to get inside people's heads as best you can. That's extremely difficult. It becomes more difficult when you are dealing with people who do not engage in continuing activity. When you are dealing with supervisors or their managers or the people at the very center of the organization who spend their days administering, meeting, phoning, and reading, it's all much more static, tacit, and hidden. So you have to learn as best you can what people do – and what people think they do – from as many sources as you can get your hands on. And of course interviewing then comes into its own.

Question: Can you talk a little bit about how in choosing sites you balanced practical issues against analytical issues such as the nature of the territory being policed?

Hawkins: The practical issues that you clearly have to take into account in any empirical project have to do with the resources at your disposal. We had a certain amount of money to fund this project out of the Center's core Social Science Research Council grant. But clearly one had to operate with some degree of self-restraint. That required selecting research sites that were not so distant from Oxford that it became very expensive and time consuming to get to them. So resources compelled a focus on reasonably nearby research sites but still one could maximize what seemed to be theoretically interesting contrasts in the various sites. I chose two sites within fairly easy driving distance of Oxford that offered a range of different kinds of pollution problems and widely divergent environmental settings. What I wanted to do was to maximize contrasts in the sites which my inspectors would have to work, the kinds of problems they would have to face, and so on. That would presuppose different levels of enforcement activity, different characters in the environmental problems, and literally different characters in the sense of the kinds of people they would have to deal with.

Question: How difficult was it to gain access to the selected water authorities?

Hawkins: It was fairly straightforward getting access in both water authorities, really very straightforward indeed. I went about it in a fairly gentle manner. I tried to present myself as not wishing to intrude upon their work routines and timetable any more than I had to. I made it clear that it would not cost them anything other than a bit of their inspectors' time. And to be blunt I've no doubt that it helps to come from a university that people know of. I made sure I wore a tie when I went along to talk to these people and presented all of the social cues that I assume would be regarded as desirable in those settings. I made sure I wore a jacket as well as a tie, and presented myself as someone who was keen to learn, and keen to understand the sorts of problems they typically faced in doing their work.

Question: To what extent did the framing of the research question and your preparations inform what you looked for and recorded when going into the field for the first time?

Hawkins: There are things that emerge from one's general reading about the research question. There are certain features, themes, and key questions that I'm sure you go into the field already conscious of and sensitive to. But when I first went into the field I genuinely tried to keep as open a mind as possible, just to learn as much as possible about what was going on, as dispassionately as possible. I tried to go in treating things as anthropologically strange and as unburdened with preconceptions as I could. As time went on I tried then to focus more, depending on what I had learned. So gradually one would try to develop and refine based on the emerging experience in the course of the participant observation. As you go on things become very familiar. You see and hear things again and again. Things become repetitive and you begin to think you're not learning anything new. You have constantly to remind yourself that the sheer repetition, the sheer regularity, the sheer persistence of a feature is itself intrinsically interesting and important. Exceptions always capture the interest and the imagination. You always want to have some explanation for the exception, but the regularity is every bit as important. So I constantly tried to remind myself of the importance of patterns and regularity and would try, wherever possible, to explore what would become taken for granted, as far as my research subjects were concerned, so that I could understand why they would regularly behave in this way rather than that.

Question: You spent time with quite a large number of inspectors over the course of the project. Did you have particular techniques for putting people at their ease?

Hawkins: Before I went into the field I would try to get some sense of what I thought would be the difficult or sensitive topics and the kinds of questions that might prompt concern. I always left those to the end of the interview session or the end of the period of participant observation. By then I would have got to know the particular person reasonably well, or the person would be reasonably comfortable talking about the job and their attitudes.

When I went to do participant observation I genuinely wanted to learn. There are things you have to learn about the area you're going to, the sites you're going to visit, the people you are going to encounter in the regulated firms, quite apart from the person you'll be working with. So you cannot but portray yourself as someone who needs to learn and that immediately casts you in a dependent role so far as the interaction is concerned. In a sense that gives your research subject the whip hand in the interaction. So they feel a bit more comfortable and that they are running the show to a greater extent than perhaps they might be. It puts them at their ease. You can gradually work toward the more sensitive and searching questions. If you've organized your time well, you have two or three days of participant observation with an individual, or two or three hours if you're interviewing.

The people that I was researching are people who get out in their cars in the morning, driving around, inspecting sites, and talking to industrialists and farmers during the day. They probably have a fairly lonely lunch, eating sandwiches in a pub somewhere, and then repeat the process in the afternoon. Then at some point during the day they would go into the office to catch up on their paperwork. It's a fairly solitary kind of activity and I think the great majority of them are really happy to have some company. And of course there are very few of us whose egos are not massaged by having someone asking about them and their work! I think everyone, with very few exceptions, will be very happy talking about themselves and who they are and what they do and why they do that.

Question: How did you organize your time and how long would you routinely spend writing up your fieldnotes when in the field?

Hawkins: I would typically go on a Tuesday morning to be able to conduct research on the Tuesday, Wednesday, and Thursday. Then I would return to Oxford on the Friday. I would follow that pattern week after week after week. When I was doing the fieldwork, I would spend the working day with the inspector. That generally meant being picked up in the inspector's car in the morning when they began work, and spending the whole day with them, including lunch in the pub or wherever. That was always a good time to talk to them, when they were feeling a little more relaxed. I would sometimes write notes during the day because the inspectors might have periods when they weren't driving or when they were sitting and looking at a river or whatever. I would take that time just to jot in the briefest possible way some key words to help me remember important things that had gone on that day so that I could come back later and amplify them. But most of the writing up had to be done in the evening. I would be dishonest if I gave you the impression that I sat there in a sordid bed-and-breakfast place every evening diligently writing up one hundred percent of my field notes from that day's work. I didn't. I just didn't have the energy because it is incredibly tiring. When you work the whole day, concentrating very hard so that you don't miss anything, and then you have to keep your mind in gear in the evening to exploit as best you can what you've learned that day, that is actually very physically tiring. Week after week of that is extremely demanding. But I did what I could and I filled out the rest of the notes as soon as I could thereafter while my memory was still reasonably fresh.

Question: How did you go about analyzing your data?

Hawkins: This was in the days when computers were still steam-driven. One simply ended up with binder after binder of field notes, painstakingly written out longhand. I collected all of my data together – the interview data (which I did manage to get transcribed in the Center), my field notes, other notes taken from the documentary analysis, the case file analysis, and any other original source material that I could lay my hands on. I just read the stuff over and over again, particularly my observational data. I read it through thoroughly and I read it through thoroughly again. Clearly there were already ideas I had in my head about what were the important themes I wanted to pursue. But, as I read, other things would emerge, which I noted. It was essentially a question of developing the existing ideas with new ideas and embellishing them with data, with illustration, whether drawn from the case file notes or the interview transcripts or the notes from participant observation. Gradually I built up a set of relevant insights, all of which spoke to the research question generally.

I have to say, the data analysis was a fairly banal thing. There was nothing romantic or adventurous or intriguing about it. It's just very banal reading the data so that you are utterly familiar with it, so that the patterns and regularities become really very clear. I knew of no other way except a constant reading and rereading of the stuff.

Question: How long did that take?

Hawkins: I did it over a fairly lengthy period. But research is a messy business. Data collection and analysis do not follow in nice discrete chunks, in a very systematic way. It all tends to run one into another. I take time to scribble down some analysis when I'm actually writing up notes if it's necessary because I want to capture the idea when it's fresh in my mind – I don't want to lose it. I started participant observation in the middle of 1976 and finished it in 1978, but I went on analyzing the data after I went to work in the National Institute of Justice in Washington, D.C., in late March of 1979. I went clutching all of my data and notes and by then I had quite a lot of drafts written. I had gone to Washington to do some further research on parole board decision making. I finished the work on *Environment and Enforcement* when I was doing this other project. I posted it back to Oxford in the spring of 1980, though the book was a victim of the introduction of new print technology at Oxford University Press and did not actually appear until the spring of 1984.

Question: What was the most challenging aspect of the project for you as a researcher?

Hawkins: I don't want to overdo this, but there was a challenge in working in what felt at the time to be very much a new area. There was virtually no literature either in the United Kingdom or in the United States that I could lay my hands on and no precedent for that kind of ethnographic research, other than the policing studies. It's hard to imagine that now, given that the whole topic of regulation is so orthodox in sociolegal studies. But we frankly didn't know anything about it other than the comments on things that one picked up from reading annual reports of the Thames Water Authority or reading Kit Carson on the factory inspectorate in the *British Journal of Criminology*.

Question: With the benefit of hindsight, is there anything that you would have changed about the project?

Hawkins: It's very hard to answer that without sounding insufferably smug, but I have to be honest and say that it went smoothly and I was generally fortunate in not having great difficulties. Things that could have gone wrong didn't go wrong. I don't have any regrets about what I chose to study and how I chose to study it. I don't think I would change anything now. Of course as you go on you tend to become more confirmed in your own research preferences and your own styles and so on and probably more blind to alternative ways of doing things. Maybe I'm guilty of that but I don't think there's anything I would change.

CHAPTER 10

CAROL GREENHOUSE AND *PRAYING FOR JUSTICE**

Successful empirical research, quite obviously, depends on understanding your data. For the legal anthropologist in quest of the cultural understandings at work in people's most foundational beliefs about, for example, community and relationships, understanding one's "data" demands an unmistakable intimacy. There lie all the dangers that present in the real emotional lives of people. The ethical hazards reach their pinnacle in fully immersive ethnographic fieldwork: living among and befriending your research subjects. As shown by Carol Greenhouse's experience, learning about a community may mean navigating unfamiliar rules of social engagement as well as appreciating the ethical boundaries of managing the relationships formed in fieldwork. That Praying for Justice focuses on the added dimension of a community's deeply held religious convictions multiplies the potential problems she had to navigate.

Carol Greenhouse's reflections on the life of her project reveal a number of paradoxes inherent in ethnography. As she notes, the ethnographer is part of people's lives but also not – present but completely dispensable. Equally, the fruits of intimacy with one's data can sometimes not be secured without its opposite: distance. Though bearing the marks of the period in which the primary fieldwork was conducted, the book – published a decade later than the dissertation – represented an evolution of ideas, aided by a secondary phase of archival fieldwork. Just as ethnographers need to see their research subjects with the eyes of an outsider and yet be on the inside, intimacy with data and immersion in the field is partner to the ability to engage them through different frames and for different analytical purposes. By returning to the field after some time and engaging in archival work she was able to observe and document how the past dimensions of conflict in the community had been submerged and silenced – what Greenhouse refers to as the "ahistoricism" of social conflict. Greenhouse begins by describing the origins of the project in the early 1970s,

---

*Praying for Justice: Faith, Order, and Community in an American Town (Ithaca, NY: Cornell University Press, 1986).

amid the concerns that were driving legal anthropology in those years, before her research struck off in different directions and long before she would find the distance that allowed her to write the book.

Methodological Keywords: ethnography, participant observation, archival research, interviews

Greenhouse: The anthropology of law in the United States is now a rich literature, but at the time of my fieldwork, to my knowledge, there was nothing in print – that this could be the case seems almost incredible now. There were other anthropologists working in U.S. "fields" of law at about the same time, so this situation soon changed, and very much for the better. In some ways the difficulty in talking about *Praying for Justice* now is that so much has changed since the seventies – in the ethnography of the United States; in anthropology, legal anthropology, and sociolegal studies; in dialogues between legal academics and specialists in the humanities and social sciences; and more generally in the politicization of access to law in the U.S. over recent decades – and, in reference to this work, the emergence of evangelicals as a national political force. I went to Hopewell in September 1973. In 1972–73, when the project was in formation, the idea was simply ethnological – to fill in a gap in ethnographic knowledge about the cultural dimensions of law use in the U.S. In terms of the state of the field at the time, there was a strong sense of new questions taking shape from the cumulative work of field ethnographers all over the world, from regions at the cusp of independence where the status of "custom" was prominent as a high-stakes issue. "Legal anthropology" had the status of a subfield (long since reintegrated into sociocultural anthropology) – and part of its excitement was what we saw as its relevance in relation to ongoing transformations of law in many parts of the world. The U.S. was part of that picture. In the U.S., this same period was the high legislative phase of the Civil Rights movement, when the landmark Supreme Court opinions and congressional legislation of the previous decades were generating new law for implementation at the grassroots. Legal anthropology was framed around theoretical questions occasioned by the times – for example, as debates over the role of law in controlling social processes (between structuralists and processualists) and over the question of the coherence of informal law, among other things.

As I say this, it seems odd that questions about the reception of federal civil rights law – still recent history then – were not explicitly part of the study design. We thought of U.S. research as inherently "relevant" but the content of that notion went unstated. Perhaps it is a sign of how very localized ethnographic practice was, how distant the state was from our ethnographic concerns, how ahistorical our questions were – or how naive we (or I?) – might have been about the pervasive relevance of federal power, and local resistance to its expansion in the civil rights era. *Brown v. Board* – the U.S. Supreme Court case that had ended legal segregation in public schools – had been decided nineteen years before I went to the field, and the landmark legislation of the Johnson era followed, a decade after *Brown*. To be sure, in the early seventies, the resurgence of states' rights had not yet fully taken shape as the banner of a national conservative movement nor as a feature of mainstream political discourse; those developments came inescapably later. Even so, in retrospect, I'm struck by the fact that at the time those could be imagined to be separate issues, or settled questions, so far in the background as to be not directly relevant to an ethnography of contemporary local law use.

Question: In terms of choosing Hopewell, had you considered other potential sites? How difficult was it to settle on a particular site?

Greenhouse: I settled on Hopewell from afar, from a set of criteria that I had worked out over the course of those collegial conversations I mentioned earlier during my years of graduate school course work. Atlases and census material were my main informational resources – once I had chosen the south and the Atlanta metropolitan area. The project I went there to do would have been a community study of law use in relation to the full range of judicial institutions in the area, since, as I remember my interests at the time, they were mainly with the relationship between social distance and density of social ties on the one hand and the duration and formality of dispute settlement on the other. From that standpoint, I imagined it would be important to have a local court (in that system, a county court) as well as other state and federal courts within easy range. I chose the Atlanta area for this reason, though any other city with this combination of access to courts would have met these criteria. I chose Hopewell because it was small, its court served a single county, and it was economically diverse (especially as between rural and urban) in ways that the other metropolitan counties were not. The last step in my selection process was just a lucky guess. I supposed that there would be a historical society in a small town like this, so I wrote off blind to the historical society of Hopewell and received a lovely response, inviting me to their next meeting. I attended that meeting, and the Historical Society became my first core network for the project.

Question: Given the range of people that you were encountering, observing, and interacting with, how difficult was it to gain access?

Greenhouse: In some ways it was too easy. My own sharpest self-critique with regard to the project is that I allowed the ethnographic study to be shaped too much by the access that I came by "naturally" in the course of working through networks of networks. I was committed to an intensely naturalistic mode of inquiry. In retrospect, proceeding in that way meant that the study was prone to be shaped by those networks, and that social fissures were likely to remain out of view. If I had been more systematic, or just less reliant on my core network for introductions, I might have discovered sooner what (i.e., who) was missing – and gained a fuller sense of context around the issues central to the study. The lines of access I did not have were those that would have led me across the local color line – other than the few formal interviews I was able to arrange through my network (and in each case accompanied by the same member of the Historical Society). Relying on networks meant that I also missed the rural poor; these groups overlapped to some extent, but by no means completely. There was a black church, and a small African American community in town – its population the same size that it had been at the end of the Civil War. African Americans also lived in small rural settlements – one was called "Freetown" – created after emancipation. The black settlements I knew about were in the unincorporated area on one end of town. There were also poor white rural settlements, beyond Hopewell's town limits in the other direction. These places were part of the scenery but they were outside the geography my networks associated with the town, and I had no contact with them – perhaps one measure of their isolation, and certainly mine.

Question: Beyond the problem of finding all enclaves of the community, and getting in the door, the ethnographer tries to understand the many people from many walks of life that you did encounter. Did a better rapport with some people affect your approach to the research?

Greenhouse: For the reasons I've just mentioned, the study responds most closely to the concerns of Hopewell's white middle and upper classes (to the extent that I knew them) – or rather, their concerns to shape Hopewell's future around a particular vision of community. Much

later, I learned something of the extent to which the time just
to my arrival had been a period of tension over the new federal laws
requiring desegregation of schools and public accommodations. Now I
cannot help but see the local emphasis on reconciliation and restraint,
as well as the commercial and touristic promotion of Hopewell, as
intricate ways of ending that history, and beginning again.

The people readiest to spend time with me were women – some of
them young women my own age (some of them married with children),
others older, whom I came to know in the context of volunteer activities
in town, or as friends of friends. These were people I could easily find on
my own. It was also very easy to find a place in the circle of young men
and women roughly my own age at the Baptist Church – where Sunday
Bible study is organized by generational cohorts. I was anomalous there,
but I wasn't the only anomaly – this was also the group for Vietnam
vets (if they were single), and divorced women if they fit the age
range.

Question: How difficult was it for you to gain an insider perspective of
the Baptists, particularly because they frame the world in terms of those
who have a Christian perspective and those who don't?

Greenhouse: Oh, it was the easiest thing in the world to put myself
in a place where I was drawn into an insider perspective. It would
have been far more difficult to insist on remaining an outsider. In this
community, to ask a question about the Baptist faith was to already
have been touched by the Holy Spirit. In this sense, there can be
no outsider's perspective – to have a perspective, to seek one, is by
definition to be in the process of crossing to the inside. This was very
challenging personally (as I felt my friends' witnessing as friendship).
It was also challenging in terms of writing about what I understood to
be their experience of faith. Clifford Geertz's "Thick Description" was
published while I was in the field, so I read it only later – but it came as
both a revelation and a relief, as a solution (via the phenomenological
aspects of interpretivism) to the problem of how to recover enough of
an "outsider's perspective" so as to be able to write.

Question: To what extent did you develop friendships in the process of
being immersed like that?

Greenhouse: There was certainly a sphere of warm friendships that
shaped my understandings of the community and the church. For the
most part, those individuals do not appear in the book, although some

do – this is why, in the book, I went to some lengths to make the identity of the town and individuals deniable, for the sake of local people who might prefer to disassociate themselves from it. But to go back to something you said earlier, "intimacy" – if it's at all reciprocal – in a sense *precludes* writing. Friendship sets a kind of limit to the work. I don't mean that it's secret, but that ethnographic writing becomes something like editing a personal letter, or rewriting one's own interview responses, to restore the kind of clarity that's possible only if one is mindful of the others with whom (or about whom) one is trying to communicate – and sometimes this means reclaiming (or giving back) the privacy one forgets to hold onto in a spontaneous conversation, yet without changing the subject, and still accountable to the original exchange.

Question: How difficult is it to manage the tension between being a friend and being an observer?

Greenhouse: For me it was not difficult in the field – for the reasons I explained when we were talking about access and networks. The tension I felt was not between friendship and observation, but between these and authorship. In my case, the difficulties were the private ones I explained a moment ago. There was little or no public stake in how I resolved any role tensions for myself. I was never called on to take sides in that sense – though certainly other anthropologists have been called upon to do so in their fieldwork, and sometimes fieldwork takes extraordinary courage for all concerned.

Question: Can you say a little bit about why you decided to study the archival data and when you did that within the overall process?

Greenhouse: The dissertation was essentially framed by what I understood to be the parameters of the Berkeley Village Law Project: what is the nature of people's disputes? How do they resolve them? What are the local norms? (and so forth). These were questions I expected to be able to answer when I went to the field – simple questions, impossible to answer. Hopewell was not a village – it was a growing suburb of a major metropolitan center. Even leaving aside the original plan of following court cases through judicial levels, the material – framed as cases of dispute – was overwhelming. Antagonism (whether as social division, disputes, or disagreements – even among friends) continually produces its own forms of excess and is a ready refrain of personal narrative. At first, I imagined I should treat these stories as evidence of individual cases of dispute, to be sorted out somehow – but they were about everything and anything. Eventually I found it more productive to think of them as what they more manifestly were: stories – things people tell about themselves in public. They had thematic and formal refrains, and they resonated with the stories people liked to tell about the town's history. That these themes and resonances could travel between spontaneous personal accounts and the more rehearsed tales of the town's past was what led me to the archival side of the project.

The archival work transformed the study, opening up the question of early social divisions and their institutionalization in the town's early history, and their contemporary traces. My main interest in the archive became the question of how the specificity of events comes to be submerged in social categories – how social categories absorb the specificity of conflict so that there's simply no story left to tell other than the play of moral types in standardized dramatic forms. The book was about the de-narrativization of class from the local past and the extension of that process in the ongoing production of ahistoricism in contemporary life – in the way essentialisms function in personal narratives of conflict, and the contemporary importance placed on narrating conflict in socially appropriate ways.

Question: You went into the field to study one thing and ended up studying something else. How stressful was that? Were you engaging with your supervisor about these questions?

Greenhouse: I'm sure I should have engaged more, although the changing storyline of my project gave me a more or less constant sense of doubt that I had anything to report. After a particularly long silence at my end, my adviser called me – I can't remember his questions now, except for one: Have you made friends whom you visit at home? That I could answer "yes" seemed to make a reassuring difference. But to respond to your question, at a certain point it became apparent that it was at church where I was finding the "material" I had expected to find in the court study. The court study would not have been feasible as framed, but it wasn't the feasibility problems that determined my choice. Was this stressful? Allowing my circumstances in the field to pull me into another sense of the project was the solution to a problem, not a problem in itself.

Question: You eventually felt you needed to leave the church because it was a source of upset for some of the people who were anxious that you become converted. You mentioned earlier that any kind of inquiry by a nonbeliever is seen as a sign of the Holy Spirit acting on him or her. Did that create a tension for you as an observer, realizing that they were hoping that some kind of conversion would happen?

Greenhouse: The other side of your earlier question about friendship and observation is that, in a sense, there wasn't an observer's role for me in the church anymore – I had been mistaken to think there could be. My not being "saved" was never a problem in my relationships – the people I knew could not have been more accepting – but I feared that the long duration of what to them was my "not yet" would become a burden for them. Having heard their testimonies (faith narratives) and engaged in many personal discussions of faith within my church circle, including with young men just back from Vietnam, I became concerned that my doubts might become a source of doubt for them. Like others I knew at church, those young veterans worked hard at their faith, and their testimonies made it clear that the church was important to their reintegration into the community, and into their own lives. It was a way to stop the killing, to take the killing out of their life stories. Everyone I knew in the church worked hard at their faith, in their own ways. Being born again is not a choice, as I came to understand it, but a path that opens once it has been cleared of the conceit of intention. Once I understood that this was something my friends were working for in their own lives and mine, and realizing the situation I had unwittingly created for us, I felt I should step back from the church circle. The upset wasn't theirs, though; it was mine.

Question: In a year-long project how much time would you spend each night working on it? Did you live anything like a normal life in the field?

Greenhouse: I thought I was having a normal life, give or take the oddity of being the local anthropologist, but when I left (only as far as Atlanta), and painful as it was to leave, I remember feeling a sense of returning to my own life, so I suppose it wasn't normal. It certainly was a full-time occupation; in my case, some of the most productive time (also enjoyable) was other people's leisure time, and I spent most of my evenings with "my" group at church or with other friends.

Question: In terms of writing the book, you had different bodies of data. Can you say a little bit about your process of analyzing and synthesising the bodies of data?

Greenhouse: The local emphasis on an ethic of restraint became the connecting strand of the book. I ordered the chapters from the present to the past, and from the personal to the collective (as I understood these), and from the explicit to the implicit – reflecting my thinking then about how culture works and is worked by individuals and groups. A concept of cultural relativity in this sense undergirds the book, though I didn't think of the project as a study of a particular culture or subculture. The book's integration – such as it is – was also a product of the writing process, of discovering things in the material at the points where the text demanded or resisted transitions. There were some valuable surprises along the way from that aspect of the project, too.

Question: In relation to your Ph.D. dissertation, when did you have a sense of the thesis emerging?

Greenhouse: I remember the intensity of my effort to find a way to write about what people shared with me – yet without a travesty of exposure – whether of private conversations or public testimonies. I also had to work around the problem that I had not collected cases of dispute. Eventually I solved the latter problem by not thinking of them as cases of dispute, but as narratives of other kinds – and the former by taking the question of individual faith out of the part of the account that was about the church. Perhaps that's when the thesis began to emerge – very much in the midst of writing, when I had to confront the question of how to preserve people's privacy (and acknowledge the limits of my own knowledge as to their inner lives) in print, in a way more or less consistent with what had been the unspoken terms of our face-to-face relationships.

Question: In what ways was it helpful or a hindrance to you to be writing the book after the event?

Greenhouse: I can't imagine it any other way, for myself. Fieldwork is necessary but never sufficient – the rest must come from somewhere else: cumulative reading, the classroom, collegial conversation, the theoretical questions of the day, or something else again. "After the event," I worked in those arenas. As the seventies turned into the eighties, anthropology was rapidly opening up in a variety of ways – and legal anthropology had begun an entirely new chapter that was very exciting, and formative personally. The book could only have come when it did – its main intellectual debts were current to the period of its production.

Later still, long after the book was published, I made a brief visit to Hopewell. I was able to see then that the people whose vision of the town I had absorbed almost twenty years earlier had also, in a sense, been writing after the event – that the small town they presented to me was one that had already disappeared, except as a myth (in the rich anthropological sense of that term) that they held onto in the hope it would have enduring value as something to live by.

Question: We were very struck in the book that you had written a letter to the Hopewell residents and I wonder if you could say a bit about why you did that.

Greenhouse: I can't take credit for the idea. For all the reasons we're discussing – even that long after the fieldwork – it was hard to let go of the book, to go to press. My editor, Peter Agree, wisely sized up the situation, and in conversation one afternoon suggested that I write a preface in the form of a letter to readers from Hopewell. I wrote it that evening in one go. Breaking down that fourth wall was a liberation – crucial to the process of finishing the manuscript but more fundamentally an awakening to connections between the creative freedoms and responsibilities of ethnographic authorship that I had not previously considered.

Question: Through the many issues we've discussed, it must be that the project made emotional demands on you as a researcher.

Greenhouse: I should begin by saying that my situation in the field was not a difficult one by any objective standard. The demands I felt were the claims of its inherent ambiguities – some of which involved genuine intellectual problems, even if they felt like impasses at the time. I was steeped in the ethnology of law from my studies in social anthropology, and in questions of customary law and "law and modernization" from courses at law school at the same time – and I had done several months of fieldwork on conflict and disputes in a Mayan village (Mexico) for my undergraduate thesis. My sense of how to conduct fieldwork on law was based on that experience, and years of studying monographs from Oceania, Africa, and Central America. But those models didn't go so very far in Hopewell, for a variety of reasons even beyond the obvious ones. As a result, I sometimes had the odd sense of imitating fieldwork more than doing it – I simply couldn't imagine how I would manage to make what I saw as the leap from my daily experiences to the sorts of accounts that I had been reading, and inspired by. Rules, cultural norms, social structure – these seemed to call for precisely the kind of certainty that kept slipping away from my field of vision. I had to figure out a way to dispense with that kind of certainty, and instead to think in terms of how other people were pursuing some certainty for themselves as to the wider relevance of their own capacity for goodness.

Fieldwork encompasses everything and yet *a project* as such can only be the remainders (and reminders) of the relationships one has formed "in the field." Some of your earlier questions touch on the ways the actuality of relationships can pull at one's focus in fieldwork – this is a paradox, and an absolutely necessary one, I'm sure. I wasn't sure then, though. Looking back, I should have felt my situation as an adventure in professional freedom; that sense of adventure came later.

Mine was not heroic fieldwork in any way, and I wouldn't want to make too much of the demands of my personal experience in Hopewell. I think the most interesting aspect of the question of emotional demands in the field is what an anthropologist does with his or her emotion – since even when we made more of objectivity in the discipline than we do today, objectivity was never indifference. Part of what makes anthropology so alive today is its openness to engagement.

Question: With the benefit of hindsight, what would you do differently?

Greenhouse: I've had some thirty-five years to reflect on this one. I remember vividly the work of crafting the book's introduction and conclusion around some recent reading, and regretting that I had not engaged those resources – particularly Weber – much sooner and more thoroughly. Some second thoughts went into the comparative book I wrote with David Engel and Barbara Yngvesson. As for mistakes of judgment in the field – I've mentioned the main ones, I think, and no doubt there were others. Some elements of hindsight became clearer in the book's local reception. I found I had underestimated the extent to which my historical analysis might be painful for some people, for example. But all of that is hindsight in the narrow sense. If we're really going to entertain the full fantasy of hindsight, this would have been a study of local experiences of desegregation in the midst of the region's incipient uptake into the migration flows of "globalization" – the latter not yet visible in Hopewell in 1973 but on the horizon by the time I began the book in earnest. Certainly the strong federal assertion over state and local jurisdictions was all around us in 1973 – hidden in plain sight. I don't know if the project would have been feasible framed in that way, but it's what was happening. It would have taken me to the same locations and conversations, as well as to others I've long since realized I missed. I've tried to make use of that realization in my other work but that doesn't cancel the critique.

CHAPTER 11

JOHN CONLEY AND WILLIAM O'BARR AND
*RULES VERSUS RELATIONSHIPS**

In the past two decades, continuing the quest to understand how law "really works," Law and Society scholars attached increasing significance to the dialogues and narratives of people involved in disputes or people experiencing "the law" in their lives. The emphasis on language and discourse has been shared by scholars coming from backgrounds in political science, sociology, and law, as featured in the work of Sarat and Felstiner (see Chapter 17) and Ewick and Silbey (see Chapter 19). Conley and O'Barr, the team perhaps most identified with the study of legal language, reached the subject through linguistics and anthropology after their own idiosyncratic path to collaboration. This interview highlights some of the differences of emphasis produced by the disciplinary toolbox, though many concerns – such as observing and listening in as nonintrusive a way as possible – are shared in common.

Perhaps not surprising for scholars interested in conversations (albeit of a legal variety), their attention to the quality of conversations is manifest in the work itself. For one, their approach to squeezing meanings from language involves subjecting texts to dialogue itself, using discussion as an analytical tool. Second, their desire to speak across disciplines and to those outside of academia, especially, drives a passion for the words' use in reporting their research. Can a sophisticated understanding of how language and culture shape the legal world be rendered simple enough to reach a wide audience? To the extent that Law and Society research begins from a desire to engage the world, the answer might not only be "yes, it can" but also "you should." The exploration of Conley and O'Barr's approach to the study of legal language begins with the birth of their long-standing collaboration.

Methodological Keywords: conversational analysis, interviewing, field observation

---

Rules versus Relationships: The Ethnography of Legal Discourse (Chicago: University of Chicago Press, 1990).

Conley: The beginning of this was very idiosyncratic and, I guess, almost accidental. I went to Duke as a graduate student in physical anthropology. At that point Mack (O'Barr) was a junior faculty member and known as an Africanist. All kinds of things were happening in my very brief career at that point, including the faculty member that I came to Duke to study with, the late and infamous John Buettner-Janusch, having just announced his intention to leave Duke and go to NYU. So he was leaving but I didn't want to go with him. I was kind of an orphan. Somehow Mack, in consultation with Ernestine Friedl, who had just come to Duke as the new chair of the department, identified me as a prospect for a graduate student to work with on his project. I said yes. The way it worked out I was going to go to law school as well. I was going to get to keep my physical anthropology fellowship and apply it to law school. So the beginning of this had all sorts of factors at work that had nothing to do with intellectual logic.

O'Barr: From my point of view I had spent my years in graduate school preparing to be an Africanist. I had just spent two years in Tanzania, where I had studied old men under trees making decisions and what passed for tribal law in postcolonial Tanzania in its early years. In 1972 I went back to Tanzania to continue that work. I found out that I was most unwelcome by the government and by the university because the politics of the country had changed to such a point they didn't want foreign researchers. They especially didn't want American foreign researchers. So I decided that some of the questions that had concerned me in my first period of fieldwork in Africa could probably be worked on theoretically in other places. So by hook and crook I started to figure out what to do in order to continue working on some issues about law and language that I had got very interested in when in the field. I managed to convince the National Science Foundation's program on Law and Social Science that I should do an ethnography of law that focused on linguistics in the American courtroom. This was sort of a lick and a promise because there was no literature whatsoever to link this to. The original grant that I was given was much more about, "Well, it sounds like a really interesting idea. Why don't you go try this?"

I had money in that grant for a graduate student to work with me on the project. We were trying to persuade John not to go to New York and he had this substantial interest in law. So, basically not having studied this very much, he took up the study of law and anthropology and he got into this pretty quickly. He was bringing his interest in and his perspectives from the early years of law school into a collaborative project that was accidentally brought together. I was focusing heavily on linguistics and he was focusing heavily on law. The two things came together, each of us being kind of an expert in one of these things and always talking in the middle about how the two connected. So it was fortuitous, accidental, totally unplanned.

Question: How did you get to this early formation of the *Rules versus Relationship* project?

O'Barr: I had spent a sabbatical at Oxford's Centre for Socio-Legal Studies in 1982 to 1983. At that point conversational analysis was a big thing in the study of sociolegal matters in the U.K. I went to work specifically with Max Atkinson, who has written about how juries respond to the rhetoric of lawyers in the courtroom. While I was there I got interested in how people tell stories. This is what the conversational analysts were doing. When I got back from England I said to John, "We have to study how people would tell legal stories – if the law would let them." The Brits were calling this "trouble talk." It was about how problems that come up in life get discussed. We sat down and talked about this and John said, "Well, you know this is the small claims courts issue because when people go to court they get to tell their story. It is as untransformed by law as you're going to find in a legal situation."

That fall I went to the American Anthropological Association (AAA) meeting in Denver. I had a long conversation with Sally Merry on the Sunday morning. We went to lunch in this dumpy little restaurant. The food was inedible but we had the best conversation. She was incredibly supportive and helpful. And the bottom line is that for the next three days I went across the street very close to where the AAA had been held, sat through a small claims court. I brought the tapes home because they cost seven dollars each. John and I sat down and listened and followed the method that I'd seen at Oxford, which was to take little pieces of conversation or parts of stories, and for each person in the group of at most six or eight, to contribute what they understood about this, or what they thought, or to discuss their perspective on it.

It turns out that those discussions were dynamite for us because when we started doing this we started seeing the rudiments of the things that you see in *Rules versus Relationships*. Oddly enough the case of Mrs. Rawls that plays such a central role in *Rules versus Relationships* was the very first case I heard that very first Monday morning in Denver. I didn't understand it in that particular way. I just sat there thinking, "What a silly old lady she is and what a mess this court is." But as we thought through this and looked at what was happening and tried to understand it by repeated hearings, a very different understanding on this started to emerge. We went back to Denver two or three times, collected more cases, got another grant, went off to other sites like Philadelphia and North Carolina.

Question: What drove the case selection?

Conley: We went to Philadelphia because they had this system there where nonlawyer clerks do intake interviews and help people prepare their case before they go in and see the judge. So you have Denver and North Carolina where people just walk in off the street and then we had Philadelphia where this structure was imposed and it was a multilevel process. We chose that because the structure was different and in North Carolina we had an opportunity to get an urban/rural mix.

O'Barr: We also sent two people back to Denver. Their role for us was to go around and talk to people who'd filed cases and hadn't yet gone to court. They'd then go back after they went to court and talk to them about what happened later. And we were able to get the transcripts of what happened in court because Denver did that. What was important theoretically about this is we were able to hear the case at the time of filing or in the period before trial, then we were able to hear it in court, and then we were able to talk to people after the fact and hear what they said about what happened in court. This seemed to us to be a beautiful way to hear the processual unfolding of the case.

Conley: We were influenced by a couple of precedents there. One was the whole processual legal anthropology thing of the 1960s and 1970s. Another was Felstiner, Abel, and Sarat's "Naming, Blaming and Claiming" article about the evolution of disputes.[1]

Question: In a sense, then, given the stress of recordings, you didn't need to be present at the sites. Were you nevertheless there and observing together when making these tapes?

[1] W. L. F. Felstiner, R. L. Abel, and A. Sarat, "The Emergence and Transformation of Disputes: Naming, Blaming, Claiming ..." *Law & Society Review*, 15(3/4, Special Issue):631–54 (1980–1981).

Conley: Not always, but usually we observed together. I think, in relation to everything we wrote about, at least one of us observed it, except for the student interviews. We didn't actually observe those. The conversational analysts whose methods we relied heavily on are, almost by definition, not present at the conversations that they record. They are limiting themselves to the evidence of the language. As anthropologists, we thought the language was the central piece of it but we were also interested in the whole context – what did the whole scene look like and feel like? That also gave us opportunities on occasion to chase down people and talk to them – litigants, judges – and that proved to be interesting. So the linguistic texts were the core piece of evidence but we were interested in the larger context.

O'Barr: John and I wrote a book in 1992 – which John likes to joke is more rare than the Gutenberg Bible because virtually nobody bought it although it is one of our best pieces of work – about the culture of people who manage great sums of money in financial institutions.[2] We used very open-ended interviews, where we had twenty-five topics written on the back of an envelope that we wanted to hear about. What we tried to do was set an environment in the interviews that would open-endedly invite people to talk about topics like the ones we wanted to hear about and when they didn't manage to bring it up we would only then ask about them. It was that we tried to be as nonmanipulative as possible, because we both believe that the conversation is a product of the interviewer and the interviewee. We thought if we could find situations where people were talking on their own without us managing that conversation, we would be much closer to studying culture as it works in everyday practice. The beauty of studying the smalls claims court in *Rules versus Relationships* was the fact that we didn't need to do anything. In fact in the Colorado courts where we first started, the tape recordings were made for the record by the court and all we had to do was pay seven dollars per tape to get a copy of it. So except for being present in the courtroom and saying nothing, our presence didn't really change the system very much. I think throughout all our work we have hoped to be as unobtrusive as possible in the production of the information.

---

[2] O'Barr, Conley, and Carolyn Kay Broncato, *Fortune and Folly: The Wealth and Power of Institutional Investing* (Chicago: Irwin Professional Publishers, 1992).

Question: When you were out in the field, was it difficult to explain to people what you were doing?

Conley: In all of our projects we've had the advantage of naivity when going in. The short answer to people was, "We really don't know what we're interested in specifically but we're trying to understand this world." With the small claims litigants, when we were asked we said, "We're trying to understand how people think about and explain their cases. Nobody really knows much about that so we just want to listen and hear from you." When we went to the investment people, the answer was, "Nobody's looked at how investment people talk about what they do and how they think about it from a cultural point of view, so we can't tell you exactly where we're going with this but we just want to hear from you, talk about yourself and what you do."

O'Barr: And oddly enough this particular offer to most people turns out to be just something that they love. Most of these folks who work in law and in finance almost never have the opportunity to reflect on what they do. So when two anthropologists come along and say, "Can we just talk about what you do?" the response we've got is, "Can you be here for a couple of other days, not just this one?" I mean, they want to talk forever! In fact, we had problems shutting people up once they got started. We found, in general, people absolutely loved to talk to us about the questions that we'd ask. I can't remember being refused.

Conley: Just to reinforce the point, I have been doing some phone interviews recently with lawyers as part of my legal profession stuff. These are people who bill by the hour. So they give you an hour, that's money right out of their pockets. But you can't shut them up! It gets to three o'clock in the afternoon, they could be doing five hundred dollars there and they're talking to me and I have to hang up on them!

Question: When did you decide fieldwork was at an end?

O'Barr: I have a very simple answer to this: when you start seeing that the conclusions and interpretations and data repeat themselves, you've got it, that's it. And until you find that, you're not finished.

Question: To those less familiar with your approach, and the anthropological approach, a notion of representativeness – and thus sample size – might be a first concern.

O'Barr: We've always been building models. We've never been enacting numbers. So in *Rules versus Relationships* we lay out models of how judges and litigants approach the legal system. Numbers are not the point. Somebody else can count.

Conley: We're interested in distribution, not frequency.

Question: To what extent do you take an interest in the distribution of the observations – the sample as it were?

O'Barr: We were more interested in the possibilities than we were in the frequency. I'd make the argument anthropologically that this is a little bit like studying hunting and gathering bands. There are not many people in the world who live like this now, probably practically nobody, but the point is that theoretically it's very interesting. So we try to approach it like that – not "What is the most frequent way that people do this?" but "What are the ways in which it can happen and what does this way lead to?" "What does that way lead to?" and so forth.

Question: When you talk about methodology in *Rules and Relationships* was there any sense in which you were responding to potential criticisms or concerns that the methods were not going to be seen as valid?

Conley: Yes, I view this as a response to Law and Society. In general, most of our most significant publications have been written not for an anthropology audience but for a Law and Society audience. We had a number of experiences submitting papers when the reviewers would come back and say, "OK, this is interesting, but when are you going to code it?" I'll never forget giving a paper at Emory years ago and some old fart said, "Well, this is interesting pilot research." I said, "Pilot research? This is three years of our lives!" So what we tried to do was explain to the quantitative side of the Law and Society world why this was important, why it was not preliminary to quantitative work. The two of these things are complementary. Both are essential. We tried to walk a fine line between dealing with these criticisms preemptively, giving the explanation we wanted, and being defensive.

We had a much more positive experience involving David Trubek. In the 1980s, *Law and Contemporary Problems*, which is housed at Duke Law School, put on a conference on empirical studies of the legal profession. In the law school world "empirical" means quantitative, and it means law and economics. We were doing some of our small claims stuff for this conference and, understanding who the audience would be, we bent over backward to explain why this was empirical. As soon as we finished, David Trubek of Wisconsin jumped up irate. He said, "You don't need to be defensive about this. This is great. Let the law and economics people go to hell!" So that was the other side of this.

Question: What would you admit or see as a limit or self-criticism of your approach?

Conley: I guess there was some inevitable frustration because we couldn't figure out a way to catch the very beginning of a dispute. Even if you pick up cases as they're filed the dispute very likely has a long history before that. We didn't have a way to solve that problem.

O'Barr: How do you find the beginning? Where is the beginning? These things sort of ferment. They move from here to there. People finally decide they're going to do something about it. But at what point can the anthropologist logically think to come into it? All we can ever do is, at the point when it becomes a formal dispute, we can begin to measure the thing, begin to see people talking about it. Before that you maybe had to be sitting in the kitchen listening to a man telling his wife about it or standing next to the lawnmower in the backyard listening to people talking about problems that each of them have had. It's very hard to imagine how to get beyond where we went.

Question: What was the relationship between data collection and data analysis? How did that unfold?

Conley: In all three of our major fieldwork projects "iterative" is a good word to describe how we did it. We were either watching cases or interviewing people. We were making recordings, getting transcripts made on an ongoing basis, and spending a lot of time analyzing them. So we were developing hypotheses as we went. We were refining them, sometimes throwing them out as we got deeper into the analysis of the transcripts, and all of that was informing the further fieldwork and interviews we were doing. I actually like to think of this as one lifelong project. We happened to be for a while in formal courts with juries, for a while in small claims courts, for a while in the investment community. But really it's an ongoing study of how language is used and how it appears to matter in settings where power is the central concept.

O'Barr: I completely agree. I think that's exactly what the situation is. I feel like we've been engaged in a long-term collaborative set of questions that have looked here and looked there but have always been at the bottom-line issue of "How does the law not deliver on what it promises and how does power enter into the legal system?" "How do some people get more of the benefits than do others?" I think those basic questions inform all the work that we've done and our method is subtle. We've tried to look at how the stuff plays itself out in language partly because we find it very interesting and secondly because nobody knows anything about this. I think it's no more and no less than normal.

Question: In the introduction to *Rules versus Relationships* you describe the method of analysis as "deceptively simple." Simple in theory but a bit more difficult in practice?

O'Barr: When I was in Oxford for that year I went to weekly sessions where the conversational analysts would all sit round the table. There would be eight or ten of us and somebody would propose an "extract for discussion" – that was what it was called. The extract would then be played for us and we would be given a one- or two-page transcript of it. After hearing it two or three times each of us would take five or ten minutes and write "notes" about it. This was so open-ended and really aggravating. But the amazing thing was it was a brilliant process because everybody would mention the things that they saw in the small amount of text which seemed to be really important and worth talking about. We tended to focus on somebody's story in court, the litigant, the respondent, a witness, and we would choose that because it seemed "interesting" to us. Through a lot of long sessions, a couple of hours at a time, we would find these to be sometimes incredibly productive, other times leading nowhere. But it was a totally empirically based method where people would simply contribute what they had to say about it.

I learned from doing that. That's where John and I started. We would basically just do exactly what I've described. It was really out of that that *Rules versus Relationships* was born. We saw the difference when we looked at "this way of doing it" versus "that way of doing it."

Conley: Over and over again "these people are talking about rules" and "these people are talking about relationships" but each group was deriving a concept of justice from that starting point.

O'Barr: It really was ethnographic analysis. I don't know how to do something more ethnographic than that. From our point of view it was incredibly productive and we were just basically taking insights that came out of the stuff, not one time but repeatedly. And as the analysis would do the same thing again, and we would see it over and over, it sort of – I hate to say it – intuitively emerged. It was almost like that. I feel like if you look at the data carefully then things emerge from it. That's what happened in that process.

Question: Is that something that's reproducible by, say, a student (an advanced undergraduate or a graduate) working with a piece of text? How much does it depend on that sense of the group listening and working together as opposed to just being able to sit down alone and think about your data?

Conley: Well, there is some synergy from having multiple heads at work. You have more people with more perspectives, you see more things, you argue more things, you get a better result. But I think it's certainly a worthwhile exercise for an undergraduate honors student to try to do this. I have students who do projects like this all the time and they invariably come up with really fascinating stuff.

Question: How easy was it to move from your conversations about analysis to your own written text?

Conley: I think we work outwards from the text. The process of analysis produces what you might call "canonical text." Mack was talking about seeing and hearing the same thing over and over again. As we analyze we begin to develop a set of core texts that are the best examples of what we think are the recurring concepts. So each concept perhaps becomes a chapter and the outline of the chapter becomes the four or five texts that illustrate the permutations of the concept. So you arrange the texts on a table and then the writing task is pretty simple. At the start of the chapter you introduce the concept and then you fill in the details, the introduction and the analysis that follow each text. So the texts really tell the story themselves, helping the reader to do what we've already done – that is, to tease the theoretical story out of the texts. A great efficiency of this kind of work is that, when you do the analysis of the texts, the account that you're going to publish almost writes itself. What we're giving the reader before, between, and after the texts is really a summary of the arguments that have led us to tease the concepts out of the texts.

Question: Is it possible for that shared, collaborative conversation to be carried through to the process of writing, or does one person take the lead?

O'Barr: What we basically did was we would take up a particular topic and we'd outline all this at the beginning. Then we would both read the text. We would argue enormously about it until we had a common point of view, until we saw this in a certain light, until we identified the points. We were sitting there with notepads, writing this stuff out, and then we literally sat in the room with two computers. I would write a few phrases, then I'd give John the disk and he'd write some more. It's impossible for us to say that somebody drafted the first version and the other changed it because it was really the coproduction of the ideas every single time, and it worked. We were constantly engaged in dialogue, conversation, and common writing.

Question: I would presume there is a remarkable degree of closeness to be able to write together, passage-by-passage.

O'Barr: I think the thing that's interesting about the project, and the humor of it all, is that John and I are just such different people.

Conley: We have nothing in common. We agree on nothing. You can't overstate the differences. In every dimension you can conceive of we are different. The thing that epitomizes it is that for twenty-five years I've gone to every Duke basketball game with Mack's tickets that he wouldn't think in a million years of using and I wouldn't figure in a million years of missing. And we have these differences at intellectual levels too.

O'Barr: Exactly. The fact that we're so different and we have such different interests has been probably the basis of the synergism. We look to the other to offer us very different suggestions about how to look at things. I really don't think that two people who saw the world the same way would probably produce anything nearly so productive.

Conley: So what I would say to potential collaborators is: find somebody who's very different from yourself.

Question: It may be, as the cliché goes, that a camel is a horse produced by committee, but your teamwork has produced particularly clear prose in the end.

O'Barr: In deference to John, I think he produces words on the page that I think are beautiful and I love to look at. He can write language that would floor most people. Sometimes what happens in the collaborative process is that I bring up the contrary ideas, the really radical things, and the beauty of the language to explain them to someone else often comes from him. I don't know anyone with a larger vocabulary than John, and what I'd always say to him is, "If this word is not in the *Reader's Digest Dictionary*, it doesn't go in this article unless we explain it." He now says the same thing: who is more popular than *Reader's Digest*, and if it's not in there, then we try really hard not to use those words. When people say, "I want to tell judges what I know, I want to tell litigants what I know, I love to speak to people in positions of power. How can I do that best?" maybe the answer is: write in language they understand? I've always thought that the major job of an anthropologist is to take the message of anthropology to other people. I don't need to talk to other anthropologists, that's not the point. What matters to me is whether I can make an impact on the things that I care about, and to take the deep, serious messages in the places where people can use it politically and practically.

I think our best version of all this stuff is in *Just Words* because in that book I think we captured, from our point of view, the essence of all the interactions, the linguistics, and micropolitical issues that help us understand how the larger legal system works.[3] But we tried really, really hard to see if we couldn't just say it in simple, everyday English. I've loved Law and Society as a field because people there haven't been so concerned with just saying it to each other. The very important uniting force is that all of us are trying to talk about how the law actually works as opposed to what the law says it does.

[3] Conley and O'Barr, *Just Words: Law, Language and Power*, 2nd ed. (Chicago: University of Chicago Press, 2005).

CHAPTER 12

SALLY ENGLE MERRY AND *GETTING JUSTICE AND GETTING EVEN**

Our understanding of the role of law in society has been shaped powerfully by research from exotic locales or unfamiliar cultures. The classic anthropological studies of conflict and disputing, in particular, looked to the Tobrianders of Papua New Guinea, the Tiv of northern Nigeria, and the Barotse of Zimbabwe.[1] In the past few decades, however, Law and Society scholars have focused on notionally "familiar" settings closer to home, such as David Engel's journeys to Sander County (Chapter 8), Carol Greenhouse's study of Hopewell, Georgia (Chapter 10), and Patricia Ewick and Susan Silbey's examination of four New Jersey counties (Chapter 19). How well does the past generation's methodological and analytical toolbox travel? The importance of that question stretches well beyond the work of anthropologists, but to all researchers seeking out new settings in which to test and develop theory.

For Getting Justice and Getting Even, Sally Merry drove to the urban communities of Massachusetts, but the journey only began there. Intellectually, her working hypotheses utterly failed to explain what she was finding on the ground. Methodologically, a large urban setting challenged the received approach to ethnography. Yet, a tension between a received framework and a new situation is an invitation to creativity. In this interview, Merry reflects on the conceptual and methodological puzzles she confronted, her resolution of which advanced our understanding of the power of legal consciousness. In her prior

---

*Getting Justice and Getting Even: Legal Consciousness among Working-Class Americans (Chicago: University of Chicago Press, 1990).

[1] Bronislaw Malinowski, *Crime and Custom in Savage Society* (New York: Harcourt Brace, 1926); Max Gluckman, *The Judicial Process among the Barotse of Northern Rhodesia* (Manchester: Manchester University Press, 1955); Paul Bohannan, *Justice and Judgment Among the Tiv* (New York: Oxford University Press, 1957). Although spatially less distant, one may note the exoticism behind Karl N. Llewellyn and E. Adamson Hoebel, *The Cheyenne Way: Conflict and Case Law in Primitive Jurisprudence* (Norman, OK: University of Oklahoma Press, 1941).

research she had found that youths in a low-income housing project, many involved in crime, were going to court to fight one another.[2] At a time when alternative dispute resolution (ADR) was expanding, she was primed to think about the uses of law in American cities.

Methodological Keywords: ethnography, participant observation, interviews, surveys, court records, archives

Merry: I started using Gluckman's framework about "close-knit" and "loose-knit" social networks. My theory was that people who are engaged in close-knit social networks would be interested in compromise and that people in loose-knit social networks would want to go to court. So I wanted to look at how mediation worked in a close-knit neighborhood and in a loose-knit neighborhood. I also wanted to look at different kinds of mediation – one much more conciliatory, community process, and the other court-based. The real question I was interested in was, "Under what conditions are people interested in reconciling and under what conditions are they interesting in adjudicating their conflicts?" I had a suspicion at the time based on my previous research of American urban communities that people's willingness to conciliate was not particularly strong, that people who lived in small communities conciliated because they had to, with social pressures on people to go along. It seemed to me that when people moved to urban areas, they were actually choosing a more autonomous private life where they didn't have to go along.

I was not sure how much conciliation would happen, but the conversations at the time, in the late 1970s, which were part of an antilaw movement, were all about notables who mediate cases. I realized that the unarticulated premise of the movement in the U.S. was that if people in close-knit communities were willing to mediate cases instead of adjudicating them, and if law was the problem, then if mediation was introduced perhaps those kinds of communities would be created. So I began this book looking for local notables – people who would be informal conflict resolvers – and for cases where this was happening naturally in communities. But I couldn't find them. I interviewed priests and community leaders. Nobody was handling conflicts. So I started studying these two different mediation programs.

[2] Sally Engle Merry, *Urban Danger: Life in a Neighborhood of Strangers* (Philadelphia: Temple University Press, 1981).

Question: As a subject for research, how easy was it to gain access to mediation, which on the one hand is not public in the sense of open court, yet is less formal and more experimental?

Merry: There was a mediation program that was a ten-minute drive from my house. I went to visit it to see if they would let me study them. I walked in and it was a very cool atmosphere. They were very hostile and negative to me. At the end of this interview they said, "see, look at this story" and they held up a newspaper story in which they had been criticized. I decided I couldn't study that mediation program. It was frustrating but they were defensive.

I found another mediation program. It was an hour's drive away but the person who was the director was very open, friendly, and happy to be studied. The distance from that neighborhood made my ethnographic research much more difficult. The second mediation program was again run by a very experimental, open group of people. There seems to be a distinction between the innovator who sets something up and then the administrator who continues it. I was working with innovators in both cases who were actually quite interested in having some research done and thinking about the mediation process and how to do it. So the people I ended up working with were the ones who thought this was an interesting idea. Finding organizations that are open to being studied is absolutely key. If there's any suspiciousness or hostility before you start, it's going to be difficult down the road.

I asked the mediators and the people in the mediation programs if they minded if I sat in. After a while the mediators got used to me, and nobody ever objected. I just sat in the back of the mediation session and took notes. One day one of the mediators didn't show up and they asked me if I would mediate because I had gone through the training. I refused to do it. It is so different to actually try to do it than to observe how it got done. One of the challenges in doing this kind of ethnographic research is that pretty soon the people you are observing put you in the status of expert. They would say, "Well, was that a good session?" and "Did we do well?" and "What did you think? Should we have done that?" It's really important to resist answering those questions. Once you've become the expert and start judging them they're going to feel uncomfortable about having you, the judge, there.

Question: What provoked the shift in focus from mediation to the courts?

Merry: What became clear to me was that mediation programs were not actually conforming to the rhetoric of being a totally autonomous way of handling conflicts based on neighborhoods. Mediation programs were solutions in search of a problem. It was very difficult to persuade people to go to mediation. These mediation centers were searching frantically for cases. Instead, people wanted to go to court – people put up with their problems as long as they could and then went to court. The whole appeal of mediation was fairly limited except for mediators. It turned out that the mediation programs worked very closely with the courts. One of the mediation programs got its cases because people went to court first and then they got sent to the mediation program. The other one started picking up cases in the small claims court because they were a more community-based program but couldn't attract cases from the community. It defined itself as a dispute settlement center, but the staff would spend a lot of time fielding problems that didn't look like disputes to them – somebody couldn't get a social security check or someone had a problem with the city. Constructing the market for mediation cases was very difficult. As a result, mediation programs turned to the courts to get cases.

So I got interested in how adjudication and mediation were not distinctive processes but were really quite similar. I started looking at what happened to the mediation cases when they went to court. Of course, they weren't being adjudicated by the courts. They were being mediated by the attorneys in the hallways, or by the court clerk. The similarity in these processes became quite notable until I noticed that people didn't even distinguish them. Some thought that the court was handling their case even when it was being mediated. So, this was a book where the hypotheses I began with were all collapsing around me.

Question: Did the move from mediation to courts require you to adapt your methodological toolkit or your strategies?

Merry: My unit of analysis was the case. That was the disputing framework. The whole notion of disputing said that the social unit of analysis should be the trajectory of a case – the way it gets changed over time – in order to make it more rooted in the social system. So I was following cases and looking at how they were embedded in social systems. Using ethnographic methods, I spent a lot of time trying to understand the social relationships in the neighborhoods I studied. I hung around the mediation programs. I followed cases. I did some interviewing. I interviewed probably a hundred disputants. I sat in and observed the mediation sessions. I must have observed a hundred and some mediation sessions.

But of course, ethnography was designed to deal with villages and when you adapt that methodology to a more complex urban situation it's always difficult. "Close-knit, loose-knit," what do these terms mean? That hypothesis collapsed because I selected three neighborhoods to study and none of them was close-knit. None of them had the kind of close-knit intimacy that all the anthropology on conflict resolution in villages talked about. That was a kind of forced "close-knit" where people are interconnected with each other through kinship and economic ties. My neighborhoods were urban areas where people dealt with their conflicts by building walls and moving away.

How you do ethnography in these worlds is challenging. You still need a place where people are, where people interact with each other. So the courthouse and mediation program became my sites. I would then follow people as they moved in and out of these sites. But in tracking a dispute you can't be there all the time. If you're in a village collecting disputes you are there all the time when things are happening. One of the challenges of this kind of urban research is being there because, although I use a lot of interviewing, I believe that observation is the best way because then you can actually see what's happening. If you rely on interviewing people about events and experiences you clearly have to get multiple perspectives on what happened and triangulate them as much as possible. I did try to do that and, of course, the various participants I talked to did have different views. In a way I've spent my career trying to rethink how you do ethnography in a variety of contexts and places outside the village.

Question: Because you were interested in rooting the disputing in the social system, how do you get a sense of "the people" in the urban village?

Merry: This is not an easy thing to do. You can't really study a suburban neighborhood by sitting there, so finding places where people are is one of the big challenges of this kind of research. I remember driving around and trying to talk to as many people as I could who lived in these neighborhoods. I would interview them and talk to them about their conflicts and ask if there was anybody else I could talk to. You may meet them in community centres. You sit and talk to people in stores. You talk to somebody in any place you can find them. Then also, if anybody came through the mediation program who lived in one of my three neighborhoods, I would be sure to interview them. I also talked to community leaders, looked at statistical data, census data, and so forth.

I dealt with a lot of difficult people and interviewing these people was challenging. Some were strange and some were troubled. And when I say "interview" it suggests a formal discussion. But I'd hang around with them. I'd go to their houses, I'd visit with them. Fieldwork is a process where you become the research instrument. It really depends a lot on your social skills and your empathy and your willingness to listen to other people. That's the sort of thing I like to do but it does mean that you're very personally engaged in the process. You have to move outside your comfort zone a lot. You talk to people you wouldn't talk to otherwise in places you wouldn't normally go.

There were a lot of times when people would turn me away and they wouldn't talk to me. I had a very low moment in this project. One of the things I wanted to do was to do a ride-along with the police to see how police handled conflicts. I went to the police station in Cambridge because I was looking at two different neighborhoods in the city, one of which was a working-class white neighborhood and one was a black neighborhood. I asked the police if I could do a ride-along. I was eight months pregnant at the time, and they just looked at me with such disdain and told me to go away. It was November, it was sleeting, it was humiliating. It was just this awful moment.

One of the things I did was to hire people from some of these neighborhoods to be my research assistants. I hired them to go out and do some interviews. Then we would meet and we'd talk about their interviews. That's actually a very effective thing because they'd describe this interview and who they talked to and of course they knew the neighborhoods themselves and they liked the idea of being a researcher. That provided me with a lot of good insight into these neighborhoods. In a way it was collaborative and was really quite productive for getting a feeling about the neighborhood.

Question: One often envisions ethnography as a solitary enterprise – the lone ethnographer in the field. What kind of challenge is it to use research assistants?

Merry: Oh, enormous! It takes training. You don't quite know how much you can rely on them. There's a capacity for being warm, empathetic, socially skilled, and courageous that not everybody has. You have to find somebody who does that. I find that I always put more emphasis on the data that I've collected myself. What the research assistants provide is the context in many ways. The cases that I wrote about in this book are all cases that I observed. I talked to the people. But the research assistants can be very valuable in providing you with a framework of how typical a case is, how often it happens, what the larger structure is within which these things happen. And sometimes I will use the research assistants as informants themselves. They usually know more than they necessarily wrote down. The other model of having somebody do all the research and you come in and put it together is much more difficult to do. It's very hard to do ethnography that way.

Question: What investment of time was necessary to do this work? How long would you spend per day in the field?

Merry: It varied a lot. I had two small children at the time which was not the easiest way to do fieldwork. I would spend much of a day if something was happening, if I was following a case. The mediation sessions usually lasted a couple of hours. They would pretty regularly be on Wednesdays and Saturdays and the trick was that people would come back to court. So I had to go to court whenever they were there and there was often a lot of hanging around. They might be in court for several hours or I might sit in a clerk's hearings for several hours. So I would probably spend two, three days full-time in the court.

I spent a lot of time hanging around the court and they got to know me. Time is absolutely central. The first time you arrive nobody will do anything for you. It's the whole process of building rapport. You keep coming back and back and they get to know you as a person. People would generally come to trust you and let you in. There's also an interesting social class dimension. These court clerks were dealing with relatively low-status people and had relatively less interest in protecting their privacy. With high-status people there's more interest in protecting their privacy. So the court clerks wouldn't necessarily ask the people if they minded if I'd listen, although I had told them they should.

One of the things about ethnography is that you have to spend a lot of time typing up your notes. If you don't type up the notes then you forget. For each five- to six-hour session I would spend in the courthouse talking to people and interviewing them, I'd have to spend at least six or seven hours typing all the notes up. And then you go back and you reread the notes and you see things you didn't see before. I would then go and interview people, sometimes for an hour and a half, two hours in coffee shops and public places. So it was very unpredictable timewise.

You can't just say I'll be there nine to five. It's more like, I'll show up when something happens, I'll stay there as long as it's going on, and I'll meet you whenever you want to meet. It's a very serendipitous thing. It is very hard to combine with any other kind of activity because you have to be ready to go whenever people are ready to talk to you or something is happening that you want to see.

Question: Did you always envisage using the neighborhood survey as an additional tool?

Merry: Yes. I was influenced by the Civil Litigation Research Project, which began in the early 1980s and was trying to map the shape of disputing in the world. The neighborhood surveys were partly an effort to see what that world of disputes looked like and how the group that ended up in court differed from the total population of disputes. I had done a similar kind of project in my earlier study, where I had done an ethnography of the neighborhood, gotten to know a lot of people, and then did a survey about how many crimes people experienced and what their attitudes toward crime were. It seemed clear to me from that study that the best approach was to do an ethnographic observation first so you know what the categories are and you know what people think about. Then you do the survey so that your survey includes their categories, not yours. For example, in this earlier study I was interested in the relationship between the fear of crime and actual victimization. There was a great deal of survey research on the fear of crime at that time but relatively little ethnography. So I spent several months talking to people who lived in a high-crime neighborhood about what they were afraid of and whether they thought their neighborhood was dangerous. Some people would put bars on their windows, never walk alone at night, and take many protective steps, but when I asked them if their neighborhood was dangerous, they would say not at all. Clearly, a survey question would not address the complexity of these views about danger and the risk of crime.

Question: How did you go about analyzing it and synthesising the different bodies of data – neighborhoods, mediation programs, courts?

Merry: It's very hard. I always see this as a foreground-to-background problem. What is the central piece, and what is the explanation in the edges? When I wrote this book I had a lot of data from a lot of different programs. I see the problem as a kaleidoscope where you try different ways of foregrounding something and backgrounding something else, deciding what's your core problem and what's the framework within which you think about that core problem. It's a matter of experimenting to see which one works. Anthropologists have developed the concept of head notes. We talk about the importance of writing down field notes, but we recognize that there's also this phenomenon of head notes. You're constantly developing theories as you go along – theories about what's going on, what's interesting, what's important. In many ways the model that you use to analyze the data is one you have constructed as you've been doing the research.

In a way I would say it was kind of intuitive. One of the things I did was to talk about the therapeutic, the legal, and the moral forms of intervention. That just came to me one day. I think it was probably a headnote because I had been sitting there listening to the court clerk saying, "This is really not a legal problem." Suddenly it emerged in my consciousness that these were the categories that were being used by the court. So one of the tricks of ethnographic analysis is to think about what are the categories at play in your social scene that you're observing. It means being attentive to the categories of the people you are listening to. Then you go back and you look at the material you have and see if it falls into those categories, to see how people use the categories, if they make sense.

Question: Was it a disappointment to have begun looking for social networks and communities, and ending up in court institutions?

Merry: Ethnography is so serendipitous. I had no intention of studying the court. I was really just going to study the mediation programs and the neighborhoods, but the court turned out to be so important to the litigants. I didn't find the local notables; I didn't find the local conflict resolution processes; I didn't find people voluntarily mediating their cases. I found people putting up with difficult situations until they could no longer stand it and then going to court. It ended up being more institution-based than I might have liked, but I had already discovered that finding communities was hard.

Yet, the part of the project that I found most interesting was actually looking at how these cases got handled in the courts. Mediation as a phenomenon became less interesting to me than how legal systems regulate a person's life and when they intersect with people's lives. I became curious about how they affect what people do and think and how the law does and doesn't serve to shape people's lives. It was that problem that really became most interesting – the question about the state and the individual. That question is probably why mediation struck me as an interesting problem in the first place – because it promised to retheorize the individual and the state and argue that mediation was a return of authority and control to local communities, away from the state. But what I found was that people actually were turning to the state for solutions to their problems, then getting frustrated because they lost control of their problems.

Question: That shift meant that not only did your initial hypotheses collapse, but your theoretical frame for understanding disputing was in flux. That must have created havoc with your attempt to write a literature review.

Merry: It was stressful. I was trained in social anthropology, and the kinds of frameworks that I've been talking about all come from British social anthropology – groups and networks and structures. But in the 1980s Marxism was getting fairly popular in the Law and Society Association in the U.S. There was Critical Legal Studies and that was a very different framework for thinking about power and the allocation of power, and about the courts as structures of power instead of just as processes of conflict resolution. The whole disputing metaphor also was very oblivious to power structures. It was about trajectories of disputes and how people make choices about how to follow them. I was part of the Amherst Seminar. We were reading about Marxism and thinking about power, and that seemed a much more fruitful way of looking at my data. And I learned a lot from Susan Silbey as we worked together on this research. Now, collecting data with one theoretical framework and using it to get at another is a difficult way to do work. It was challenging to rethink my material in the middle. I spent six months writing the introduction, which was really the time I spent trying to rethink my material from the categories I started with.

I know graduate students are told to write the chapters and then the introduction of a dissertation. In a way, it's good advice. But on the other hand, you can't write the rest of the chapters until you know what's going to be in the introduction. I make an effort to come up with an introduction first. But you don't have to finish it. To focus on totally refining the introduction before you've written the rest of the book is a mistake. My strategy is to make a crack at the introduction to figure out what it is that's the core problem in the book. You have to decide that before you can write the rest of the chapters. But then after you've written the rest of the chapters you go back and revise the introduction to really fit with the rest of the book.

Of course we were also beginning to think about legal consciousness. As an anthropologist I liked the consciousness idea rather than culture because culture in my understanding is a kind of collective shared expectations and understandings. But the idea of consciousness connected that set of cultural understandings with individual experience. I thought it was an important move to add the focus on consciousness to that on culture. Now, the concepts of legal culture and legal consciousness are still very ambiguous and mean many different things to many different authors, but I've continued to be interested in how experience shapes the way people think about the law and use it.

Question: Does recognizing a frame mean you then have to leave out a lot that, while interesting, won't make it into the book?

Merry: This is such an important problem. Throwing stuff out is so difficult and so essential. I had enormous amounts of information I didn't use, lots of mediation cases I saw but didn't include. I interviewed lots of people. To force yourself to pick the highlights and toss everything else out is really hard. I just picked some but had to let the others go. They'll be sitting in my files and they'll never see the light of day. It's hard to let them go. I still should have thrown out more than I did from this book. Of course, it is important to do all that extra research in order to know what is important to include.

Question: In retrospect how might you have theorized or analyzed the data differently?

Merry: I wish I had done more thinking and defining of what I meant by legal consciousness in this book. I don't think I did as much work theorising what it means as I could have or should have. When people cite legal consciousness literature they tend not to go back to this book as much as they do to Ewick and Silbey's *The Common Place of Law*. It was one of the issues I was interested in. But you can't do everything.

The problem that I have gotten most criticism about, that I didn't see, was the way I talk about the cultural domination of law. That may have been too much Marxism. It may be a little over the top. I think I would tone that down if I were to write it now because it was a more nuanced problem: people did get something but they didn't really get what they wanted. How much power the state was actually exercising over them I think is questionable. I think maybe I overdid the way the power of the state was coming down on people's heads. The pattern that I saw was more one of lenience, the lack of power exercised by the state. It was a case of "I'm a citizen but the court is not paying much attention to me" rather than that the court was heavy-handed. The court was often indifferent to small injustices in these interpersonal cases, although it did develop its own definition of the problems regardless of what the litigants wanted. Overall, the litigants lost control over their cases, and from time to time the courts intervened to shift the balance, so there certainly was some exercise of power by the legal system. In the end, my hope is that people will find the book provocative and a way to think further about law and people's everyday lives.

CHAPTER 13

TOM TYLER AND *WHY PEOPLE OBEY THE LAW**

The raison d'être *of the Law and Society movement has been the shared appreciation of interdisciplinarity – the recognition that one has much to learn from scholars of other disciplinary backgrounds who unite around a common interest in "law." Though numerically a smaller presence in the field of sociolegal studies, for over a century psychologists have contributed much to our understanding of legal phenomena, from police discretion to jury decision making, from memory to insanity. More broadly, the turn toward behavioralism in the 1950s inspired others, such as political scientists, to employ psychological models and methods in the study of those – from judges to citizens – touched by law.*

In this interview, Tom Tyler points to the cross-disciplinary conversation that ties his undergraduate experience in the 1960s to a decades-long research agenda into the legitimacy of law. What methodological challenges lie at the core of the psychologist's approach to studying law? To some, psychology's distinctive place in the social scientific study of law lies in its common use of experimental methods. However, Tom Tyler's choice of large-scale surveying for Why People Obey the Law *puts him squarely "in the field" alongside all who seek to understand people in their relation to law, whether or not they do so quantitatively (see also Genn, Chapter 20). It is apparent, rather, that Tyler's need to theorize and operationalize Law and Society questions before collecting most of the data places a particular premium on planning and attention to detail. The fieldwork cannot generalize the theory but must follow it. The significance of* Why People Obey the Law *as a piece of scholarship is due to the care exerted at the earliest stages of planning, a disposition reflected here in Tyler's candid appreciation for the things that still fell short of ideal.*

Methodological Keywords: interviews, surveys

**Why People Obey the Law* (New Haven, CT: Yale University Press, 1990; rev. ed., 2006).

Question: The title of the book asks a classic question: why do people obey the law? It's a problem of imposing scope, a great challenge to take on, and as important as any in the field. Did you begin with that question?

Tyler: I will have to be completely honest and say that I never gave the book that title. When I sent the manuscript to Yale University Press there were two things that they changed about the book. They changed the title and they came up with a new idea for the cover. I don't remember what the title was going to be but it wasn't *Why People Obey the Law*. I can't take any credit for that.

I agree, however, that it's a classic question. But I didn't make it a classic question. I just recognized that everyone was saying it was a crucial question. People who were writing about the relationship between citizens and government were seeing as the fundamental question the general question of what we want out of people in relation to law. And, the answer was, "We want people to comply." Lon Fuller, for example, has written about that – follow the law, obey the decisions made by legal authorities.[1] Now the ironic part is that if we asked that question today I would think we wouldn't have the same answer. People writing today do not think that the primary thing that we want out of people is compliance. It would be more, "Why do people cooperate with legal authorities?" There's much more emphasis now on how, for example, you get people to turn in criminals in their community. How can you get people to participate in neighborhood watch, to go to meetings and work with the police, to identify crimes in their community? The real challenge, I think, is how to get people to be actively involved in government, in politics, with legal authorities in helping to maintain order in their communities.

Question: What sparked your interest in that problem?

Tyler: The core concept of *Why People Obey the Law* is legitimacy. I think the origins of my interest in that were my undergraduate years at Columbia University during the period when there were student riots. It was the height of the era of student discontent about the war in Vietnam. We had the experience of being told by the government that it was our responsibility to fight in a war that many of the people in my generation thought was illegal and immoral. So it makes you think

[1] Lon L. Fuller, "Human Interaction and the Law," in *The Rule of Law*, Robert P. Wolff, ed. (New York: Simon and Schuster, 1971).

about obligation, responsibility, and the nature of legitimacy. All of my cohorts were very much focused on such questions – when is it OK to disobey the government? Is it wrong to break the law?

The other important idea in the book is the notion of procedural justice. You can't really read the social science literature on legitimacy without starting to get the idea that procedural justice is really important. David Easton and Murphy and Tanenhaus wrote about the Supreme Court, about the dynamics of authority, and they all talk about procedure as the basis of legitimacy.[2] They don't necessarily use the words "procedural justice," but if you were familiar with the literature on legitimacy in political science and sociology you would immediately recognize when you read psychologists writing about procedural justice that they were all talking about the same thing. So I noticed that the ideas flying all over the place in the social sciences in general matched some discussions that were going on in psychology that were more technically focused on the nature of justice.

Question: In attempting to take a large problem, and given the methodological tools you prefer, how do you build up to the full-scale collection of data?

Tyler: The theoretical framework is what really matters in a project. A strong theoretical framework is what makes the difference between A-plus research and research that doesn't have as much impact. You really ought to be spending most of your time thinking about what you're going to study and why it matters. It can be nebulous and frustrating, but I think that's the most important part. When you're designing the questionnaire you have to keep going back to your theoretical framework. You have to keep thinking, "Am I asking questions that are addressing the theoretical questions that I have said are important? When I get this data, will I be able to address these questions that I said I thought were really important?"

The book was published in 1990. Between 1984 and 1988 I was designing the project, getting the money, doing the research, and writing up preliminary papers. There is a *Law & Society Review* paper on

---

[2] See, for example, David Easton, *A Systems Analyis of Political Life* (New York: John Wiley & Sons, 1965); W. F. Murphy and J. Tanenhaus, "Public Opinion and the United States Supreme Court: A Preliminary Mapping of Some Prerequisites for Court Legitimation of Regime Changes," *Law & Society Review*, 2:357–84 (1968).

defenders' evaluations of their experience in court.[3] That was kind of a prototype study for the book. So I had it sketched out. I had done some research to make sure that the basic ideas were reasonable, that they worked. Then I got the money from the National Science Foundation and the American Bar Foundation to actually do the large-scale study and the book is based on that. At each of the stages of the book I made an effort to review the literature to identify instrumental and normative models and then think about how to assess the components of each of those models. There's a lot of discussion in the book about how to measure legitimacy. At that time there was a lot of grand theory but not so much about what you actually say to somebody to measure legitimacy. In fact, I think when people look back on the book they say that some of that operationalization could have been better. We've now had a lot more literature, but at the time I wasn't working with very much content. People like David Easton or Talcott Parsons, or Murphy and Tanenhaus, talk about it but they don't really measure it. So the trick was to go from these abstract theories down to some concrete operationalizations.

Question: When drafting a survey to do that, how do you gain the confidence that you have a sufficient instrument – that the questions will in fact give you the data you need?

Tyler: With every survey that I have ever done I have had a lot of pretesting and done a lot revising. A number of the questions haven't worked well in the beginning and I've had to rewrite them. Every time I go through an extensive pretesting process, where I interview people using the instrument then rewrite the instrument. I did that several times with the survey for *Why People Obey the Law*. Even though that's true, I made a lot of mistakes in the design of the survey. I think it's just a long learning process of making lots of mistakes and adjusting for those mistakes.

One mistake that I made with *Why People Obey the Law* is that a number of the questions was yes-or-no questions, like: "Did the police do anything that was improper or unethical?" or "Were the police dishonest?" That was a terrible idea. If I were doing that over again, there would be scales: "Would you say you 'agree strongly,' 'agree,' 'disagree,' or 'disagree strongly'?" That was something I learned because

---

[3] T. R. Tyler, "The Role of Perceived Injustice in Defendants' Evaluations of their Courtroom Experience," *Law & Society Review*, 18:51–74 (1984).

some of the distributions of the responses were bad. We got perhaps sixty or seventy percent of the people in one category and thirty percent in the other. From a statistical point of view that's really bad. I just didn't really think about how the analysis would go when I made those questions. I was focused on trying to get the right questions in there without thinking enough about the right response format.

Another mistake was the response categories for behavior. I knew the results of the first wave when the second wave was designed. If you look at wave one and wave two, you'll see that they changed. That's because nobody wanted to say that they broke the law. So in the second wave the scale is something like "almost never," "practically almost never," "absolutely, completely never in my life." It's a scale that tries to differentiate between people over at the "I don't do anything wrong" end. That's because the distribution in the first wave wasn't good. I also changed the legitimacy questions. The way I did this was not to change the questions that were already there but to add additional questions. If you look at the legitimacy scale in wave two you'll see it's longer and that's because legitimacy didn't work as well as I had hoped it would. I think it was because there wasn't a lot of literature to draw upon when I was trying to figure how to measure legitimacy. So in the second wave I drew some questions from other material that I had found and I improved the scale by adding more questions.

Having said that, if the survey question contains a good idea, my experience is that there's enough power in there that you still get an effect. To have used scales, or better scales, wouldn't have changed the results a lot because in those studies in which I have used better measurement I've gotten more or less similar results. I just get stronger results – they explain more of the variance, you can see more differences in subgroups. So I think there was enough in there that the story was right but I acknowledge that there were mistakes.

Question: What is the standard or the litmus test in that process? Do you pretest on the same population as the intended survey respondents or do you also send it to your mom to see if she understands it?

Tyler: Well, I think both. First my mother and then people I know – or students – then the survey research group does interviews with a sample that really is the population. It's amazing to sit and listen with headphones to interviews on the telephone. It's really scary because you realize how much people don't understand the questions that you've written. I think the general thing that happens is that the question become less "jargony" over time. Often you can tell when the respondents don't get it. So you have to rewrite the question and speak in plain English. I think education is a big issue. You can tell who's been to college because people who have been to college get the idea of scales; they just answer them. People who haven't been to college hear the question and then start talking to you. For example, you might ask, "Were the police honest?" They say, "Well, let me tell you what he said to me..." So then the interviewer has to say, "OK, that's great thanks, but would you say he was very honest, somewhat honest, not very honest?" People can have a lot of trouble with that concept. But it's very important that everyone understands the questionnaire, so we have to keep trying to simplify both the content of the question and then the response format. We now often use broken-up scales. For example, "Would you say the person is honest or dishonest?" "OK, you said they were dishonest. How dishonest would you say they were? Very dishonest, somewhat dishonest?" So what you're doing is you're making it easier for the respondent to answer the question by breaking it up into a set of smaller questions.

But I don't think there are any magic bullets there. It is not like you are going to get any clear sense that this question is completely bad or completely good. You have to listen and take your best guess. I think it's intuition. I think you just have to go with what feels right.

Question: You've been criticized for the kinds of criminal behavior you asked about in the survey. Why, for example, did you not look at drug use or other types of criminal behavior to measure compliance?

Tyler: If you do criminology research you ask about things like: "Did you rob banks? Did you steal cars?" If you call up a thousand people in Chicago none of those people will have done those things. That's why criminology studies tend to focus on populations that you can identify in some way – like they're in prison, they're at risk or something. I didn't conceptualize this project in that way. I thought this project was about ordinary, everyday citizens. So the range of behavior I asked about was really dictated by the nature of the population surveyed. I had to think about what kind of behavior ordinary, average, everyday citizens potentially involve themselves in where they were breaking rules or breaking laws. What kind of behavior could I ask you about where you might actually break the law?

Question: Downloading music from the Internet?

Tyler: OK, well nowadays, illegal use of music, or movies maybe. The equivalent in my mind would be something like parking or speeding, behaviors you might reasonably think that ordinary citizens would actually engage in that are against the law. I don't think it would have been possible to do what some people have suggested: to focus on serious crimes. It couldn't be robbing banks or stealing cars. In fact, if you look at the worst thing asked about in the study it was stealing things from stores. Nobody said they did that. I think you have to make a choice – what's the group you're actually interested in studying? For example, to me the difference between the Law and Society Association and the American Society of Criminology revolves round the question, "What's your target population?" Is your target population criminals or is it the average person and the ordinary citizen's relationship to the law and legal institutions?

I think the biggest weakness of the book is the focus on self-reporting. I make the best case that I can make for its validity but the fact is it would have been a lot better to have had some actual evidence about people's behavior. But it was not possible or I couldn't think of a way in the framework of this project to get evidence about people's real behavior. I have subsequently done studies where I have focused on behavior as it's been identified by other people. So, for example, in a recent article, I used police reports as the variable.[4] That's an effort to look at the same kind of idea but to use a better form of data. If I had had that better form of data I would have loved to use it in *Why People Obey the Law*. I think it would have been a better book.

Question: You had the survey conducted by telephone. Did you consider alternative methods?

Tyler: Certainly not written surveys. You get terrible response rates for mail questionnaires. Written surveys are thought the least-effective method in terms of response rate. The best approach is to do in-person interviews but the cost was completely prohibitive. I couldn't get the money to do it so I did telephone surveys. Telephone surveys have gotten a lot worse in the years since the study was done. Many more people now have cell phones or they have answering machines. At that

[4] T. R. Tyler, L. Sherman, H. Strang, G. C. Barnes, and D. Woods, "Reintegrative Shaming, Procedural Justice, and Recidivism: The Engagement of Offenders' Psychological Mechanisms in the Canberra RISE Drinking-and-Driving Experiment," *Law & Society Review*, 41:553–85 (2007).

time this methodology was considered to be pretty good – not as good as "in person" but pretty reasonable. Whether telephone surveys remain a viable methodology is a really important question and I don't know the answer to that. I think people are so barraged with calls and callers have been so dishonest. You can't even say, "We're from a university." People won't believe you. I have worked now with a group called Knowledge Networks. They identify a random sample of Americans and basically pay them to be a panel. Essentially, they are paid respondents. That may be a new thing that we end up doing more of.

Question: Could you say a little about the relationship between yourself and the survey company that conducted the work for you. Quality control must be an issue. How was that relationship managed?

Tyler: To me there are two aspects to this that are really important. One is checking very carefully the reputation of the people with whom you are working. The University of Chicago helped me to identify the people that managed the surveys. I had a lot of confidence that these people would do a good job and that they would care because if they didn't do a good job they wouldn't just be upsetting me, they would be offending this institution that was important to them.

And, second, I spent a lot of time with them at the beginning going over the survey. I went and listened to the pretest. I think it's really important to show you care. So you show up at night, you sit and listen to the interviews, the interviewers can see that the investigator is there, is interested, cares about what they're doing, listens to them, and listens to the feedback sessions with them about what's wrong with this survey. I tried to pay a lot of attention to the comments that they made, both because I thought the comments would be really helpful but also to show that I was very invested in this and that it was very important that it be done well.

Question: How big is the gap between what you might expect from a professional survey firm and what you might expect from graduate students you employ to do the data collection?

Tyler: I think you can tell the difference. Survey firms have professionals – people who have more experience. You can see in the pattern of the data that a survey has been done better. If you get really good interviewers the coherence on a scale that ought to be coherent will be stronger. That shows that they're keeping the person more focused on the interview. They're better at keeping them on task and focused on what they're doing. It's easy if you're an interviewer to just want to get done. It's so frustrating to keep saying to the respondent, "Thank you very much for telling me your opinion but would you say you agree strongly, agree, disagree, or strongly disagree?" You have to do it over and over and over again. You have to keep bringing the respondent back to the response scale. People want to tell you their story. A common problem is if you let the person talk about their story they feel like the interview is finished, but of course it isn't. So if you're a good interviewer you have to get the right balance between letting the respondent talk and getting the survey questions answered. You can't just shut them up, but you have to somehow get them to stop and go back to the questions. Those are skills that people really have to learn. It just takes time. Professionals are trained to do these things. You get something for the money that you pay to a professional survey firm. I think you get better quality data.

Question: Social scientists seem to have different attitudes toward manipulating data. Some create models by formulating index variables until they find something that works and gets the maximum R-squares, for example. Others are more inclined just to run the data and stick with those results. How did you view the possibility of manipulating the data, and massaging it?

Tyler: I think if you're going to use nonexperimental methods – and surveys are obviously very nonexperimental – the biggest danger is that you would manipulate and massage the data. So I tried really hard not to do that. I tried to have clear ideas in advance and basically to test those ideas. You have to look very carefully at what anyone does when they're analyzing survey data. We now have this amazing but very dangerous software that is an automatic interaction detector program. You just put the data in and they find the biggest effects for you. Then you make up a model. I did not want to do anything like that. I wanted the book to be very strong from a theory-, hypothesis-driven approach.

Question: The book built on separate articles that you had already published. Did the process of writing the book generate a different thesis than would have emerged separately had you just left them in separate articles?

Tyler: The truth is that I think it's unusual that I wrote the book at all. Psychologists don't usually write books. But from my point of view it was fantastic. I think it really created a coherent argument and it shows why psychologists ought to write books. But that's the unusual part – to take the articles and stitch them all together into a book. The book basically takes the same theme – normative and instrumental approaches to law – and runs it through: "You think that people obey the law because they think they'll be caught and punished? Well, actually, these normative values are more important. You think that people are instrumental in their response to their experiences? No, they're not. Actually, procedural justice is much more important than outcomes. You think that people think about fairness only when it helps them? No, they don't. They have ethical criteria." So basically the book is framed around the idea that at each stage the data supports this normative model. That would never have been so apparent if you didn't have all of that in one place.

Question: You mentioned earlier that a weakness of the book was relying on self-reporting of criminal behavior. Did you anticipate criticism about that from reviewers, and were there others you anticipated?

Tyler: Yes, that was the criticism I thought it would get. The one criticism that I didn't anticipate came from Austin Sarat. He wrote a critical review saying that I should have found stronger race effects.[5] He suggested there's got to be something wrong with the methodology because we all know the race effects are there. But the book doesn't find them. I'm a psychologist and psychologists really believe in data. So I feel that if I didn't find the differences it's because they weren't there. I guess that line of criticism suggests I should have done an in-depth study with a very small group of people that I talked to at length. Then I would have discovered more differences than I did with survey research. The reason I didn't want to do that is because I didn't consider that to be the real focus of the book. I would have been changing the methodology to address a question that wasn't the question I really cared the most about. I mention race differences but they're not really the focus of the book.

Question: What is the greatest challenge facing you with this kind of research project?

[5] A. Sarat, "Review Essay: Authority, Anxiety, and Procedural Justice: Moving from Scientific Detachment to Critical Engagement," *Law & Society Review*, 27:647–71 (1993).

Tyler: The biggest problem with surveys is the question you forgot to ask. Once you've gone out and interviewed a thousand people, that's it. So you have to get the outline of all the things you want to measure in advance. You have to think about how to measure them; you have to do pretesting to make sure you do a good job. You only have to screw up on one idea to really weaken the project. Psychologists, especially, are great at data analysis, so that's not the problem when psychological projects falter. It's the framework that I think is really hard. If you create problems it's hard to fix them.

Question: In hindsight, did you discover any significant problems you wish you could go back and fix?

Tyler: I made one mistake that I would like to change. The book has a section on personal experience. I didn't ask people whether they accepted a decision made by the police or the courts. The book is focused on legitimacy – how going to court and having an experience in court or dealing with the police shapes your views about the legitimacy of the law. But making that its focus, there's a disconnect with a lot of the literature in the procedural justice area which focuses on the notion of fair procedures leading people to accept decisions. So I wasn't able to address that literature when I wrote the book and that's a weakness in it. I fix it in my later book, *Trust in the Law*. That book is all about decision acceptance, but if I'd done it right in the first place I could have saved the energy. I wouldn't have had to do a new project and write a new book.

Having said that, no single project ever settles any question. What you do is a series of projects where you try to address different aspects of the general questions that you're trying to deal with and you build up a case over time. There's no project I've done that you can't criticize on some grounds but if you take all of the research I've done I think there's no criticism you can make that applies to all of the studies. What you want to have is a program of research that over time addresses these concerns that you have.

CHAPTER 14

DOREEN McBARNET AND "WHITER THAN WHITE COLLAR CRIME"*

"Have tape recorder, will travel" – *it might almost be stamped on the calling card of the qualitative social scientist. The open-ended interview, distinguished from a survey with "closed" questions requiring a person to choose an answer, is one of the most powerful tools in Law and Society research. Interviewing has a lot to offer, including the ability to tailor questions to small but potentially important differences among research subjects and to probe interesting avenues that are discovered along the way. Interviewing also allows one to discover worlds that may forever be closed to direct observation, allowing one to hear people report their perspectives and describe their behavior.*

Successful qualitative interviewing requires a degree of preparation that allows the researcher to explore, conversationally, topics of core concern. Yet researchers who remain open to pursuing new avenues that serendipitously arise in interviews can discover whole new worlds. For more than two decades, Doreen McBarnet has used extensive interviewing to capture how law and business work in action, understood through the details of complex banking, securities, tax, and bankruptcy transactions. Focusing on corporate tax practices in the United Kingdom, "Whiter than White Collar Crime" reveals the kinds of discoveries one can make when successfully balancing detailed preparation with curiosity.

The complex arenas of corporate law, such as the one discussed in this article, remain ripe for exploration by Law and Society scholars. The trail of inquiry brought McBarnet down the road less traveled after the publication of Conviction: Law, the State and the Construction of Justice *(1981), a well-regarded study in the criminological tradition. She begins by tracing that journey in her early career from "blue collar" criminal law to "white collar" corporate behavior.*

Methodological Keywords: interviews, documentary analysis, observation

*"Whiter than White Collar Crime: Tax, Fraud Insurance and the Management of Stigma," *British Journal of Sociology*, 42:323–44 (1991).

McBarnet: The *Conviction* project was my Ph.D. I was teaching deviance at the time so I wanted to do something in that area. The idea was to observe trials in court and see how events that were by definition disputed became constructed into a clear enough conclusion for a verdict to be reached. But almost immediately I was struck by the fact that the legal goings-on in court did not correspond with my commonsense understanding of how legal rights and courts worked. For example, in jury cases previous convictions were introduced as part of the evidence. I started asking lawyers how that could be done. What did the law require? But I could never get a straight answer. Their answer to "What is the law?" was to come out with a string of cases: in case A the decision was X, in case B it was Y – nothing was unambivalent. This may have been old hat to a lawyer but as a sociologist it caught my interest. It suggested that there was more flexibility in law than I had anticipated. I began to get an understanding of law (this was well before critical legal studies or postmodernist concepts of law) as a shifting, moving thing. I started to see that you could do things with law as a lawyer and a judge in a criminal court.

But surely that meant that other people in other legal contexts could also do things with law? As a sociologist I was interested not so much in law per se as in social structure, power, class, and ideology. I began to think about how I could explore the role of law in relation to those big questions. From *Conviction* came this wish to explore business as a manifestation of class and power. Some people have described me as a Marxist. I don't know that I am a Marxist, or any other kind of "ist." I've always resisted pigeonholes. I like to follow my own curiosity rather than be led by pre-existing frameworks. But I'm interested in who pulls the strings in society – how power works at a very micro level – and that carried me to the project which produced, "Whiter than White Collar Crime" and a series of related writings like "Law and Capital: Legal Forms and Legal Actors" or "It's Not What You Do But the Way That You Do It" – the notion that law was a substance you could do something with, but that you needed power to do it.[1] Who are the people who have the power and what might they be doing with the law?

[1] "Law and Capital: The Role of Legal Form and Legal Actors," in *International Journal of the Sociology of Law*, 12 (Special Issue: Law and Capital):231–8 (1984); "It's Not What You Do but the Way that You Do it: Tax Evasion, Tax Avoidance and the Boundaries of Deviance" in *Unravelling Criminal Justice*, David Downes, ed. (London: Macmillan, 1992), pp. 247–68. Numerous other publications came out of this research, many of which explore the technical legal work involved in

I decided to look at business, where you have power of a different kind. In the lower criminal courts the context is the state having power versus the defendant. But of course it could be the other way round. The power may not lie with the state but with big business. At the same time as I was turning my focus to business, people were writing a lot about law and capital. But nobody actually looked at what that meant in terms of the nitty-gritty. What do we mean when we talk about capital? What does business actually do with law? Law may facilitate business but how does business make law facilitative for it? I didn't want to study crime; I wanted to study the manipulation of law. What interested me were the boundaries between crime and legality: how do you make what you want to do legal? I focused on tax because tax avoidance was a recognized concept. It was something I could go and talk to people about as something that was a bit ambivalent. It was recognized that there was something else going on by the very notion of tax avoidance as opposed to tax evasion. It was an irony that I got money under an ESRC research program on crime and criminal justice to study non-crime.

Question: Taking on this new project, it would mean moving from a large project based on observation, with *Conviction*, to interviews.

McBarnet: The *Conviction* project was literally sitting, observing in the courts. But how do you observe legal transaction work? You can't. You can only try and do it indirectly. Maybe you could conduct participant observation, but given that some deals take months to go through I'm not sure that would get you anywhere. Sometimes I have had access to lots of transaction papers and that has been interesting and useful. But it is a rarity that someone is going to give you access to that kind of material. So interviewing was really the only possibility. You're still observing of course – the body language of your interviewee can provide important clues too. And you are always, at the same time as participating in the interview, in some sense standing back observing the way it is going.

Question: How did you start? Did you know what you were looking for? Were these ideas already well formed?

McBarnet: No, they weren't. There were some hunches there but essentially in everything I've ever done the ideas have always come out of

the manipulation of the law. They are collected in *Crime Compliance and Control* (Aldershot, U.K.: Ashgate, 2004).

the data. My approach has been not so much about reading other people's work and creating hypotheses from it, but more about letting the ideas flow from the data. And it's looking at things from the bottom up, rather than just the structure. Once I was out there interviewing and thinking about responses, new questions would begin to emerge. Some of these were also a result of just being one of those irritating people who is always asking, "But why? I don't understand that. What's going on there?" You don't necessarily stick just to the six questions you thought you would want to ask. Questions arise out of the process of interviewing itself. The data would lead me down different routes and from those routes I was getting into hypotheses – for example, that people who can afford really expensive lawyers must be able to manipulate law quite a lot, so let's go and see what's going on there.

Question: In the "Whiter than White Collar Crime" project you interviewed a broad range of people – solicitors, barristers, judges, merchant bankers, insurers, Inland Revenue officers, tax scheme promoters, and so forth. Ultimately you conducted 105 interviews. How much of this interview approach was planned in advance? Did you have an idea of how many interviews you would conduct among each group?

McBarnet: No, I didn't plan to do 105 interviews, as such. That was where I stopped rather than what I had originally decided. I started with accountants and lawyers, getting a sense of how tax-avoidance schemes were put together. But from this set of interviews I realized I needed to widen my net. Merchant bankers were also really important. Some of the most interesting information came from them. Similarly, the insurance business was also playing a very important role in the construction of devices. Expanding the pool of informants in this way was interesting. For a start, it told me that legal work was not all done by lawyers and accountants. It was being done by others. In a way, if they were the ones constructing the deals they may have been doing the most interesting stuff. So it was a case of "why not keep on going until I get a full picture of what is going on?" The numbers were less important than getting to the horse's mouth, if you like – getting to the people that really would have something important to say, something insightful to provide.

Question: How did you approach people for permission to be interviewed?

McBarnet: In terms of approaching organizations, you don't go in at the very top because if you get a "no" you can't go anywhere else. So unless you know you're going to get a "yes," you don't go in at the top. You have to find a middle way somehow where if you get in that's good and then you can work outwards, up and down, and if you don't you can try again somewhere else.

More importantly, it was rarely a cold call. My approach would often be primed by getting someone to call my "target" first and ask whether he or she would be willing to be interviewed. You cut the rejection chances significantly by having it done that way. The intermediary might be someone you know on the outside, perhaps a practicing lawyer that you have some connection with through a context that has nothing to do with the research. You could ask whether he or she would be willing to ask certain clients if they would be interested in participating in a piece of research. And because it is being done through an intermediary like that, you are more likely to get a "yes." So it's being sold for you rather than doing a cold call yourself. But of course you have to get the intermediary to see the project as interesting and worth doing. In my case, in relation to the Inland Revenue, I happened to know that a friend of mine had a brother who worked there. I talked to him informally over a cup of coffee and told him what I was interested in and asked if I could come and talk to him and some of his colleagues. Once into an organization or professional circle of course you can "snowball" – ask one contact to suggest or introduce you to others.

Another technique which I developed quite consciously in the tax world was to go to professional practitioners' conferences, run as commercial events. Once you're there, you're an insider. You have your card and you go and chat to someone over coffee. You tell them you're doing this interesting research and ask whether you can come and talk to them. They then give you their card and you're in because they've got a face to put to the name. They know you smile and you're quite chatty and friendly and said something vaguely interesting at the time. Those were the sorts of techniques I used and I didn't get many rejections. Sadly but usefully, I suspect that for this kind of elite research, the Oxford University brand was also a help in gaining access.

Question: How difficult is it preparing for interviews in this area in terms of your grasp of the subject matter? It involves very complex legal issues and you are not a lawyer.

McBarnet: I just had to learn. I can't claim to be an expert but I pass as a lawyer quite often – though in fact many academic lawyers wouldn't actually be up on current cutting-edge practice anyway. The trick is to focus. You do a few interviews to try and get a sense of things. And you read a lot of the journals and magazines that those in the business are reading, to see what are the interesting things on the go. Long before Enron or the subprime mortgage crisis I homed in on off-balance-sheet financing because it very clearly involved business and the professions scrutinising legal definitions and manipulating them. Within that broad area there are many specific techniques, so it is important to home in further on two or three key techniques, really know the background, really learn about the area. Then you can interview people about that and have a fair shot at asking sharp questions rather than accepting what they say and being too scared to challenge it. With enough homework, you can feel confident enough to say, perhaps a little more judiciously, but in effect, "Come off it, tell me what really happens."

Question: With the sharp questions, you are an academic asking them to open up about practices that may invite criticism, and they must be mindful of both their clients' interests and their professional interest, their status. How do you warm them up to talk about these things?

McBarnet: I would say two things on that. The first is that these are really esoteric matters of which the people doing them are pretty proud. They are not criminal actions. It is clever legal work and they are doing their clients terrific favors. But if they turn up at a cocktail party and try to talk about these interesting things they have been doing all day everyone glazes over and moves on to the next drink. With me they had someone who was sitting there willing them to talk and absolutely enthusiastic about hearing every last technical detail of these strategies. And I don't think anything I have done has been what you would call a polemical exposé. It has more been analyzing what people are doing and describing it fairly neutrally, fitting it into some kind of analytical framework. The professions and business have taken on board the concept of creative compliance. So far as I know they don't see it as polemical, and the regulators have taken it on as something that needs to be addressed. Of course, I didn't actually go to someone and say I'm studying "creative compliance." Indeed that concept didn't exist at the start. It emerged as a way of understanding and capturing the practices researched. But in any case I introduced the research as a study of "tax structures" – neutral language – and analyzed what emerged.

The second thing is that I think the interview has to be a conversation. There has to be a rapport. It has to be looking people in the eye. There has to be a certain amount of trust which you must not violate.

So I've had some very interesting information I have never printed because it would have been violating that trust. And very frustrating that was too when it was really, really interesting material! But if it was remotely recognisable then ethically I felt I could not publish it. I had gone in on the basis that it was confidential and to describe it in a way which would have revealed who or what it was would not have been right.

The important thing with elite interviews is to establish that you are a peer – that you can ask cheeky questions if you need to. But you've got to feel your way into that. For some interviewees that would be easier than with others, and maybe it is better to ask such questions later on in the interview rather than at the beginning. And I think that's where stupid things like power dressing come in. You go in looking like someone that they have to take seriously. I think when you're young and fumbling, you can get away with it because you don't look as though anyone needs to be frightened of you. And when you're older then maybe you are accepted as trustworthy because you've been doing this for years and no one's sued you!

Question: Did you go into interviews with universal questions, things you're going to ask of all interviewees? Or is it a purely conversational approach, just letting it go wherever it runs?

McBarnet: A bit of both. There would be half a dozen key issues, but how they were addressed would vary with the role of the person and the sector they were in. But that said, once the ball rolls and it takes you off in some direction you hadn't anticipated, you just go with it. That's more important. Getting the new information that you didn't know to ask questions about is much more important than making sure your planned questions are answered. After all, that's how you learn what you don't know. Finding questions is the most interesting thing, isn't it? If you come out with a different research question after six months, you've done research, you've learned something you didn't know beforehand. I think the breakthroughs come from coming up with the things that you wouldn't have thought about beforehand until you actually start doing the research.

Question: How did you schedule your interviews? How quickly did you move from one set of informants to the next?

McBarnet: It was done fairly gradually over a period of time. As the project developed I could schedule two or three for a week but to begin with I was always learning from each interview before I did the next one, thinking about what were the implications of the previous interview and how I might reformulate ideas and questions and do more homework for the next. For example, I could beef up on a particular technique of creative compliance and go into an interview with that as one of my questions. But then the really interesting thing was to get into all the other techniques that weren't in the public domain. I couldn't prepare for that. I had to find those out and then I would learn something about those issues in order to pursue them in the next interview. So it was an accretion of knowledge from which to keep constructing the questions. At each stage you're learning something. The last interview would probably be very different from the first one. I didn't think that mattered because you were acquiring knowledge all the way through. It wasn't a matter of whether "seven out of ten people said this." It was the learning about what was going on out there that wasn't common knowledge.

Question: How difficult was it to get consent on an individual basis to record what interviewees would say?

McBarnet: I didn't use a tape recorder in the early interviews at all and I don't know whether or not that helped people be open. It's amazing that people do take you on trust and they take your institution on trust as well I suppose. I go in and I say this is confidential in the sense that both the individual and the firm will not be revealed, but that the material will be used. I have never offered, when I have used a tape recorder, to go back to interviewees and have them read the transcript or approve my analysis. Sometimes interviewees will say, "You know, maybe we should switch it off now," or something like that, but it's amazing that people do take you on trust.

Question: Did you ever come across situations where interviewees were reluctant to talk about certain issues during interviews? If so, how did you respond to that?

McBarnet: There were one or two in the early stages. Interestingly, it wasn't the practitioners in their role as practitioners who were a problem. Essentially, if they agreed to talk to you, you were already in there. It was people in the tax world where I wanted to talk about the profession's view of something. They were, then, speaking in the role of a spokesman for the profession and that was a much stickier situation.

I actually never did that again. I don't think I ever used what they said. I was definitely getting ideology. It wasn't useful as data on practice. It could, of course, be useful as ideology in other contexts. I tell my students this. It's important to recognize what you're getting. Are you getting practice? Are you getting opinion, or PR? If it's the latter it may still be useful data about what people think they *ought* to be saying and what that tells us.

Question: Where does one go from interview notes, ultimately getting to the article?

McBarnet: Quite often the interviews would be the starting point. That is where you would learn what was interesting. You would then go and see how it was based on the law – what businesses were doing with the law. So it was often not the approach you might intuitively think of where you start with the law and then go and ask questions about it. I was trying to find out practice, which wasn't general knowledge. I would find out the practice first and then have to do the digging. Informants might refer to, let's say, section 5 of an Act and then I would quite often have to do a hell of a lot of digging to work out what it was they were talking about. And when you find it you say, "Ha! I see how they used this bit of law to do that." So it was working backwards very often.

Then it's just a lot of writing and rewriting of material and organizing into different categories – going through the notes, annotating with numbers and categories, marking a quote as interesting for raising some point in my mind. It might not at that stage be a clearly formulated idea, but it would have raised some question. Then you start seeing more instances of that and you start creating a concept or issue out of it, collecting those bits together. It was just going over and over the notes, writing them down in lots of categories, letting the categories emerge – very painstaking and slow.

To start with I found it very hard to figure out how to write up the material. It gradually becomes easier as you create formulas for how to do it. One formula that emerged was to describe the device, then how it was done and what the implications were. But to begin with it was a bit more of a struggle.

Question: Law and Society research is inherently interdisciplinary. Did you have any dilemmas about which audiences you should write for and how to present it so that it will be understood? Was the desire to influence policy ever part of your ambition?

McBarnet: I've had a real problem, I think, in that a lot of people only know isolated segments of my work because it's been directed at all kinds of different audiences. Some will have been read only by accountants. Some was published in legal journals, some in sociology journals, some in ethics journals, philosophy journals, or books. The different audiences can be a bit of a problem unless you always publish in places like *Law & Society Review* or the *Journal of Law and Society*. I think this is a problem within interdisciplinary areas such as sociolegal studies. As for it being understood, insofar as I've read references to my work, people seem, on the whole, to have seen what I was trying to get at. And it seems to have become useful in the range of tools used by scholars of regulation. I have occasionally seen someone describing what I was doing and thought, "Oh my God, I wasn't doing that at all! It's the exact opposite from what I was doing."

I always wanted to do work that I felt was relevant to what was going on in the world. I wanted my work to be able to be used. But I didn't want the research questions to be driven by what policy makers had decided was important at that particular moment. Very often they would not be focusing on the things that I found really interesting. If you just followed the given line you would never do anything that was thinking outside the box. And, interestingly, having policy relevance can be counterproductive. *Conviction*, which if anything was as an indictment of the criminal justice system in terms of it taking away the alleged rights of defendants, was used in the Royal Commission for Criminal Procedure as evidence that it was alright to widen the formal legal powers of the police because they already took these powers in practice anyway.

Question: Do you find yourself emotionally invested in your projects?

McBarnet: In the research for *Conviction* I certainly was because I used to get quite involved through interviews with defendants in the lower courts. I used to get quite upset about situations, not because I thought all the defendants were innocent but because you could see the way people were being railroaded, and often feel their powerlessness. I was conscious of the ethics of interviewing, being a sympathetic person rather than another figure of power – not in order to get information out of people, just not to give them another bad time. I was very cautious about not being a distant academic who came along and acted insensitively. Dealing with the powerless rather than the powerful is always harder.

It's not quite the same in the business world. But I certainly had an emotional involvement in why I chose the topic. I wouldn't research something that I didn't really care about. I'm driven by more than an abstract intellectual curiosity. I do things that interest me emotionally and morally. I try not to *write* about them emotionally or morally but I'm driven to particular issues by my own sense of morality and justice.

Question: How well did the project go to plan?

McBarnet: I don't know that I had a plan as such. You have to make it up as you go along because you have to take the opportunities that you either create or that come your way. You learn as you go along and then construct the next stage from that. It was always a quest driven by curiosity and a sense of "what do I not know?" It's like that moment in the first Indiana Jones film where someone asks Harrison Ford, "What'll we do now, Indy?" He looks at the camera and says, "I don't know, I'm making this up as I go along." Doing qualitative research is a bit like that, isn't it?

CHAPTER 15

GERALD ROSENBERG AND
*THE HOLLOW HOPE**

It is the dream of every scholar or budding academic to be relevant to others – to influence how others think and understand the world – or even "to make a splash." Few books have done that quite in the way that The Hollow Hope did. The book has generated much subsequent research and debate, and it is frequently used in the classroom, but the measure of its impact does not end there. As Gerald Rosenberg discusses in this interview, it was the surprisingly unprofessional response of some academic audiences that marked his entry, as a graduate student, into academia. What had he done? The answer gets at the calling of the researcher, to ask an important question and seek out the best available data. Yet, as he recounts, the process of inquiry was not as simple as question-data-theory. Would the data speak to him, and was he listening?

The researcher is a product of an age and is not free of all the limits in vision that accompany that. It is an imponderable question of whether The Hollow Hope could have been written any earlier than it was – can one even identify the presumptions of the current faith, to question them? He began work on the dissertation that would become this book at the cusp of the 1980s, when a conservative legal movement was rising to power, challenging the belief in courts as appropriate tools of social change. Although Rosenberg did not share their commitment, he was prepared to be led by his data. That obligation to be honest to oneself led him to even more troubling conclusions – and then he would have to be prepared to follow through on the social scientist's conviction.

Like the legal historian's quiet days with old documents (see Friedman, Chapter 5), Rosenberg's detailed and even tedious data collection may not have seemed likely to have set off particular controversy. He begins here by describing the challenge of even finding a topic about which he was passionate.

---

*The Hollow Hope: Can Courts Bring About Social Change? (Chicago: University of Chicago Press, 1991; rev. ed., 2008).

Methodological Keywords: documentary analysis, public opinion survey analysis, media analysis, government documents, congressional debate, political speeches, judicial opinions, biographies, autobiographies, diaries, letters

Rosenberg: I was in graduate school and looking for a dissertation topic. I found that very hard. It took me two years to come up with a question that I wanted to write about. I remember trying to bring two academic worlds together: law school and social science. I was a refugee from law school at that point. I had done a year and hated it with a passion. There was an arrogance to law school that drove me nuts. It seemed to me at the time that the model of the great American law school was where arrogance meets ignorance. It just drove me crazy. I took a leave of absence from law school to spend two years at Oxford – to see if I liked political science instead. I fell in love with it and went to Yale to do the Ph.D., though I also ended up finishing the law degree. So I found myself caught between two worlds. Law school and legal training seemed totally oblivious to social reality. But at the same time it struck me that a lot of social scientists did not understand how judges and courts operated.

I think, like many graduate students, that I actually wanted to write something that somebody would read, something that mattered. I wanted to ask an important question. Yale had an approach which was: you ask a big question, you offer middle-level theory, and you test it with empirical data. I kept spinning my wheels looking for an important question. I was living at the time with a group of other graduate students. I had a particularly brilliant housemate. I was explaining to him some idea I had about the legality of union organizing in the U.S. and the like and my heart really wasn't in it. Finally he looked up to me and said, "Do you care about this?" And I said, "No." He asked me, "What do you really care about?" It seems liked an obvious question, but nobody had ever asked me that before! I told him that what I really cared about was whether courts can help the relatively disadvantaged. He said, "Good. You have a dissertation. Now leave me alone." It ended up as *The Hollow Hope* many years later.

Question: That was the spark, but how did you develop the idea from that starting point?

Rosenberg: The first thing I did was to answer my own question: can courts help the relatively disadvantaged? On the one hand, my year of legal training and my growing up in the 1960s led to an obvious answer:

Of course they can! *Brown v. Board of Education* is the great symbol of the ability of courts to help racial minorities by knocking down legally required school segregation. But, on the other hand, my studies at Oxford suggested it was unlikely that courts could have such a profound impact on society. As I thought about it more, the first question became: did *Brown actually* end school segregation? I was naive because I was stunned when the data showed that segregation did not end after *Brown*. Indeed a decade later, only one in a hundred black kids in the South was in a school with whites. That surprised me. However, I then said, "OK, clearly that's not the end of the story. Courts may not be able to have direct impact but surely they have indirect impact? Surely they change how people think about things? They put issues on the agenda, they affect politicians. So I'm going to write a dissertation that says 'courts may not change things overnight but they have these important indirect effects that can't be overlooked'." That's the dissertation I started to write.

But the damned data weren't coming out right! I looked at media coverage. Obviously media coverage of civil rights was going to increase after *Brown*? It didn't. Well, I thought, "What else can I look at? Oh, let's look at what happens in Congress. There are bound to be lots of civil rights bills introduced after *Brown*." There were not. The number of civil rights bills introduced dropped after *Brown*. Some people advised me to read the debates on the 1964 Civil Rights Act. Surely, senators were going to talk about *Brown*? Well, I read the debates and to my amazement *Brown* was hardly mentioned. So I hired two graduate students to read the debates independently of me and each other. They found the same result: senators didn't talk about *Brown*. This was not planned! I kept scratching my head and saying, "This makes no sense. I've got to look somewhere else to find evidence of these interactive facts." So I kept trying lots of different avenues, lots of different hypotheses. Maybe it's this, maybe it's that, but I kept coming up empty-handed. And I was really depressed. My whole dissertation was collapsing!

Then, literally one morning I woke up and realized, there's nothing wrong with the data, it's the theory that's wrong! And then, of course, all the light bulbs went off. So what got produced in the end was not what I intended to write.

Question: When you were beginning the dissertation you were entering a venerable area in political science, the "impact study." What had you been reading as examples of impact study? What models did you have in mind?

Rosenberg: I remember looking at the literature and being disappointed. I found it atheoretical for the most part. It was very hard to find testable hypotheses in it. And it didn't pay much attention to what I called "indirect effects" – effects on people's thinking, on agenda setting, and the like. I remember saying to myself, "I've got to be able to do better than this." This is probably not the best advice to give, but I didn't start from the literature. I started with the question and then went out and read the literature that addressed the general idea. I'm not sure that's the best way for graduate students to proceed, but I'd found something I cared passionately about.

Question: When you were having this critical dialogue with yourself, about the meaning of *Brown*, to what extent did you brings others into the conversation?

Rosenberg: My dissertation committee (David Mayhew, Bob Dahl, and Rogers Smith) was really wonderful. In particular, Rogers Smith was supportive but demanding. He was an unknown assistant professor at Yale at the time and I was his first, or among his first, graduate students. I remember in particular a single-page typed set of comments he gave me at one point when I was floundering. He suggested that I argue that courts can never produce significant social reform. While in retrospect I don't think that's accurate, and I'm sure he didn't believe it, it was particularly useful because it provided me with a framework around which to structure my argument. It got me out of a rut. I tried to correct the argument in the book but at least some critics suggest I didn't succeed.

I also benefitted from a particularly talented group of graduate school classmates. We were a very cohesive group. We'd always eat lunch together, do sports together, go to the theatre together, go to New York to watch baseball games, etc. Through the social interactions we'd always talk about our work. In the best tradition of friends and colleagues, they were supportive but skeptical. In fact they all thought I was nuts. They'd always say, "Well, what about this, what about that?" We had this tremendous interplay and they pushed me to keep searching for data to respond to their skeptical prodding.

Question: The section on *Brown* in the book is 169 pages. It is almost a complete work in itself. But you went beyond that and explored other scenarios. Why did you do that?

Rosenberg: Well, the next question was, "OK, *Brown*'s unique. After all, it concerned segregation. We had slavery in the U.S., we fought a civil war, so is *Brown* a unique case? Surely the argument won't hold for anything else?" Well, the next case to do was clearly *Roe v. Wade*. *Roe* proved very interesting because *Roe* did produce change. This was great because it made the project more complex. Actually, the dissertation did not do a good job with *Roe*. What I tried to do, essentially, was to deny there was change, to fit *Roe* into the analytic structure I developed for *Brown*. I was never completely comfortable with that argument and for good reason – it was wrong.

But then it's time to turn it into a book and people say, "Look, *Brown* and *Roe* are really unique. You can't generalize on *Brown* and *Roe*. What about all the other wonderful things the courts have done for the relatively disadvantaged?" It seemed to me the clear and obvious ones in the U.S. were reapportionment, the environment, and defence of the rights of criminal defendants. So I looked at them more quickly. I was just looking for the kind of cases that someone would say, "Oh, if only you had looked at X, you would see your argument doesn't hold." Now obviously there are a gazillion cases but I was trying to do the big ones, the critical case studies.

I had actually written a couple of hundred pages on criminal defendants and I remember John Tryneski of the University of Chicago Press taking me out to this really nice lunch when he had the manuscript. I knew something was coming. We were just chatting away and it was not till the end of lunch that he said, "We really want people to read it, but it's too long." And so we cut out almost all of the criminal rights stuff.

Question: Did you have a clear plan for how long the project would take?

Rosenberg: Oh yes, sure! I was going to take a year and a half to two years to complete the dissertation and then a couple of years to turn it into a book. But it took four years to complete the dissertation then six more years to finish the book. It took forever!

Question: What most affected the reality of the pace with which it came together?

Rosenberg: A few things. One was I had this tremendous cognitive dissonance problem with the dissertation. As much as I had hated law school, it had obviously gotten to me. I believed courts were important agents of social change and I could not accept the fact that I couldn't find evidence that that was true. Readers of the book don't know that. They think, "Here's this guy who thinks courts are irrelevant and they can't do anything. And, boy, he writes this without doubt!" That's not how it evolved at all. So that was one problem, I was always fighting.

Number two, getting this evidence was really hard. It took a lot of time. For example, I have a table on the number of legal abortions. Well, putting that together took forever. I had to negotiate with the Alan Guttmacher Institute. They didn't want to release the data. It was just very hard to get these kind of data. It took a *very* long time. I also remember doing something I'm not sure I would have done now: measuring the coverage of civil rights in the *Readers' Guide to Periodic Literature*. I'm sitting in the Library at Congress with this little print. I go through a page and I write down the number of entries. Then I'd go through it again. Well, most of the time I'd get a different number because the print's so small! I had a rule: I would only go with the number if I got it twice in a row. I could only do this for about an hour at a time and then I had to do something else because I'd get a headache. These nice tables in the book look very simple but often they represent many months of work.

Question: Were the challenges in converting it from a dissertation to a book any different from the challenges in writing it as a dissertation in the first place?

Rosenberg: Yes, they were quite different. The dissertation challenge was making an argument and gathering the data to test it. As I turned to the book, the challenge was to make a contribution to theory as well. In doing so, I had to get distance on the dissertation. I actually put it aside for about a year and a half. That was very important because I could then come back to it, scratch my head, and say, "What was I thinking when I wrote that?" The dissertation was much less nuanced, much less complex, and much less theoretical. Senior colleagues at the University of Chicago helped a lot, particularly David Greenstone. What David kept stressing was a more complex model. He kept pushing me to specify conditions, to talk about different competing approaches – what became the dynamic court and the constrained court models – to offer a theory of the role of courts. Then another senior colleague, Cass Sunstein, said, "What's really going on in abortion based on your reading is a market method of implementation." So that became condition three.

So making the argument more theoretical and more nuanced – though "nuanced" and *The Hollow Hope* are words that don't go together well for many people! – moved it from the dissertation to the book.

Question: Although this might have delayed you even further, did you ever consider interviewing key actors – those who could attest to the importance of *Brown* or *Roe* in the field – as part of your methods?

Rosenberg: I thought long and hard about whether I should interview people involved in the civil rights struggle. I decided not to. The reason was I didn't know how to disentangle what they thought in 1957 from what they were going to be telling me in 1987. I thought there would be too much time lapsed. I didn't know if I'd be getting what they really thought back then or the way in which the society and culture has reinterpreted the events. Instead I read dozens of biographies, auto-biographies, and letters home from civil rights workers in the South, mostly written at the time the events I was examining were taking place.

Question: Are there any methodological choices that, with the benefit of hindsight, you would change?

Rosenberg: I didn't do any content analysis of the media and that's something where I've been criticised, I think correctly. That would have enriched the book. I simply had coverage numbers – how many stories there were, without analyzing them. I don't think it would have changed what I wrote but I think it would have enriched it. Another thing I didn't do was look at the black press. I have since done some work on the African American press and how it covered *Brown* and it's a shocker.[1] It didn't give it very much coverage. I would have done that for the book but I was under pressure to get it out. And it was already too long so I went with what I had. You can't do everything. You've got to say "All right, enough," and then move on.

Question: The title of the book has a memorable ring to it. How did you come to that?

Rosenberg: I got to my title largely through Rogers Smith. I had some horrible name like "The Inability of Courts to Help Blacks." Rogers said,

---

[1] "The Supreme Court, the Civil Rights Movement, and the African-American Press" (Paper presented at the 1992 Midwest Political Science Association Annual Meeting, with Thomas E. Thress).

"No, no, no. Why don't you call it '*The Hollow Promise*'?" I said "Rogers, that's a great idea but you've got no sense of the English language. It's '*The Hollow Hope*'." He didn't like that but I did. Then, when I was done with the book manuscript I found the funniest graduate student I knew and I took him to lunch. He was a guy named Rob Eisinger. I said, "Rob, I need chapter titles. I need names of models." We brainstormed for a few hours. He came up with "dynamic" and "constrained," I think. He came up with a lot of the chapter titles. I think titles do matter.

Question: What was most difficult aspect of the project for you?

Rosenberg: I think what was most difficult was developing a theory of the role of courts in producing significant social reform, synthesising data into hypotheses or conditions going beyond my data, saying, "Well, who cares? Why are these data really important?" And that's what I think makes anything worthwhile reading. Unless you care about the particular data, what's important is the hypothesis or the hypotheses it generates. That's what I think is the difference between an article that five people read and something that gets read, taught, argued about, and actually gets people thinking. So that for me was clearly the hardest. Data gathering takes time, but once you know what you want to get, it's not, I think, intellectually difficult.

Question: Did you have a sense of the kind of criticisms you might get when the book was published?

Rosenberg: I had a sense of the intellectual criticism. In fact I remember being very worried that I wouldn't be able to get the book published. In fact I actually sent it to multiple presses. The criticisms I most expected and I most feared was someone saying, "Boy, your data are wrong: (a) you counted wrong in this and it makes a difference; and (b) if only you had looked at this, you would see . . . " I was very paranoid about that and I tried to be as careful as I could. I think there's almost none of that kind of criticism.

But what I did not have any sense of was the emotional criticism, particularly from within the legal academy. I hit a raw nerve. To many older lawyers and law professors, here was this young kid who's telling them their academic careers were worthless. These were lawyers and law professors who understood their life's work as training the next generation of social reformers who have made this country great. I was telling them, "No, they haven't." I had a casebook thrown at me at a talk. I had a garbage can thrown at me at a talk. I had people scream at me in the middle of talks, interrupt talks, and walk out slamming doors. The vehemence, it was really stunning. I understand it now but I was taken aback by the kind of visceral, emotional response I got from the legal academy.

The first time I got an inkling of this kind of reaction was actually the first time I presented my initial work, at an APSA conference. It was my first take on the *Brown* stuff. It was a very long paper, embarrassingly long. I was on a panel with two professors and two discussants. The first discussant says, "Well, there are three papers here. Professors A and B have done fine jobs and I really don't have anything to say. But Gerry Rosenberg's written an embarrassment and a disaster. I need to save him from this project so I'm going to devote my twenty minutes to telling him what's wrong." Then the second discussant does the same thing. So I'm more than a little shaken. Then they open it for questions and I'm the only one who gets questions. Most of the questions consist of people yelling at me. Now, I'm a graduate student. It's my first conference. I have tears running down my cheeks. I'm just devastated. I can't move after people are leaving. Then I look up and there are two people standing in front of me. One says, "That was brilliant. They are all full of it," and gives me a hug. She says, "My name's Lee Epstein. I teach at Southern Methodist University." And then the second person says, "That's terrific. This is a great project. My name is Larry Baum. I teach at Ohio State." They took me out and gave me a pep talk. I had never met them before and it was truly remarkable because I was devastated, absolutely devastated. Indeed, Rogers Smith warned me that I might not get a job with this dissertation. In fact, even though I was on the job market for two years I was only offered one job, thankfully at a great university.

Question: There is no question today that even those who were strongly critical of the book in its implications have taken it seriously.

Rosenberg: Well, one of the things I was disappointed about is I thought I had interesting things to say about *Roe v. Wade*. For example, I was stunned to find that there were nearly 600,000 legal abortions in the United States the year before *Roe*. I thought I had a neat argument about why *Roe* worked in contrast to *Brown*. But nobody ever talks about that, everyone focuses on *Brown*. So I've kind of been disappointed about the lack of interest or reaction to the *Roe* stuff. That surprised me.

Question: Did any of the criticisms hit home, that is, you felt were valid?

Rosenberg: To me the most telling criticism, or maybe more a suggestion, came from someone who has become a friend – Michael McCann. He said that I should have done more of a bottom-up approach. I think that would have enriched the project. I tried, without having that vocabulary, to do some of that in chapter four where I was looking for the effects of *Brown* on activists by reading biographies and autobiographies. But I think I could have done more of that kind of work.

There was one set of criticisms that wasn't made very widely. I think Peter Schuck at Yale did the best job on this. He basically said all my analytic categories were really slippery and I think he's right. Fortunately not too many people have picked up on that! But I think that's really quite telling. He says, for example, my second constraint, "Courts lack judicial independence" – well how do you measure that? And maybe it's not really a constraint. It's saying, "Look, courts aren't very likely to do this." Well I think that's right but what are the conditions under which they will? Well, I don't think I'm very clear or precise on that.

Question: Were you motivated at all by wanting to make an impact outside academia?

Rosenberg: Yes, I was naive. I really hoped groups and lawyers on the left, those working for progressive causes, would change what they did, would only litigate when conditions were met. Pie in the sky! It clearly hasn't happened. For example, I've been very disappointed with same-sex marriage activists. I think that, particularly after Hawaii and the Defence of Marriage Act, it was crystal clear that you don't litigate. But they kept litigating and so we now have twenty-seven constitutional amendments that ban same-sex marriage. I think they've set their cause back and I find that very disturbing.

I have become more and more concerned about the ideological influence of so-called progressive lawyers. That is, progressive lawyers are clearly well educated, which means they're middle or upper class. By litigating, in effect they hijack social change movements away from organizing people on the streets (to produce movements that can make political change), to this focus on abstract rights which, if I'm right, very seldom make change. So rather than furthering movements, they hinder them. This is a real example of class bias at work. It's a lot easier for a lawyer to write a brief and argue before another upper- or middle-class lawyer (the judge) than to go out and hold meetings and organize ordinary people who often lack much formal education. So I think lawyers can play this very negative role in supporting class structures and in deemphasizing and destabilizing working-class organizations.

Question: With the benefit of hindsight would you do anything differently?

Rosenberg: I wouldn't do much differently. If I were doing it from scratch I would certainly make very clear and emphasise more what courts *can* do. But the fact is that this book works. People tell me it works very well in the classroom because it gets students angry! It gets people thinking. So when you got something like that, you don't want to mess with it too much. There's also a tone question. A lot of people go after the tone of the book. They say, "The flypaper court? Come on!" But I think the tone works even if it's a little over the top. It gets readers going. It's effective.

CHAPTER 16

MICHAEL McCANN AND *RIGHTS AT WORK**

Law and Society research, born in the 1960s and a successor to legal realism, has roots in a tradition of "engaged" scholarship, connected to progressive politics and the concerns of marginalized people. But with one foot in the social sciences, there remain disagreements about the position scholars should have in the field, either in advocating for change or living lives of engagement. Certainly, explicit political commitments can complicate research in a number of ways, such as through bias that can affect the questions asked or the answers reached. On the other hand, political commitments can strengthen the researcher's position, providing enthusiasm, energy, and access.

Michael McCann's research into pay equity mobilization and litigation brought him to the heart of that problem. By his choice of topics, Rights at Work *reflects his prior investment in union politics. Once in the field, he was drawn into a more active role than most textbooks on research methods – imparting a veneer of neutrality – describe. Yet the sympathetic academic does not have an uncontested position. In this interview McCann reflects on how race and gender affected his interactions with his research subjects and with the way he framed the project as a whole. Unavoidably we must ask how the identity of the researcher might affect research projects such as this.*

Even further, it invites the question of what it means to be an academic, not only as those in higher education define themselves but in what the people who are research subjects expect and ask of researchers. What do "we," as researchers, tell them and what impact do we have in their lives? Elite and nonelite populations naturally present different contexts for these issues. Although these questions do not admit of easy answers, McCann demonstrates attentiveness to methodology and a healthy appreciation for his status and position – important attributes to bring to difficult fieldwork. The interview

---

**Rights at Work: Pay Equity Reform and the Politics of Legal Mobilization* (Chicago: University of Chicago Press, 1994).

begins with him recounting the intellectual progression that led him into empirical field-work.

Methodological Keywords: interviews, surveys, participant observation, engaged research, epistemology

McCann: I came into Law and Society research very indirectly, kind of walking backwards. I was lucky to find a job doing research at the Center for Law and Society at Berkeley. I worked for Bob Kagan on a book that he was writing on regulatory legalism. I didn't know much about it but I was intrigued. I then took a graduate course with him. I was working on two tracks originally. One was a more traditional political theory type of work. But then I was increasingly doing work with, to me, this new community of Law and Society scholars and I found a lot of overlap. So I developed an interest early on about law and the struggle for social change. My doctoral dissertation really grew out of the work I was doing for Bob Kagan and his book on regulatory legalism. It was about the public interest law movement in the United States. I melded that into my own interest in the history of political social movements in the United States. I treated it as a new phase of middle-class reform politics. What was really new was the faith in lawyers and litigation as a strategy and a resource of social change.

Then, on the University of Washington campus, I got involved in organizing clerical workers and nurses on the campus. I had a long history of interest and involvement in union politics. There had been a couple of court cases that had been lost by those who were proposing wage advocacy. That fit very well into what I was already writing about – critical perspectives about the politics of litigation.[1] So I wrote a paper about why a legal strategy using equal protection and civil rights law to try and promote wage equity for women and minorities was likely to be a losing cause in the courts. It was an argument saying it was a noble campaign but the legal strategy was not going to work. I was using a quasi-Marxist Critical Legal Studies conception of legal ideology, which is rather unlike the sort of everyday legal consciousness approach to legal ideology. I delivered the paper at a conference. I remember Marie Provine asking: "Why don't you go talk to these people? You are arguing here that the strategy is not going to work but why do these people keep going to court?"

---

[1] Michael W. McCann, *Taking Reform Seriously: Perspectives on Public Interest Liberalism* (Ithaca, NY: Cornell University Press, 1986).

When I went back to the University of Washington there was a rally on campus around wage equity. I talked to one of the leaders there, an amazing scholar activist named Helen Remick, while we were waiting around in a room one day. I asked her what she thought of the lawyers and the litigation strategy. She had been very active nationwide on the pay equity issue. She gave me this very complex and quite sophisticated, subtle analysis: "The litigation's probably not going to work but if it wasn't for the litigation we wouldn't have this movement. And the lawyers in the union movement have been really terrific. They've been very strong allies and we've been able to organize around this campaign." That was a different perspective. So that's really where the idea came from – both realizing the first tack I took was a one-dimensional approach to the issues and then just very serendipitously running into one of the major leaders in the movement who had a very different cut on it all.

As soon as I began talking to activists, especially the nonlawyers, about how they thought about the lawyers, about the litigation, about the legal rights claims, I began to really see it differently. I had a sense that this was an opportunity to do a much more social-movement-grounded study. I had a keen interest in the history of social movements. Social movement theory in the United States in the 1980s was really developing some momentum. So one of the primary goals from the beginning was to merge social movement theory with various forms of legal mobilisation theory and add some legal consciousness angles. It was this kind of bringing together of separate traditions. I don't remember ever really designing it that way, it just happened along the way. I remember my NSF [National Science Foundation] proposal was very different from what turned out.

Question: How was that grant application structured?

McCann: Well, it was much more of an impact study, a little bit more along Rosenbergian lines. I had some narrowly defined measures of effectiveness. It was framed in a very instrumental, strategic way: here's a legal strategy, does it work, does it not? I had some hypotheses that were to be tested in six case studies. I don't remember what they were but it had this very neat design to it. But in every one of these places, as soon as I arrived and began interviewing people, I found a much more complicated story than had been told in previous studies. The original six cases had been carefully designed to be quite different so I could compare and contrast different outcomes. But they looked much more similar in terms of these indices of how organizing women had been advanced, whether the law suit had been successful or not, advances in collective bargaining and other routes that accompanied litigation. Also, I increasingly found women talking the language of a critical rights perspective and that seemed to be uniform. So I kept adding new case studies. I would study one place and people would say, "Oh, you should go over there and talk to those people." So I would do that and then add another case study. I ended up with twenty-three or twenty-four cases from the original six. From a research perspective what I found was, on one hand, disappointing. I didn't find the variance along the dramatic lines I had hoped to find to make a nice neat study. It was the similarities across the board that really became the story.

Question: Your case studies brought you to many sites, which might have threatened to stretch you thin. How did you plan and prepare for that?

McCann: I would usually choose geographical areas in which there might be several sites of activity that would be close to each other and I would try and do a couple of cases within those different regions. It was really more of a snowballing procedure – the more I would interview people and study cases, I would find out about new cases that had not been written up or had not really caught my attention before. There was a very clear criterion for the original choice of case studies, but after that each case study just led me to a new case study.

I tried to get as much background as possible. Then I would usually call up a handful of people in advance and tell them I was coming. I would ask them who I should talk to and I would usually go into a site with maybe eight or ten interviews lined up. Then along the way I would almost invariably run into people. Often when I would go to interview somebody who was a local union leader I would be sitting in an office. I would chat to the receptionist or a secretary or someone passing through and sometimes I would turn it into an interview. Or I would say, "Can I take you to lunch?" and we would talk. So I had probably three or four times as many interviews as I actually treated as formal interviews quoted in the book. I didn't record or I didn't transcribe them fully but I would take notes. I was always looking for opportunities to get alternative and unorthodox views. I tried not to just speak to the people who were the appointed leaders and activists, though I didn't find as much variance as I might have expected.

177

Trips were usually ten days to fourteen days; some places I visited several times. Once I ran out of NSF money, there were still places where there was a university and I could get invited back to give a talk, and I would do follow up interviews. I eventually had to do some interviews by phone, and those are really awkward. At a certain point I just ran out of money and time and energy to keep studying more cases.

Question: What were the methodological foundations that guided your approach to the fieldwork?

McCann: Well, I shouldn't admit this but I never took a formal methodology course in graduate school. I was a political theorist. I've had no training for anything that I've done. It was very much making it up as you go along. But I think that's mixed, you know. I'm not sure it's a good prescription to offer to young scholars, but in my case it's been kind of liberating. It means a lot of work if you have to develop the methodological expertise as you go along, but it's not that hard in some ways. After all, I learned a great deal just by reading lots of empirical social science studies and talking to fellow social scientists for many years.

In terms of this project, I had studied epistemology and legal theory, especially language theory and theories of knowledge in various modes of traditional political thought. So I had thought a lot about how we know. I wanted the project to be interview-intensive from the beginning because I wanted to hear the accounts of people. But I also realized the limitations of interview-intensive approaches. First there would be a limited "N" and so how representative would it be? That's always the question. So I also developed a more formal, formally structured survey. I designed different kinds of questions for that, ones that would make sense if I aggregated them.

I also wanted to compare the interviews with how the interviewees had filled out the survey response. That was very useful to me. When I asked questions and gave people a standard five choices about how useful they thought litigation was, it was interesting to compare the long interview answer with how they filled out that form. Often it was almost opposite. Somebody would say litigation is "very effective" but then in the course of talking to them you discover that what they meant by that was not what one would naturally expect. People's views about litigation being a waste of time would often come out of great momentary frustration with some encounter with lawyers, but when we began to ask the question, "Do you think litigation's been useful for the movement?" they would say, "Oh, we wouldn't have a movement if it wouldn't have been for the lawyers and for the litigation."

Question: Without prior, formal training in methods, what was your experience learning interviewing in the field?

McCann: Quite early, after I had done a few interviews, I said, "Maybe I should go back and learn how to do interviewing," but I found that what I had been doing was actually pretty good "textbook" stuff. I had never really studied that. There was some new literature from social psychologists on interviewing in a much more conversational style, really probing and pushing people. That made a lot of sense to me and was working very well for me as a style in the interviews. There is a real divide between a classic scientific posture of reserve and distance versus a much more interactive dialogic approach. I think in some of the early interviews I tried both strategies and generally found that my interviewees responded far more to a much more informal, interactive dialogic kind of process than a more formal interview process.

At least in the early phases I was learning as much about the questions I needed to be asking. My questions continued to expand as I went along but I always started at the same place. One of the strategies I had learned from the dialogic interviewing was to begin the interview by saying, "How did you become involved in this?" Usually the person would talk for forty-five minutes. I would have a set of questions that I wanted answers for and I would usually find that in that first long narrative half of my questions would be addressed. Telling their personal story broke a lot of barriers. One of the things that was surprising to me, especially given that there was a lot of academic discussion at the time about scholars being elites, imposing themselves, and doing damage to others, was how much people wanted to tell their stories. One of the reasons I like to interview people who are engaged in struggle is they want to tell their stories. A large number of women began by saying, "Well, I went through a divorce and all of a sudden I was a single wage earner making very little money, pissed off about guys, beginning to see in different ways the ways in which the world is full of guys who are kind of giving us the shaft." I think divorce became a major pathway toward the development of a feminist consciousness and made them available for activism. The interviews I remember most were women who talked about their divorces and I could just see how that played into eventual politicisation. I had planned to write a separate article just about this interesting dynamic, but I never got around to it.

179

With rank-and-file people I learned lots of techniques. Taking them to lunch or buying them breakfast or coffee was often a really good thing. I also learned to deal with silence. A lot of the discussion would be very painful for them either because they were frustrated or because they didn't want to reveal some of the interpersonal conflicts, ideological conflicts, or organizational conflicts. I found silence was often the most useful tactic to let the person sit there and really go through in her mind how she wanted to say it and whether she wanted to say anything at all. Silence was often much more effective than me trying to pry out an answer.

I'd often look for a seeming contradiction. I'd want them to explain how they could hold two views: for example, "I hate lawyers but lawyers are really important" or "Litigation's a waste of time but we wouldn't have a movement if we didn't litigate." I think a lot of the interviewees found that to be useful. They would have these seemingly contradictory views and in thinking them through they often seemed to come to a different place in their own reasoning. Usually I felt best about and probably drew the most on the interviews that were most initiated by the interviewee. I could just get clarification on points and steer the discussion on one direction or another but say very little. That was a kind of measure: the less I interrogated the more productive the interview was probably.

Question: How did you develop trust between yourself and your interviewees, so that they felt able to speak so openly?

McCann: Very quickly after I did one or two case studies, I became known among activists around the country. I also became involved in a lot of places because a lot of times I would show up and they were about to have a rally. They said, "Would you come and give a talk at a rally? You know more about what's going on than we do." So all of a sudden my whole relationship to the subject of research was really quite different. But in doing that, I won a tremendous amount of trust. I still did have moments where clearly I was being treated as an outsider and, I think, as a male and as an educated white guy. There were many moments when that was quite palpable to me.

During the research, there was a series of court decisions which didn't kill the movement but certainly placed important constraints on it. Activists were becoming more and more frustrated that the doors were closing on them. Some of that frustration would occasionally be displaced on me. I think many people, especially in later stages, thought that I was a big advocate of litigation and at that point there was a growing frustration with lawyers and legal strategies. I usually didn't try to say, "No, that's not my position"; we would do the interview and then later on I would, if they wanted to know where I stood on that. I think that gender was only part of a series of issues that were all related to power to some degree and how I was perceived. But mostly I had become sort of a conduit of knowledge among different activists to some degree and I think that helped me overcome those barriers of gender and other kinds of distance that were sources of distrust and scepticism.

I realize that some people might find that such engagement would really interfere with my objectivity and impartiality. That's where I was reading a lot of feminist standpoint theory. Nancy Hartsock was a colleague of mine and she had developed this idea of feminist standpoint. I took a position that was a sort of postpositivist – that this would be written from the perspective of the activists themselves and I was neither an advocate of this cause nor a critic. I had in the process shifted from scepticism to being much more supportive of the cause, but this was not a book where I was advocating pay equity as policy. It was really trying to understand the struggle from the activists' point of view in all of its complexity.

Question: You had to broach potentially sensitive or aggravating issues in this project. What were the most difficult issues for you?

McCann: I think the most difficult issues and ones that I did not adequately deal with and have greatly lamented not doing more with, were issues of race – how race cut deeply through some of these case histories. It was certainly true that I could get access to white women workers much more effectively than I could to African American, Latina, and nonwhite women. I learned early on that that was not an issue that I was going to get very far with. There was far more skepticism and mistrust of me by women of color than white women. I sensed that all along but I didn't come to grips with it until too late, I think.

I don't know what I would have done about it and I've thought about it a lot of times and how I might have offset that. Probably about a third to a half of the way through the research I began making a more concerted effort to really identify and to generate interviews with African American women. That was generally not very successful. I had the greatest success in Los Angeles and that was mainly with Latina leaders and activists. There I had some of the most amazing interviews I ever generated.

In terms of issues of power and equality and subordination, I would say the race issue was the most sensitive and difficult issue. It was also clear in many places from interviews with white women that there were significant racial issues but that they did not want to talk about them. I would try and encourage them to talk about it but with little success. I also felt I think that if I pressed that issue, they would close down and that I would not be able to get to anything else. I didn't really sufficiently grapple with that in the process of writing the book and I should have. Getting close to the race issue tended to be paralyzing for the project in its own terms. I mention racial divides a lot in the book and I give some evidence of it but if I would have really tried to develop that, I think I would have not been able to really develop the rest of the book. That should have been a story in itself. I think I had to close that down a little bit to enable me to continue with the rest of the project. It was only later that I fully realized that. A couple of critics have rightly pointed that out that there's a background of racial issues that are not really addressed in the book. I put on the cover a picture of activists that prominently feature African American women that kind of invites that critique. I was aware of that. I thought that was a good thing. It was my own way of making race more prominent on the cover than I had managed to make it in the book.

Question: You did a survey as well as qualitative interviews. Did either of those bodies of data work better than the other?

McCann: A lot of people didn't want to fill the survey out. One of the very first times I went to interview a local union leader I said, "Did you get my survey? I want to do the interview now but the surveys are also important." She replied, "Oh yes, I gave it to my assistant to fill out." So I said, "But the point was to have *you* fill it out because I really wanted your perspective." She goes, "I just hate doing those things." So that was a bit of a challenge. I didn't want to push people. If they're going to do it under protest, what are you going to get? A handful of times after I conducted the interview, the person would say, "Before, I said I didn't want to fill out the survey, but I would like to fill it out now." For whatever reason the scepticism or mistrust in me often dissipated after talking through the issues.

I'm much more keen on the dialogic interviews because that's where I best came to understand and develop the most important insights. But on the other hand the survey instruments were really useful because I could aggregate them. One of the standard questions I had was something like, "Was litigation very effective, somewhat effective, or not at all effective?" I could show that, let's say, sixty percent of women said "very effective" and very few said "not at all effective." That's a good starting point for getting into the interviews about what that means and all the ways in which they thought about what is useful. So I think that they ended up being very complementary.

Question: When you left the field you had a mountain of data. Where did you start and how did you manage that?

McCann: I had never done anything like that before and I've never done anything like it since. I should say that the research was really exhausting and I really don't plan to do something like that again. I had a very crude system. I believe strongly in developing a project where one constantly has to be imagining the study's architecture. So very early on I would imagine the chapter-by-chapter structure and the themes that would go into that. But every day I would be rewriting that outline, constantly rethinking the structure. I was getting all this information so I could put it into boxes and I was constantly moving it around in those boxes. But at least I had boxes. I was reconstructing what the boxes themselves were about. Technologically it was very crude. I would transcribe the interviews and in those days do a lot of cutting and pasting, literally. So I would have a box on legal consciousness and that would be broken down into five or six different categories. I would just fill in all the quotes and my observations and ideas and would often put in scholarly articles, archival materials, whatever. By the time it was written up those categories were often reconstructed in new ways. I ended up with eight big boxes of just interviews and probably another eight big boxes of other materials. I'd have sections in them I kept moving around.

We tell ourselves that we have a research question and we have a set of hypotheses but in the process of developing that book, the questions were changing all the time. Anybody who does research will have these moments. All of a sudden you have this epiphany. You wake up in the middle of the night and see something new and go write it down. Next morning you say, "Well, that's what I've been working on all the time." I see doing research as more and more trying to figure out and develop and thicken the questions rather than just having a simple question and then finding the results than answer it.

Question: When did you gain confidence about the analysis that you were building out of the data?

McCann: For me the writing process is really about organizing, about trying to put it all together. I don't know when it was that I developed a sense that this book might be a good book. It was really unsettling to me. Sometime late in the process, probably when I'd written a number of chapters, I went back and read Stuart Scheingold's *Politics of Rights*, which I had not read since graduate days.[2] That put me into several days of depression. I thought I was saying absolutely nothing new, just providing a lot of data showing that Scheingold was right. But then I got out of that and realized that I was doing a lot of things that Scheingold didn't do – complicating a lot of his ideas, developing quite a different view of ideology, adding lots of new dimensions. I got a grip and realized that I was certainly building on what he had done and working within that tradition. But it was also, I thought, going to be a significant original contribution – although I was never sure.

I think that the entire manuscript probably took about between a year and a half to two years to write in draft form. From the NSF proposal to my final involvement in the production of the book was probably five or six years. The biggest challenge was figuring out what to do in the concluding chapter, which originally was a very long engagement with Critical Legal Studies – fighting my earlier self about the limitations of CLS approaches.

Question: It seems that the demands and the exhaustion of which you've spoken were of different kinds.

McCann: It placed personal demands on me because I had a wife and two children and it meant I had to be gone for significant periods of time to do the research. I also think I was extremely invested in the book. A lot of aspects of the research were new for me. I had never really been trained to do empirical research and I felt like I was making it all up as I went along. That meant that I was constantly critically analyzing what I was doing and never very certain that I was doing it right somehow. There was also a concern that there were too many projects in one and that it was not really manageable. I was working theoretically at this intersection of bringing legal mobilisation literature with social movement literature with this growing attention to legal consciousness. I tend to really work at organizing – that constant process of reworking

---

[2] Stuart A. Scheingold, *The Politics of Rights: Lawyers, Public Policy, and Political Change* (New Haven, CT: Yale University Press, 1974); 2nd ed. (Ann Arbor, MI: University of Michigan Press, 2004).

a very detailed outline and shifting folders around in my boxes and just pounding on it until it took enough shape. That was demanding.

It was also demanding because I was dealing with real people in lots of struggles. While it was taking a toll a little bit personally in my own family, it was not at all like the people whom I was often interviewing. I think the project meant a lot to me in a lot of ways and not just professionally.

It really absorbed a huge amount of me. That's one reason, I think, why I haven't done the same kind of project again. It's just too demanding too often. I'm still very mixed about that period when working with the graduate students because most of them do case-study qualitative work. They tend to go out into the field and do quasi-ethnographic interview-intensive case studies. I try to alert them that that takes a lot of time and energy, and it's difficult. They will labor in tremendous uncertainty and confusion much of the time. They have to be willing to constantly be reconstructing their question, and it's not easy. I think it would be very difficult for a graduate student to try and take on a work of the scale of *Rights at Work*. There's a lot to be said for simpler versions of that approach. The agenda needs to be a little bit more manageable, both to conduct the research and to produce a book. I have been very fortunate to work with many gifted graduate students who developed more realistic boundaries for their terrific projects than I did.

Question: Did anything in the process not go to plan?

McCann: What plan? Certainly the book that was produced was very different from the original NSF proposal. The process of developing the NSF proposal required simplification and formalisation and a certain amount of reductionism in specifying relationships in fairly simple causal terms hypothetically. That isn't really how I think about power and relationships. But one of the things I learned is that such a process is very useful. It is important to develop a good formal research design, while at the same time recognizing that, once you go out into the field, you have to be very willing to adjust, reconstruct, adapt or maybe even throw it out. But you need to come in with an organizational framework of understanding and analysis and expectations.

So I suppose things worked according to plan in those ways. It began in one place and ended up somewhere rather differently but it was a quite logical and well-scrutinized path from beginning to end. And a lot of serendipitous things happened along the way. The book would have never happened if I hadn't run into Helen Remick at a certain moment and asked for an interview with her. People that I met and interviewed often were not part of a plan I started with. Often when I went to a site the most important interviews were not the people that I originally was told I should interview. But I suppose that it is building a plan that allows and encourages such things to happen. My approach to research is looking for the unexpected to some degree. And complexity's good. That makes research laborious, but also much more fun and gratifying.

CHAPTER 17

AUSTIN SARAT AND WILLIAM FELSTINER AND *DIVORCE LAWYERS AND THEIR CLIENTS**

Where is law most "in action" in society? Very often, it seems, where it is difficult if not impossible to observe directly. Courtrooms can be observed, though private offices can hide bargaining and discretion. Judges may provide written opinions, but their psychology remains a black box. And so it goes. For scholars of the legal profession, a significant obstacle to penetrating law's power has been the office door, behind which lawyers and clients engage in dialogue, bound by the claim of "lawyer–client privilege." But all the clues received from aggregate data to anecdotal evidence, not to mention academic instinct, drove researchers to break down these barriers.

Bill Felstiner and Austin Sarat, among those who succeeded in challenging the boundaries, found a wealth of data in the interactions of divorce lawyers and their clients. On the path to Divorce Lawyers and Their Clients, Felstiner and Sarat confronted the scientist's paradox that observation itself may change the behavior of the observed – and the subsequent problem that the publication further exposes to embarrassment or critique what was once hidden. In a number of ways, this research project could have been stifled by obedience to the most formal or cautious standards for research ethics. It may be easy to conclude that the lessons of this book validate their judgments, but it offers an opportunity to consider whether the ends of observational research into legal phenomenon always justify the means. When and how should scholars, someday exploring different contexts and legal settings, exercise restraint?

This interview, like others in this volume, also touches on the joys and complications of collaborative research. With fieldwork on opposite coasts of the United States, and through a period of analysis and writing lasting over a decade, their complementary partnership survived. The interview begins with an account of the birth of this project, at the tail end of an earlier joint project.

* *Divorce Lawyers and Their Clients: Power and Meaning in the Legal Process* (New York: Oxford University Press, 1995).

Methodological Keywords: interviews, participant observation

Felstiner: Austin and I were already working on a large government-funded project on the costs of civil litigation. I was at the University of Southern California at the time and Austin was at Amherst College in Massachusetts. We temporarily moved to Madison, Wisconsin, rented Malcolm Feeley's house together, and were working to write the stuff up intensively. Austin was going through, or had recently been through, a divorce. We used to talk about how the nature of a dispute would change over time depending upon who entered the picture, who his wife was talking to, who he was talking to, and so on. It was those kinds of conversations that led us, with Rick Abel, to write the "Naming, Blaming and Claiming" piece.[1] That was a kind of speculation about the way things go. So having done that, we thought, "Well, let's find out if there's any real content to it." We decided to do an empirical project in which we would focus on the transformations in disputes over time. We wrote a grant proposal, got the money, and started to do the work which led to the book fifteen years later.

Question: How did you come to choose divorce and divorce lawyers as the substantive focus?

Felstiner: We thought about it a lot and our main concern about the whole project was access. Before doing the research in the communities in which we would eventually be working, I think I talked to maybe a half dozen divorce lawyers in Los Angeles. I distinctly remember one of them said people would never let us sit in on the conversations because there were so many intimate details going back and forth between lawyer and client. We said, "What, you mean about sex?" And she said, "No, nobody cares about sex. I mean money!"

Actually, while our application to the NSF [National Science Foundation] was pending, the *Law & Society Review* published an article by someone who had received funding to do an observational study on lawyers and clients but had been unable to secure access.[2] It collapsed their project. From our point of view the timing was extremely unfortunate. Part of our effort with NSF was to persuade them that we

[1] Felstiner, R. L. Abel, and Sarat, "The Emergence and Transformation of Disputes: Naming, Blaming, Claiming..." *Law & Society Review*, 15:631–54 (1980–81).

[2] B. Danet, K. Hoffman, and N. Kermish, "Obstacles to the Study of Lawyer-Client Interaction: The Biography of a Failure," *Law & Society Review*, 14:905–22 (1980).

had a better way of doing it – that we were going to succeed where they had failed. Thinking about access we thought that divorce lawyers would give us a good shot because we knew that a lot of lawyers involved in divorce law were unhappy with it. If we could persuade them that the result of our project might be to make their lives easier or make the lives of people like them easier, it might work. In the long run I don't think it made any difference. We might not have been able to do it if we decided to look at lawyers with big corporate clients, but as long as we were studying people whose clients were individuals I think we would have been able to do it in any field.

Sarat: Divorce seemed particularly promising as an area in which to work because of the interplay of the usual stuff of law – money, property, rights – with emotions. Even when the legal rules say that divorce is no fault we thought that emotions might play a large part in the work of divorce lawyers. We were interested to see how the emotional context influenced the way lawyers and clients interact.

Question: For another major choice at the early stage – where to locate the research – you chose two "university towns" in Massachusetts and California. Could you tell us how you weighed practicality versus the other theoretical concerns?

Felstiner: We did the fieldwork where we lived. We didn't have a choice really. Nobody was giving us any money to take time off to do this. I was living in Santa Barbara so that's where I did the fieldwork. It didn't have anything to do with theory, it was just convenience.

Question: When you got to the communities in which you'd actually do the research, what was the reception from the lawyers you approached for access?

Felstiner: It was difficult. It took us a couple of years. We didn't hold up the research waiting to get the number in each community that we wanted, but the time between when we first starting talking to people in the community and when we started observing the last case may have been eighteen months to two years. The first thing we did was to see the presiding judge in the local court in each community. We didn't want lawyers to say, "Let me think about it," and then talk to the judge and the judge say, "What the hell is this?" Then we had to figure out what the population of divorce lawyers was. I had lived in Santa Barbara for about fifteen years. I talked to a couple of divorce lawyers and asked them for the names of other divorce lawyers and we kept doing that until we weren't getting any new names. We also had a formal list of divorce lawyers. Over time I called up every one of them. Sometimes I would go see them in their office. More frequently I'd take them to lunch. There wasn't anybody who was reluctant to talk to me. It's a small town and there wasn't that much going on. They got a free lunch. One or two lawyers were people I'd had a social relationship with before, which helped. There were some oddballs, you know, people who said, "Yes, of course we'll do it, but I'll have to charge you my normal rate to sit in."

But in many cases it was a long process of wooing the lawyers. Nine times out of ten they'd agree to do it and the arrangement was that when they encountered a new client whom they thought might be willing to cooperate in the research they'd call us. We wanted to follow cases from as close to the beginning as possible. Well, after six weeks or so they'd call back, "Oh God, I forgot all about it." Sometimes we did that kind of thing half a dozen times. I think in some instances it was just luck that a few days either before or after our call there was a client that they thought, "Oh, maybe this guy would be willing to cooperate in the research." And we wanted, if at all possible, to do two cases with each lawyer. Once we got the first one then the second one was much easier.

Sarat: Much like Bill's account, the Amherst-Northampton bar is relatively small. It was pretty easy to identify the lawyers who did divorce work. And like Bill once that was done there was a period of cultivating their good will. I did less lunch buying than he did, but spent some time hanging out in the probate court introducing myself and some time hanging out in a restaurant right next to the courthouse where the local lawyers ate. The probate court judge was very interested in the research, and he introduced me around.

Most of the lawyers seem flattered to be approached about the research even if they were not exactly clear about why we were doing it. There is a high boredom factor in local practice. That helped. Our research project was something to break the routine.

Question: How were the clients approached?

Felstiner: Essentially the lawyer would say, "Hey, there's this guy in town doing research on divorce. I'm happy to cooperate. Would you talk to him?" That's about as much of an introduction as we got. The process of talking the client into it was a bit of a challenge. I can remember sitting down with clients in very odd places and describing the research. But normally, once we got a lawyer willing to introduce us to clients, they would keep at it until we got a client.

Sarat: Like Bill, I relied on an initial introduction from the lawyer. I also recall working hard to cultivate the clients who they referred for the project. Among the things that I did were driving one woman so she could do several errands and helping another hang laundry. This was hardly the stuff I'd been trained to do in graduate school.

Question: Did you have any difficulty in any case maintaining access?

Felstiner: Yes. Sometimes these cases went on for a year or longer. That was a big problem for me. I was working in Santa Monica which is 85 miles or so from Santa Barbara. So I needed at least two hours notice of any kind of meeting. What I tried to do was make friends with the lawyer's secretary. I'd always stop and talk to them, try to make sure they understood that this research was going on and that it would be a calamity for me if the lawyer and client actually got together and I wasn't there. During those years I actually took different kinds of vacations than I normally would. Normally I might go away for a month or so but I tried not to do that. And when I knew I was going to be away and that there was a likelihood that there was going to be a lawyer–client conversation, I would leave the tape recorder with the secretary and ask her to remind the lawyer to tape it.

Sarat: In my site maintaining access was a real chore. Many lawyers did not have secretaries. And remembering to let me know when there was a meeting was not a high priority. So I would regularly call or check in with the lawyers and the clients: "How are things going in the case?" "Is there an appointment scheduled?"

Question: Given the difficulties you experienced in getting and maintaining access, did you ever get to the stage of thinking it wasn't feasible?

Felstiner: No, we were going to do this work. I'd had a lot of experience before then doing fieldwork. I'd written two monographs in the preceding years which involved really extensive fieldwork. One was on things that were done inside the criminal justice system in the U.S., but were done outside the criminal justice system in Europe. In the other one I studied a neighborhood justice center in Dorchester, Massachusetts, which required me to sit in a little office for well over six months, all day every day watching what was going on. So I was used to "nose to the grindstone" kind of fieldwork and really enjoyed it. I mean, I loved doing it. Both of us loved doing this divorce lawyer project. The variety of behaviours, the way people would act, it's fascinating kind of stuff. In the beginning we were scared about whether or not we would get access but we were determined to keep at it. Essentially what the process amounts to is converting a stranger into an acquaintance, even sort of a light friend, so that eventually the lawyers were in the position they felt that they had to do something for us because we'd been so persistent and so interested in their work. We'd even been spending money taking them to lunch. We thought it was important to get inside that room and see what was going on.

Sarat: I had not had Bill's fieldwork experience. I had come to this work with most of my experience being with surveys. While this was more fun by far, I lived in fear that the whole thing would fall apart, that the research subjects would change their minds, that when I was in a lawyer–client meeting that the tape recorder would fail, etc.

Question: How did you put the clients at ease? It was a difficult time in their lives.

Felstiner: Yes and no. Not everybody in a divorce is in some maelstrom of emotions. Sometimes people have been separated for a significant period of time and were just going through the motions. We had relatively few cases which involved children, which is probably when a lot of the emotional turmoil comes. My experience in general is that though it may be difficult to arrange for the initial part of a conversation, once people start talking it's hard to stop them. Some of the stuff just comes on out. It was all quite easy to establish relationships with most clients. If the typical case involved six or eight lawyer–client conferences, we would probably have talked to a client around ten times or so.

Sarat: People in crisis like to talk. And they exhaust their friends, kids, families. And we were there to listen. We were always interested, and they did not have to pay for our interest. And driving them to meetings, hanging their laundry, being ready to listen to them complain about their spouses, their lawyers, etc. – I think that all played a part.

Question: Were the conversations with clients easier than those with the lawyers?

Felstiner: They were much easier. The university has a lot of prestige. I think they were kind of awed by professionals. In the long run a lot of these clients got a lot out of having us there. Their time with their lawyer was somewhat rationed because they were paying by the hour. A lawyer just blocks out a certain period of time, talks to the client for however long it is, then brings the conversation to an end. There may be a lot going on in the client's mind or a lot of ways that the client wants to vent about their own life situation, but the lawyer doesn't listen to them. But we'd listen to anything, so we would very frequently see the client shortly after the meeting with the lawyer and listen to them, sometimes for hours.

Sarat: Yes and no. I think the clients mostly came to like having the attention and the lawyers liked something to break the daily routine. But there were many times when the anger, or hurt, or fear of clients came pouring out. That was hard. I was not trained as a therapist and often felt a bit overwhelmed by the neediness of the clients.

Question: Were there any ways in which you sensed that your presence affected the interaction in the field?

Felstiner: Yes. We had a relatively naive view of what kind of physical arrangements were typical in a lawyer's office. I've been a lawyer in quite a nice law firm. So I had thought that the lawyer would be behind the desk, the client would be on the other side of the desk and somewhere off in the background there'd be a sofa where we'd be and that the client wouldn't even see us – they would lose awareness that we were in the room. But there are lawyers' offices that are about as big as an ante room where you're sitting across the desk from the lawyer with the client and your knees are touching. So yes, of course, our presence had some kind of an effect.

Occasionally there was some direct evidence of this. I remember one time I was walking down the main street in town and I ran into a lawyer whom I had known socially. She said, "I've heard about the research you're doing and I know you're doing it in such-and-such a case. I'm the lawyer on the other side. I used to work for the lawyer who you are observing." I didn't say whether we were, but she was right. Now this lawyer was always responding on time, didn't lose anything. She said, "I know Paul, that's not his normal way of operating so I figured out that must be because you're following the case." So the lawyers probably were better organized, more responsive, better prepared, more solicitous, and more supportive in their behavior toward the client than they would have been the normal case. Our feeling about it was, "Well, look at what goes on even when they are on their best behavior."

Sarat: Frankly, not much. I had the sense that the lawyers and clients kind of forgot about me once things got going. Though there were a couple of occasions on which I thought the clients were getting lousy advice and I had to bite my lip.

Question: Did the collaboration ever take the part of observing each other's sites? Did you sit in on the same client meetings?

Felstiner: Only when we were preparing for fieldwork. In our application to the National Science Foundation we said we would not tape the lawyer–client meetings, that it was too much of an intrusion. We said we would just take notes. So when we got the grant, Austin came out to Santa Barbara. We wanted to make sure that, in observing these interactions, we'd both be recording the same things so that the notes that one or another of us would take would be reasonably comparable. We worked out this little playlet. I got a friend who was a lawyer to play the lawyer and my wife to be the client. The notion was that Austin and I would sit there in the room, they would have a meeting that would go on for an hour and we would then compare the notes we had and see how close they were. Well, within fifteen minutes we both gave up. There was no way we could keep up with this stuff. We just stopped the thing and said, "Well, we've got to tape record these things." And so during fieldwork, as soon as an interview was over, we made duplicate copies of the tapes and sent it to the other person. We each had a complete set. As soon as I got Austin's I would listen to it and vice versa. So if there had been any situations in which we were going off in radically different directions, in a way that would pose a problem for the research, we'd catch it pretty quickly. At this stage of the game nothing was typed. We would just listen to the stuff and maybe make notes about what's going on. So we were each always current on what the other was doing.

Question: How did you manage the collaborative aspects of data analysis?

Felstiner: We had actually been awarded a second grant from NSF in which we persuaded them that in order to write the book we needed to spend a year together. So they came up with our salaries for a year. I arranged that we would each have fellowships at the Centre for Socio-Legal Studies in Oxford. The idea was that we would go to England and we wouldn't do anything else. A short while before we were due to leave, Austin called and said he wasn't coming, that he was going to law school instead. So I went to England. But I decided that I wasn't going to do this thing by myself so I spent the year investigating asbestos litigation in the U.K. Austin came over every six weeks or so and we talked about the project, but we never sat down in one place to analyze and write. As you can see, it took us another ten years in fact to produce the book. I was in Oxford 1985 to 1986 and the book was published in 1995.

During that period I went to the American Bar Foundation in Chicago. To help us analyze the transcripts we hired three graduate students to work with us: Wendy Espeland, Cathy Hall, and Mindy Lazarus-Black. Frequently these graduate students were better in ana-lyzing these cases. We decided somewhere fairly early in the analysis that the best way to work with the material was to take individual cases and go over them with a finetooth comb, interpret virtually every line. It wasn't entirely at random. Because we had been there, we knew that some cases were more interesting than others, that the clients were more sophisticated, or that lawyers were complicated or interesting. We'd all read the cases. We'd each figure out what was going on in the cases, how we were going to interpret the cases, what they told us about the kind of things we were interested in. Then we'd all sit down together and talk about it. We'd spend weeks, months, reading the stuff and talking about it and trying to figure out what was going on.

We also had some ideas about themes and we told the graduate students to go off and read the five thousand pages and tell us how much of those were in there. The one example that stands out in my mind is our becoming aware of how much of the time lawyers trash the legal system in talking to their clients.

So the analysis involved attacking the data from more than one angle and over a long period of time. I was at the American Bar Foundation for four years and all that time we were playing around with this stuff whenever we had time.

Sarat: Let me add only one thing. We would read and reread the same transcripts over and over. We would send transcripts to each other when we thought they had interesting things in them. We wrote memo after memo. It was all pretty thorough and pretty tedious. And like Bill, I did other things, like going to law school.

Question: How did you go about writing the book, which pulls together all that data and a theoretical argument about the study of legal interactions?

Felstiner: Usually one or the other of us took the lead in writing. Then we'd fight about every sentence because we have somewhat different approaches to writing. Austin's idea, essentially, is that if something is worth saying once, it's worth saying ten times! I'm exactly the opposite. But he's a very powerful writer and the whole thing was a pleasure. We never had a serious disagreement in the fifteen years we were working together. I think about two-thirds of the time he wrote the first draft and maybe a third of the time I did. Most of the intellectual veneer of the project is his, not mine. I don't think we had any major theoretical intentions in the beginning except for the stuff about the transformation of disputes. I mean, if you could dig up the application we made to the NSF I doubt if you would see very much other than, "Here is the paper we wrote and now we want to try to see if these dispute transformations actually happen as we predict." Throughout the project most of the theoretical energy came from Austin. I'm not even trained as a social scientist and I was much more interested in just finding out what happens.

Sarat: It was very exciting to work with Bill. He was a great reader of the transcript and had a flair for the imaginative and revealing interpretations. There were several "Wow!" moments that kept the whole thing going. For me it was also a chance to apply some very exciting theoretical developments to a priceless body of data. And, frankly it was great fun working together. That meant that even when we didn't see things exactly the same way, we often found ourselves laughing about something. I love that two decades later he still teases me about my prose!

Question: By way of reflection, what was the most difficult thing about the research project?

Felstiner: We had a real problem with the human subjects aspect. I was working at the Rand Corporation by the time we were going to start the fieldwork. Rand's human subjects committee decided it was too complicated for them and so brought in the corporation's lawyer. We had to face this question of the waiver. Our presence, even our tape recorder, constituted a waiver of the lawyer–client privilege. The lawyer came up with a compromise. He said, "When a lawyer agrees to cooperate in the research, tell him he's to call the lawyer on the other side and say there's a researcher who wants to sit in on these cases, which constitutes a waiver, and ask the other lawyer to waive the waiver on behalf of his client." At first blush we accepted that but in every case, every lawyer we talked to said they wouldn't do that. They said that, in the first place, the last thing you would want to do at the start of an adversarial case is to call up the other side and ask them a favor. They said, secondly, no judge would ever actually enforce that kind of subpoena directed to a lawyer, a client, or us. And, third, they said, "Look, it's our client, let us worry about the client and the effect that the research will have on the client. You don't have to worry about that." So we were then in the position of saying, "OK, now what do we do? Do we go back to the Rand human subjects committee and try to persuade them that this would be OK?" We never did. We just went and did the research and there never was a problem. There never were any subpoenas or any threats of anything like that.

We knew this work was good stuff and that we had learned some things that there wasn't any other way to learn. We got a lot of attention at the time and so we thought that, now that we'd demonstrated you could do this kind of observational stuff, a lot of other people would do it in other contexts – in big law firms, in other fields of law. But as far as I know nobody else has ever done this kind of thing in the States. We were very surprised about that. Maybe Institutional Review Boards have played a part in that.

Sarat: I would simply add that I don't think we anticipated the sheer volume of pages of transcripts we would have at the end of the data collection. We put so much into the upfront design that I think the complexity of the data analysis issues kind of caught us a bit by surprise.

Question: Is there anything in hindsight you'd like to change about the project?

Felstiner: Yes, the title of the book. The title came from OUP – it certainly wasn't ours. They thought this book had the potential to sell to some parts of a trade audience. Of course that never happened. And the book's not really about divorce lawyers and their clients. It's about the creation of meaning in the legal process. I've always felt it didn't do justice to the effort we made with the content of the book to talk about "divorce lawyers and their clients."

Sarat: I agree about the title. And maybe in retrospect I would have wanted to do something a bit less academic with a bit more of a reach to a broader audience.

Question: What criticism from the academic audience did you most anticipate or concern yourself with?

Felstiner: I think we knew in advance that there would be a lot of people, particularly women, who'd be upset that we didn't pay any real attention to gender issues. But that's not what we were doing. In the 1980s there was some kind of rule or working principle or attitude, probably still is, that after some period of time when the people who gathered data had full opportunity to exploit it that the data then ought to be generally available. We would have liked to have done that because the stuff's a treasure. You could have mined it in a hundred different ways, including an emphasis on gender. But we came to the conclusion that we couldn't do that, make the data available, without going back and getting the permission of each of the people who had participated. Opening up the data had never been part of the deal. I think we tried for a while but we couldn't even find all the lawyers – they'd moved or died – and we clearly couldn't find the clients.

Sarat: We talked about the sample size and sampling issues. We thought that people might criticize our work for being unrepresentative. But we consoled ourselves that this work was the beginning of something, an opening of a research area using a strategy that was quite cutting edge. We got what seemed to us to be a rich and powerful source of data. The richness lay in the questions our work opened up.

Question: What concern did you have for the participants when you published this? The book presents one lawyer, Wendy for example, who you described as disorganized, ineffective, and lazy.

Felstiner: Well, we felt we had carefully and accurately characterised behavior and attitudes. If that wasn't the way they saw themselves I don't think it worried us very much. I think we also realised that unless we actually plonked this stuff right down in front of them they'd never see it. As far as I know nobody ever did see it, with one exception. We had picked a case to do the first kind of intensive analysis because the lawyer was someone more sophisticated than most and the client was very smart. We analyzed the case and then I went back to these two people because they were both still in Santa Barbara. I said, "Look, here's what we've done. What we'd now like is for the client to comment on what we said about the case and then for the lawyer to comment on what the client said about what we'd said about the case." We would have this threefold analysis of the same thing. They both said they'd do it. Six weeks or a couple of months passed and I hadn't heard from either of them. Then the client said it was just too painful going over this stuff, so she didn't do it. Then the lawyer said, "You're a son of a bitch." He didn't talk to me for about five years because he obviously did not like the way we had characterized him. I still run into him occasionally. He's mellowed in retirement.

Question: What about reactions from the legal profession more generally?

Felstiner: It was mixed. Articles from this project were being published when I was the director of the Bar Foundation so there was more attention paid to them by practicing lawyers than otherwise. One time I was giving a talk about the work of the American Bar Foundation and gave as an example a number of papers including our own work. This one guy got up, absolutely outraged, and said, "Well, that may be the way lawyers behave in California but that's not the way lawyers behave in Florida where I'm from. You're abetting either the mediators or the Communists!"

But on another occasion I was giving a talk to a club in Chicago which was composed of the leading members of the bar and federal judges. I was describing trash talking. A woman who was a federal trial judge got up and said, "You know, I do exactly the same thing. When I'm faced with a case which I think ought to be settled and I'm having difficulty in producing that settlement I call the lawyers in and I tell them to go back out and tell their clients, 'For God's sakes, open your eyes. Look, the judge is a woman and you know what women are like!'" The president of the American Bar Association was there at that meeting. Afterwards he came up to me and said, "Oh, I don't think that's the way my partners and I practice law." But about two months later I got a letter from him and he said, "I've been paying attention to how I talk about the legal system to my clients and you're right." That kind of external validation was very satisfying, when lawyers read about or heard about this project and it seemed to make sense when they paid attention to what they were doing in their own practice.

CHAPTER 18

YVES DEZALAY AND BRYANT GARTH AND *DEALING IN VIRTUE**

A whole generation has now grown up with "globalization" as essential part of the vocabulary, but in the 1980s Law and Society scholars could only see important developments in the legal world in terms of an older set of concepts and questions. At the time that Yves Dezalay and Bryant Garth began thinking about the mysterious world of international commercial arbitration, they had a study in "dispute resolution" and domestic courts. When they had finished, they had a book that was praised as a study in globalization and a window into an emerging global legal field.

At a time when social and political theorists had only begun debating the nature and meaning of globalization, the social scientific study of international commercial arbitration presented new challenges along with the old. Prosaically, top-drawer commercial arbitration is an exclusive club, and they would expect to encounter the sensitivities that accompany research among most elite. Also, this legal realm is among the more complex and obscure. How could one cut through the impenetrable to see the emerging field in a different light? Add to that, now that this emerging legal field served global corporate enterprises, and one might ask where do you begin and where should you end? Dealing in Virtue, in the end, examines activity as far reaching as Egypt and Hong Kong, among other places.

At first glance, Dezalay and Garth might have seemed unlikely partners to take on such a project: Garth, an American law professor comfortable with the button-down collar set, and Dezalay, a French sociologist with a verve for critical theory. Their reflections on this project suggest that their collaboration was not merely complementary in the sense of bringing different disciplines and continents. In a sense, they suggest that collaboration can be the creative, synergistic response to the problem, with the process of responding to one another and to the conditions in the field serving as a provocation to a new set

---

Dealing in Virtue: International Commercial Arbitration and the Construction of a Transnational Legal Order (Chicago: University of Chicago Press, 1996).

*of shared questions not wholly derived from one another's prior position. The interview
began with asking them to explore the genesis of their collaboration.*

Methodological Keywords: interviews, documentary analysis, relational biography, global ethnography

Dezalay: I was doing some research with a judge and a lawyer, and it was probably a distant offshoot of this ADR American propaganda but they decided to be interested in what at that time in France was called mediation-conciliation. Since they were practitioners, of course, their interest was to promote it. My interest was to use that as an entrée into the working of the courts. Their focus was with small conflicts – family mediation and neighbors – and, being the contrarian, I suggested that they look at the other side. I'd known that there was this kind of arbitration in big disputes. The judge had contacts with Pierre Bellet, then the most senior judge in France. Through Bellet I interviewed maybe twelve or fifteen people around him and I quickly realized that I had a situation like the elephant where you can only touch one leg. The first paper I wrote was on the politics of mediation around the law, more or less describing why in France it doesn't work.

Garth: I was program chair of the Law and Society meeting one year and met Yves, I think, in the annual Fun Run. Then in the next year there was a panel on Dispute Resolution where I was to critique his paper. I said, "Well, this is wonderful and interesting stuff but it's all so much about France. You really should study arbitration in a larger setting." I'd been very involved in studying mediation globally and so I had the sense that there was this community out there doing something important, sort of mystical in a way, but also that it was just impenetrable whenever you tried to read this stuff – very, very legalistic. It was the sense of "this is something important that no one knows anything about" – big-stakes ADR – so I thought, if he's interested, let's go for it. I think his response was, "There's no money for that kind of thing." We just started talking and eventually we prepared a project that we didn't think would get funded. We thought, "If they fund it we'll figure out what we're going to do."

Question: At that point, did you share a common approach of any kind? Did you have in mind that this was a study of globalization processes?

Garth: We took up the issue that lawyers debated: was this escape from the state a privatization of dispute resolution? We were, in part, looking at dispute resolution and it had an ADR component. At the time, globalization had hardly been talked about and the National Science Foundation was just moving to globalization, and they said, "We need to study this thing called globalization and look, your project lands in that category."

Dezalay: One of the problems was that in France, like many countries, the law was a fairly closed milieu. If you were outside, especially if you were a sociologist, you had great difficulty in entering it. Maybe you would be allowed to look at small topics, small clients, but certainly not looking at politics or big issues. But around the mid-1980s, when the European project was being shaped by big business and industrialists around a completely different agenda, every week planeloads of American lawyers would arrive in Brussels in their usual way – you know, "here's our visiting card" – looking around. This created huge upheaval and turmoil in what were largely sleepy markets that were beginning to wake up. So it was a great opportunity for a sociologist to start looking at what was going on. I realized that it was a fantastic tool for sociologists to piggyback on the invaders, using them as a way to explore and explode the context in which you work. And at the same time this was creating something entirely new – what the globalization of commercial justice could look like. So maybe Bryant had more of a disputing perspective, but probably because I'm a sociologist, my interest was in using these transformations as a way of getting into this professional milieu.

Question: With a global community so ill defined, even "mystical," how did you think you would break into it?

Dezalay: Initially when we devised the project we were thinking of dividing the work: Bryant would take America, I would take Europe. That sounds reasonable, and it also makes for a more acceptable budget. But what happened was both of us were very busy at the time, so we never got around to writing a questionnaire. But we had set up a window of possible dates for interview trips. We had blocked out certain periods when we were each free, and we kept to that schedule. When the time was approaching, we had prepared all the things that sociologists should do – this list of people we were going to interview – but the problem with this milieu was that it was closed. You could find lists of arbitrators but the lists were almost invalid because either they were too long or we knew that the core of the real practice was very different from the people around it. The real players were listed alongside the would-be players.

Garth: And there are people who have written books by surveying all the arbitrators listed in a big book listing arbitrators, and two-thirds, maybe three-quarters of those people have never done an arbitration. They're just there because they're looking for one.

Dezalay: We both could identify a few players who had told us that there were no more than two or three dozen real players in this milieu. They claimed that they were, and I think they were, definitely a part of this very inner group. But they had much more fuzzy knowledge about what was going on outside of Paris, Geneva, and maybe London. Even London was almost a different world and they didn't know too much about this. So at the beginning we said we were going to put together our different points of entry – do something in the U.S., travel back to Paris, explore our contacts in Geneva and the U.K., and then we'll see: how do those connect? We realized that the only way was to accumulate a certain amount of knowledge, to be two people coming from different countries, and to bring two perspectives. It was very rewarding as a research tool, so we decided that we had to continue.

Garth: We met in New York and we started with law professors. We knew a couple of them who were known for arbitration. Bob MacCrate, a former president of the ABA who was on the ABF board, had a protégé at Sullivan and Cromwell who gave us some of our first insights. He said that without a platform you can never be an arbitrator, and he started saying, "Here are some names in Hong Kong," and the like. We wrote them down, all misspelled and everything, and only later figured out who they really were. He really spoke of arbitration as a narrow area in which, "if there's a conference and I don't know who the names are, it's not an important conference about arbitration."

Dezalay: It's also interesting because when you have these problems of trying to enter a milieu which is closed and unfamiliar and has enough resources to protect itself against outsiders, you have to find some informants. There are two kinds of privileged informants. One is like this young lawyer, well connected but still a young guy. In an American law firm with clients, with disputes worth many billions of dollars (thus many thousands of dollars to an arbitrator), he was shopping around for arbitrators, and doing this kind of indigenous sociology. As a "buyer," these informants had a distrust of the "grand old man" in Geneva, using

Latin words – *lex mercatoria* – and talking about opera. And they prob-ably thought that having outsiders shed light on this mafia might make it more acceptable for their work. The other kind of informants, vice versa, was the grand old man, grand old professor, or grand old judge in Europe, who were far more fluent in Americana and American law than most of their contemporaries but were still ill at ease with the litigators who "have no respect for our grand theories, they want to fight to the end, and they bring us these bus loads of documents that mean nothing because the real issue is a doctrinal issue." So on both sides of the Atlantic there was a misunderstanding or dissatisfaction which could be used as an entrée because you could say to the grand old man, "We can put some focus on these newcomers who want to spoil your beautiful intellectual machine." By playing these two sides, you could get more insight. They might be reluctant to tell you about their own side of the game but they were more than happy to tell you all that they could about the other side. If we had each gone on our way (me in Europe, Bryant in the U.S.), the first part of the book would have had the more rationalized view of the ideology of arbitration and the inter-pretation by the grand old man, and the other part would have been the American law firms. But because we were seeing these two sides together and discussing it, we then understood how this tension could be the real fabric around which this milieu was being constructed. It was a point of entry but also an organizing principle, and it fit perfectly into Bourdieu's theory of how fields are constructed around polarized and complementary positions.

Question: Was there much difficulty, overall, getting access to arbit-rators?

Garth: It was really quite easy. I would write a letter that would name all the people we had talked to and say that they were named as a very prominent arbitrator, and would they like to talk to us. At the end of the day I even got a letter from somebody thanking me for a mention in the book, as something that helped promote his arbitration career. Most of them were very anxious to be part of that, the league of the people that we had interviewed.

Dezalay: This is a strange animal in relation to the classic criteria for doing scientific, objective work where you have a list of the potential players, you pick out one out of every ten, and then you have an answer rate that gets you to forty or fifty people. This worked in a completely different way but we were lucky, to have Sullivan and Cromwell in the American world, and Pierre Bellet on the other side, the biggest name in arbitration at the time.

Question: Often, methodologically, you are taught not to start with the biggest names first. You work your way up.

Garth: Yes, but those are the names we got first.

Dezalay: I had interviewed Pierre Bellet already, and he was quite friendly. But I would say the same to my students: don't go to the Pope first. Or get an ex-Pope if you can!

Question: All along, as Yves has signaled, the sociology of Pierre Bourdieu was the central frame that he brought to the project. How receptive were you to this, Bryant?

Garth: I had become tired of the Law and Society approach, which I saw as seeking over and over to find "progressive rights" and see how they could be used to promote social change. I thought that it had reached a dead end. So it was interesting to me to take on something that looked at the processes that produced these dead ends: Why was it that law wasn't getting anywhere? What was the role that law played? Why had all these things not transformed the world in the way that they were expected to? I was disappointed in where Law and Society seemed to be going. And here was this Bourdieu who has just been noticed in the Law and Society field and I thought this is an interesting way to get some tools that could potentially have a very high intellectual payoff. At the Law and Society meeting in Amsterdam in 1990, I said to Bourdieu, "I'm new to this game and I am only learning it through Dezalay." He replied, "There are worse mediations." I very much had to learn by doing. I found that as we talked and did things together we got the sense of what we were looking for and what the interviews ought to be.

Question: What kinds of changes did you make with the fieldwork under way?

Garth: We changed our interview style fairly early because we started by asking a lot of questions about arbitration and I think we were disappointed with getting formulaic answers. That's when we shifted to just having people tell their stories: How did you become an arbitrator? Just "tell us about your background" and walk them through, and then that would get us into the issues around arbitration. We actually found we got decent responses rather than just the sort of useless recitations and the propaganda formulas, which is often a problem when you interview lawyers.

Dezalay: We would, of course, let people talk about their vision of arbitration, and at the same, as a good sociologist, I would sometimes try to ask about themselves and "who they are" so that we could fill in this category on the "questionnaire" a proper sociologist would ask. Most of the time we got very difficult, disappointing answers, as we were taking them from their pedestal and saying, you know, "Tell us about your kindergarten and your mommy." Whereas, once we presented it as, "Give us your intellectual and professional trajectory, but please start from the beginning," it fitted in much more.

But the other thing we found was that it was much better when Bryant asked the first question. He had a nice way of saying it: "Many lawyers are from families of lawyers, so tell us, is that the case for you?" – as a way of getting back, with the first question, to something that is never mentioned in law books: families and family capital. From there you can branch out with precise questions like what kind of school they went to and so on. I had a distinct feeling that it went much better when it was somebody who was clearly "one of them" saying, almost, "We were probably in the same kindergarten, so what happened to you?" It was probably much less threatening that it was somebody more easily identified with them, because he was a director of the American Bar Foundation, he had the right pedigree to talk lawyer-to-lawyer.

Question: Two hours, on average, for the interviews, is quite long for very busy people. How did you engage people in such a long dialogue and build a rapport?

Garth: Well we never asked them for two hours, you know? But once they start telling their story they're happy to keep it going. One of the nice things about having two interviewers is in helping to keep the interview going. We could fill in if one of us started to get tired. Yves would typically ask more questions and sometimes we would play a kind of good cop/bad cop even, where I could slow it down. So I think having two people also really extends the interviews because you don't lose them, you don't bore them, or you can move them off something that is making them mad or getting them off-track.

Dezalay: After the first trip we did some homework and would focus on one country. For ten days we would interview forty people at the rate of something like four a day. People knew each other and after a while you don't have to ask big general questions. You cannot do an ethnography of this milieu, but by acquiring this sort of high-density familiarity you can fit into their daily discussions – basically the tactics used by journalists, and unfortunately not so much by social scientists.

Garth: We would say, "Other people are saying this," being free with the content but not necessarily with the names of those who'd said it. We were free with the names of who we talked to. They were OK with us sharing names, but we didn't quite go the journalistic way because there was an issue of confidentiality.

Question: How did you share the responsibilities for preparing for interviews?

Garth: After a very short period of time we did no preparation for each individual interview. We would know a little bit about them and we would brief each other on what we knew, and if there were some issues to cover, but essentially we would just take them through their story and follow leads. Not every interview was the same and it was very cumulative. So as we learned more, we dealt with different issues and could get into some of the conflicts, some of the things that divided the generations and the different places.

Dezalay: With Pierre Bellet and Paris, I knew what he represents, but when we decided to go into Sweden, it was also a very closed and small legal milieu, and we didn't know much about it. There it was very important to understand how it was structured in order to understand who those people were. When you arrive in Stockholm, Hong Kong, or Cairo, that was a completely different story, and that was how out of this project grew the interest and the methodology and the questions for the next project.[1]

Question: How did you select those smaller settings for case studies?

Garth: Well, the places were identified to us by the arbitrators as places where there was activity and I think the only choice we had to make was whether to go to Singapore or Hong Kong or both. We opted that we

---

[1] *The Internationalization of Palace Wars* (Chicago: University of Chicago Press, 2002).

just didn't need to do Singapore as well. For oil arbitrations, we found that some of the people that we had interviewed had cut their teeth in oil arbitrations. As a teacher of international law, I remembered that there were these great oil arbitrations and so we got into the notion that we could look at those by interviewing the players. That was just taking advantage of an opportunity that presented itself when we started talking.

Dezalay: When we were asking these people about their pedigree and their training, many people may mention something but the first time you don't notice it. With some luck you might say, "There might be something there." Bourdieu puts a lot of emphasis on the genesis of a field – that many things are very important because they shape the field. But they shape it in a way where you can no longer decode it. There was an interest in going back to what we perceived as the genesis of this field, but not the very distant history claimed by the Europeans – "at the end of the nineteenth century there was a group of distinguished professors who met and established..." – like how every family has to show that they have been aristocrats for at least five generations, something claimed by the Europeans but of no interest at all to most of the other players. Most of these players, Americans as well as Europeans, got a big entry into this field as practitioners through this period of the oil cases. So we deliberately decided that we were going to try to choose people that we knew were oil lawyers, all working for big companies, and we decided that we had to go to Cairo because part of the link between the European grand professor and the Gulf State was through their students who later became well-known professors and state advisors. We went to find something about this history of the early period.

Garth: We never dreamed we would get the stories that told us that the arbitrations in a sense were almost completely symbolic and that the real disputes were being fought elsewhere. I think that was one or two interviews, where they gave us the entire back story, where it was something quite shocking.

Dezalay: It's an example of where you couldn't go to the interviews unprepared. We did some systematic search into histories written about the oil companies, and one of our surprises was that arbitration was never, never mentioned, whereas for our side of the world this was the founding moment. So trying to explain this discrepancy involved, again, learning more about these lawyers and what was the structure of power of these oil companies.

Question: In addition to being sociologists of law, to what extent did you think of yourselves as writing a history of a secret field, such that the historian's tools and techniques were essential supplements to the interviews?

Garth: We received huge volumes of published materials from these arbitrators because they write a lot about the issues. For documents on the arbitrations themselves, of course, there are none. They only keep weak statistics and the count is always a little strange – there was much more written about arbitration than there actually were arbitrations. We started reading this literature and we had a chapter in the book where we related what arbitrators produced as legal doctrine about what legal issues were there to who the arbitrators were and what their position was in the field. You could explain their scholarly production exactly in relation to who they were, but the book was just too big and we just threw out the chapter and didn't publish it.

Question: It is often said that your fieldwork is at an end when you keep hearing the same thing over and over. Is that so obvious, or do you push on out of worry that with the snowball technique you may have missed a part of the field?

Dezalay: I think it was in Stockholm that we were finishing a week or more of interviews, and we were interviewing some lawyer. Maybe I was tired but I was almost answering for him and getting annoyed when he was not following the "script" that we had given! At the end of the interview Bryant said, "Maybe we should stop!"

The snowball does have this big problem but you can diminish this risk precisely as we did, not starting with one snowball but two, and then systematically trying to look in the dark corners, not so much for "Who are your friends?" but also "Who are your competitors?" You get a feeling for who they are fighting, which is an entry to a different part of the picture.

Garth: It's actually more than two snowballs because everybody we knew who knew an arbitrator, we would talk to. I had a friend whom I had known during a three-week visiting professorship in Sweden, who had a friend who was known to be an important arbitrator in Sweden.

And my aunt had a friend who is an arbitrator in America. We tried to find any point of entry. There could be a closed arbitration system in Argentina that we didn't come across, but we had the world of arbitration mapped very explicitly.

Dezalay: There probably are a few exceptions where the picture gets less clear. We didn't get into Latin America in that book, a sort of terra incognita where we assumed that there was not much, but we didn't know really. Now, in fact, we know that there were some home-grown varieties who didn't quite make it into the big league in the transnational circles for various reasons, but still they could have been considered as part of this milieu intellectually because they use the same words and do the same thing. Probably you could say the same for China. We approached some of it through Hong Kong but obviously there was activity in China that we didn't approach because we didn't have the time, resources, or the linguistic skills.

Question: How did you create a story of the global field from the national experiences?

Garth: Typically at the end of each trip we would sit down and Yves would always have some point of entry that we would start to discuss. We would produce a kind of first cut, a country-specific chapter, while the interviews were fresh in our mind. We were constantly producing stuff, and we did have a software program to analyze the interviews, which actually worked pretty well. Everybody lined up so well, that the grand old men really did all say certain things versus the youngsters who would all say certain things, and you could go through the interviews and divide them up. It fell out perfectly.

Dezalay: This was almost total immersion because not only would we have at least four interviews a day and the rest of the time in taxis, but in the evening we were tired and having dinner, a good bottle of wine, and discussing what we had heard. This whole thing was maturing, and this routine provided a sort of double check. You add new questions with each interview and after each day, like a good cop who doesn't ask the same questions once he hears the alibi of the previous suspect.

Question: When did you begin to see your thesis for the book emerging in the course of writing these chapter drafts?

Garth: I don't know. I think there were some moments in the interviews when we got great confirmations of things that were working hypotheses. We had an interviewee at the ICC in Paris tell us that his job was "routinizing charisma." He had done his sociology and here he is actually taking the position that fits the analysis we were finding, looking at the old guys. Here's the young upstart, even envisioning his role. So that kind of story of transformation was almost writing itself.

Question: What was the most difficult part of the research project?

Garth: It's just physically exhausting. One day I arrived in Paris at 7 AM, and I didn't let go of my suitcase until 9 PM, on a day that I didn't even go to the bathroom. I just did interviews in Paris that day. We would be completely spent. Yves would typically get sick after we finished. We would console ourselves and say that we were like the arbitrators who would descend on an arbitration for two weeks and work very hard. Only they would get lots of money for theirs and we would get lots of interviews.

Dezalay: But another difficult part was dragging along all the heavy literature that they were giving us and we couldn't decently throw on their doorsteps.

Garth: And I think not getting trapped by that literature. One of the things that could paralyse you writing a book like this is believing that you had to read all the literature that they gave you. There was just an infinite variety of little legal claims. We had to do enough interviews so that we could almost instantly decode the literature and figure out where it was strategically.

Question: Having become known to everyone in this closed network, did you find yourself concerned about how they would receive the academics' gaze?

Dezalay: I remember we were a little bit worried about what kind of reaction we were going to have from the milieu itself because we more or less consciously never presented anything to them until we were finished. Were they going to say, you know, "This is journalistic nonsense"? If a milieu collectively says "this is void" then you are in trouble.

Garth: We sent an article manuscript which is the chapter on "grand old men" to some of the arbitrators who were youngsters. One of them from Switzerland wrote back and endorsed it. He said it was like a great painting: "I see myself in a different light but I understand myself better." I figured with that at least we were going to have some people on our side. As it turned out, both sides used it in their own struggles against each other, claiming our book as authority for how arbitration was being proceduralized, formalized, and taken away from the purity of the old practice with this Americanization. Then the young Turks would write that it shows the inevitable process that they were making happen.

Question: How do you feel about how it's been interpreted and used within the academic community?

Dezalay: I don't think it reached outside of this law and society milieu. The story to be told around arbitration was fascinating in itself and so there was hardly the need for making a theory of it. Plus Bourdieu was still alive and he was doing the theory, so you are not going to compete with him! But people would say, "Oh, that's an interesting story about this small milieu but if you don't have an interest in it it's difficult to relate to it." We probably could have been a bit more ambitious in saying that this is a case study of arbitration but also it's a way to talk about the politics of law, about how you build and sell the credibility of law, about legitimacy, that would challenge some received view. Consciously or not, we didn't do it. Maybe you can get some inspiration and use the approach to look at something else but we don't give you clues on how to apply this kind of approach. The reproducibility was not clearly there. In Europe, with its more clear divide between the law and the social sciences, a few legal academics writing about legal doctrine dismissed the book with "If you want to have a sort of journalistic account, read that book," while no political scientist or social scientist ever used it as both a methodology and a specific thematic. Because the book after this one was formatted differently, addressed different issues, and was a bit more ambitious, even if it was limited to Latin America, it got a lot more reactions from political scientists who used the methodology as a starting point.

Question: Was there anything in the research process that hadn't gone to plan?

Dezalay: There was no plan, but at the same time that meant there was an engine, a dynamic, with the whole process being flexible. We brought from our disciplines what we might have expected but that was shaped in the course of it. We didn't find answers to questions about disputing that were Bryant's at the beginning, or questions about lawyers and politics that were mine, but because of this maturing process there was not a time when we would say, "Well, we have these questions, we have these data, too bad the data doesn't fit the question, so let's drop it." The questions were transformed very smoothly. There were these intensive one- or two-week periods, and then there were two or three months when we were doing something completely different, and so by the time you reopen the arbitration file it's almost as if you had digested everything you had learned. You had forgotten that you started the earlier step with a certain set of notions and had ended up slightly different.

CHAPTER 19

PATRICIA EWICK AND SUSAN SILBEY AND *THE COMMON PLACE OF LAW**

It may be Panglossian to say that everything works out for the best, but you could forgive Patricia Ewick and Susan Silbey for taking that view. The well-regarded book, The Common Place of Law, *did not begin as their project or even the kind of project they might have crafted. Living in Massachusetts – and with families at home – left on their own, they would not have designed a project involving extensive travel to New Jersey. Substantively the project pushed them in new directions. But the invitation to have a hand in this project, and then the necessity of seeing it through, put Ewick and Silbey at the center of currents in the field, a place to make a contribution. Even the setting – the racially diverse, understudied mid-Atlantic state – turned out to be fortuitous.*

Their reflections on The Common Place of Law *suggest comparisons with any number of studies, from the deep ethnographic approaches of David Engel, Carol Greenhouse, and Sally Merry (Chapters 8, 10, and 12, respectively) to the survey methods of Tom Tyler and Hazel Genn (Chapters 13 and 20, respectively). What level of understanding can we draw from each method? What are the limits of each? What questions remain unanswered today, and what strategies will be necessary to answer them?*

Collaborations can be an enjoyable, as well as a productive, way to approach scholarship, as made clear in many other chapters of this book. A common approach to collaboration, especially in an interdisciplinary field such as Law and Society, is to find your complement, someone who possesses a disciplinary or legal speciality that you need. Compare, then, what Ewick and Silbey brought to their joint project – not disciplinary diversity (although they do bring complementary talents in other ways) but rather, the power of two like-minded scholars engaged in a profitable dialogue. They begin the interview by describing how this chance project built on their friendship.

** The Common Place of Law: Stories from Everyday Life (Chicago: University of Chicago Press, 1998).

Methodological Keywords: in-depth interviewing, survey research, inductive coding, grounded theory

Silbey: I didn't conceive of this project in a line with other work. I do not believe that the textbook notion of how research evolves or how projects begin is in fact accurate. I did my dissertation on the attorney general's office of consumer protection in Massachusetts, although I wanted to write a treatise on constitutional law and freedom and liberty, but I didn't know how. My mentor said, "You should study consumer protection if you really want to understand how the law works, not these grandiose notions." So I ended up writing a dissertation on a topic that I had no interest in. I was never allowed really to use the law on the books as a standard for the law on the ground. I had to describe what was being produced, not that it was not what was supposed to be being produced. So my training as a fieldworker was always to try to get access to lived experience and not to use some idealistic, legalistic, theoretical notion of what the law is supposed to be. So I began as a scholar with a notion that law is what people do in the name of law.

I got a telephone call one day from Bill Chambliss, a radical Marxist criminologist at Washington University. I didn't know him, just his books, and he called me up about a consulting project he was doing for the Supreme Court of New Jersey. This came out of the sky and fell into my lap. I said, "What can I do for you?" Thirty-five years after *Brown v. Board of Education*, the Supreme Court of New Jersey, like many state supreme courts, had the intuition that their court systems were highly discriminatory. Minority citizens would not turn to law as help for their problems. Half the cases in the district courts are brought by citizen against citizen – it's a citizen-initiated judicial system. Bill was hired, along with a sociologist at Princeton, to help the New Jersey Court. So, I flew down to give them four hours' instruction on what Law and Society people call "the mobilization of law." They wanted to do a study of differential perceptions of the courts in New Jersey by minority and nonminority populations. Their design was to ask all the civil rights organizations in New Jersey why they brought suits. I started laughing. He said, "Why are you laughing?" I said, "Because you've asked the already knowledgeable and mobilized people. You are not going to find out why ordinary African Americans or Hispanic people don't bring small claims complaints."

They hired me to write an essay reviewing the literature on mobilization. I had two weeks to tell them everything that was known about the mobilization of law, so I got everything that I could find and I lined it up on tables in my office. How was I going to summarize this? I started with the methods and the minute I started it was obvious that the methods that scholars used seemed to determine their answers. The survey research people get on the phone for twenty minutes with citizens. What's the answer they get? The American people love the law, when the law is defined by having your chance to say your piece. But you look at the anthropologists who would spend six to twelve months in a community and they didn't tell the same story at all. They were constantly writing about how the people resist the law and how they learn to manipulate it.

So I called up Chambliss and I said, "Look, I'll write you a review essay but I've got an idea for how to do the research. I'll write you a research proposal and you can go do it. What you have to do is a random representative sample of the people of New Jersey interviewed in depth that will mirror the ethnographic approach but give you the generalizability of the surveys." I wrote them a proposal and they asked me to stay on it to consult and help them along.

I put Patty on the proposal because she was my friend – both a great statistician and interpretive scholar – and when I got this consulting opportunity I thought Patty should get a little piece of it too. We were friends for five or six years before we became colleagues. We cooked together. We'd go sailing together. We used to teach the same courses and we shared our lecture notes. We thought the same way. We were the same kind of sociologist. After about three or four months, I went down to Trenton, New Jersey, to see how the project was developing. I discovered that the people hired to do sampling and invitational letters were making a mess of it. And my name was on it! I said to Patty, "Our names are on this, I'm a principal investigator, and this is embarrassing." So I dropped my other projects, flew down to Trenton, and started it all over again.

Question: You were presented, inadvertently, with a great chance to collaborate.

Ewick: It was very collaborative. Susan and I had a lot of conversations sitting in offices next to each other, and driving back and forth from Wellesley to the Amherst Seminar once a month. There was just a lot of talk and we would get little glimmers of ideas. But it was also collaborative with the other members of the Amherst Seminar in a sense. In terms of other people's research, in terms of other readings, the scholars that we invited, we were really wrangling with some of these questions about legal process, ideology, discourse, and culture. And there was the work of Sally Merry, Barbara Yngvesson, and Austin Sarat. You can see the overlap in the concern about resistance and about text. So Susan and my collaboration did not occur in a vacuum. It occurred around and with a lot of other people who were thinking and studying and researching similar ideas. It's funny how the process itself in some ways mimicked the process we were describing in the book, which is to say it was very emergent, just like legal meaning is emergent out of interactions and relationships. It isn't always in some instrumental way headed toward a known goal. A lot of this was just talking about things and reading.

Question: In developing the project, did you have a sense of how your work might contribute something distinctive to the existing literature on legal consciousness?

Silbey: Our view was that the literature posed two primary conceptions of legal consciousness. On the one hand, consciousness was framed as an individual attitudinal opinion. That was the survey research. But then there was the Marxist structuralist notion that consciousness is just an epiphenomenon. But Patty and I are deeply interpretive social constructivists. The law is what people do about the law. We said that people's engagement with the law in their lives was an ongoing construction of relations. Law was just a flavor to any social relation. So in order to understand the rule of law we had to find its place in ordinary social relations. So the question was not only, "What do people do?" It was also, "What is the rule of law?" That is very important because it's the part of the book that is misunderstood ninety-five percent of the time. What we were talking about is basically the ether that we live in – it's culture. It's that which circulates, that which we draw from, the pool of language, of symbols. If you look at any room, for example, it's just littered with things we take for granted, which we're not inventing most of the time, we're just reproducing – although there are certainly moments of invention. That's what we wanted to show about the law.

Question: When you came to begin the fieldwork on the project, how difficult was it to get people to participate?

Ewick: We got a pretty standard response rate for large-scale surveys. We didn't have a disproportionate number of people who said, "No, I don't want to talk to you." But we didn't just say to people, "We're

217

interested in your ideas of law." We anticipated some of our subjects didn't have such a great view of law and maybe would be suspicious. So we thought long and hard about how to broach that. What we did ultimately was to play it down.

Silbey: The letter was on Wellesley College stationery. It said that we were professors of sociology, doing research on community services and neighborhood problems, that we would very much like to interview them to find out what life was like in the community – what they liked and didn't like about it. We said the interview would last about an hour to an hour and a half, and that we would pay twenty-five dollars. But it took a lot of work. Two-thirds of our project costs were in getting the sample. I hired my niece in New Jersey who, after we sent out the letters, would get on the telephone calling people, setting up appointments. She had all sorts of spiels we gave her on the telephone, like "twenty-five dollars, that's a movie and pizza for two people for an hour and a half of your time . . . "

Question: How were these interviews structured?

Silbey: The interview schedule had three parts. The first part was an introduction which was absolutely important because it always set the tone. We did the same spiel: "We're doing research on communities, we want to know what your life is like, what you like about it, what you don't like about it," and so on. Then the first question was, "How long have you been living here? You know anybody in the neighborhood? Any friends? Who do you hang out with?" And then came the critically important question: "What do you like about this neighborhood? What don't you like? What would you like to be different?" Those three questions set the tone for the whole thing. First of all it allowed people to announce themselves. It asked them to draw a distinction. I always teach students to ask people to draw distinctions, to make comparisons, because that's how people establish their moral order. They're letting you know who they are and they're also naming what they're not, where they locate themselves in social space and moral space. We just did it to make them feel comfortable. What they told us frequently was a preface to what would be the themes that came up later in the interview. So people would say, "What do I like about this neighborhood? I don't like it at all." So we'd ask, "How come?" And so you'd have a whole conversation.

The second part was an adaptation from Sally Merry and my previous research – a sort of inventory of what could be a case that a citizen might bring to court. We'd say, "I'm now going to ask you about things that happen to ordinary people. If any of these things ever happened to you let's stop and talk about it." That was over ninety separate probes: "Have you ever had a problem shopping? Have you ever been bothered by noise in your neighborhood? Have you ever been bothered by garbage? Fences? Children fighting? Parking?" And so on. If they said "yes" we then had lots of follow-ups: "Well tell me about the last time it happened. What did you do? How come? Who else did you talk to? Does this happen a lot?"

The third part was something we took from Kristen Bumiller. "Well, you've told me about all these problems, let's talk more about one of them. Who did you talk to? Who didn't you talk to? How did you feel when this was happening? Did you wish you had done something?" You tried to get the whole emotional thing about at least one story. That was our conversational part.

Question: Did conducting the interviews pose any particular challenges for you?

Ewick: The problem with these interviews was they were a one-time thing. They were random. We couldn't go back. We figured out that each interview cost three or four hundred dollars by the time you added up the travel money, paying the interviewer, paying the subject, and having it transcribed. So they were expensive per item and there were no follow-ups. They were each unique opportunities. It was daunting for me. This was in-depth interviewing, which I hadn't done before. Susan was a much more skillful interviewer which is why we did the first twenty or so together. I had no problem with the basic survey questions. Where I found it difficult was in asking follow-up questions, when they got to the narrative component of the interview. People tell long wandering stories that sometimes seem to be about pretty trivial things. So part of what I'd learned in the process was to relax and let the people tell their stories and try to just be inquisitive and curious and to encourage them to talk. For some people that's easier than others. On the other hand, one of the dangers is actually relaxing too much when people talk too much. It's easy to say, "Oh good, I have a chatterbox. I just have to sit here and listen." While you don't want to direct the interview, you still have to be constantly attentive and not forego an opportunity to get them to expound on something that is an important detail. You have to let go a little bit, but you have to have control, too. So it was a learning experience for me.

Question: You mentioned that the initial questions in the interview were designed in part to put people at their ease. Did you use any other techniques to do this?

Ewick: I think one of the things I learned was to listen very carefully to what people were saying and to play off of that, ultimately to remain anchored in their account. If you create a space for people to talk they're going to address most of the things you're interested in and, if they don't, then at the end you can say, "Well, there's just one or two other things I'd like to ask you about . . . "

Silbey: I also believe in engaging the people. So if they would tell me a story about problems with children and school, I might tell them a problem of mine so that we feel comfortable. Why should they make themselves naked in front of me? You also think about what you wear. I did not wear any expensive suits or silk clothes. I just put on a sweater and a skirt. And we rented a Chevrolet to drive to interviews. I could have borrowed a more expensive car and saved rental fees, but you don't want to raise class issues. You don't want people to feel bad. You are already an educated professional earning more than the median income in the United States. People are opening themselves to you. They are making themselves vulnerable. I believe that we shouldn't impose any more pain on them by issues of class and status. You can't really thank these people enough. We live off them.

Question: Yet you had to listen to some pretty graphic stories and opinions.

Silbey: Oh God, yes! You listen to a lot of racism, but you do it empathetically. It's a little bit like therapy. "Tell me more. How did that happen?" Or "I don't quite understand, I've never had that experience. Help me to understand." Sometimes if the person is very comfortable you can disagree with them. But you have to be very careful.

Question: In addition to conducting interviews yourselves, you hired people to do them. What are the challenges in managing a team of researchers?

Ewick: You do what you can to select people. You train them. What we were trying for was about fifteen hours of training for each of the interviewers. They would interview each other and they would interview us and we would interview people in front of them and mark their interviews. We basically gave little methods courses to the interviewers. But ultimately they had to go out into the world and sit in someone's living room. It's a trade-off. We could not have done 430 interviews of two or three hours each, especially when we were not living in New Jersey.

Silbey: It can be wonderful finding a talented and eager student and it can also be horrendous. I do think that the quality is variable, there's no question. You can get garbage unless you're lucky and get people for whom the training sinks in. We basically did all right. Sometimes, however, Patty and I would read a transcript and say, "Oh shit! They didn't ask them the obvious next question we would ask."

Question: Did the varying quality of interview data affect the analysis stage?

Silbey: Well, if you've got hundreds of interviews that you feel confident about, you don't need to have a thousand. When you do qualitative research, after a while you're not learning anything new. You've heard the same things over and over and over again. This kind of in-depth qualitative research is about trying to identify and map forms of variation. It cannot tell me what proportion there is in the world. Quantitative research gives you proportions.

Question: How did you decide to stop the fieldwork?

Silbey: It took three years to do 430 interviews. We just couldn't do it anymore. In the end we never did the six hundred interviews we'd planned. When we saw that we had a really good representation of the state in the sample, we decided we were not doing any more. We didn't get enough money to transcribe all 430. We transcribed the interviews Patty and I had conducted. We oversampled the minority ones and then we made sure we just randomly sampled in the other demographic categories. We also sampled on all kinds of things – lengths of interview, for example.

Question: The project produced a mountain of data. You mention in the book's methods section that you eventually decided to start analyzing your interviews by each reading through twenty-five transcripts. Had you considered other approaches to starting the analysis before you settled on that particular one?

Ewick: No, we didn't. Retrospectively it sounds like that was a plan. But it wasn't really a plan. We had ten thousand pages so we just said, "Well, we've got to read them. What are we going to do with it? Why don't we pick twenty-five and we'll each independently read them and just see what sense we make." So we said, "Before we make a plan, let's just see what we have." And so the plan probably emerged out of reading those first twenty-five rather than it generating that. You've got to start somewhere. When the end of the day comes you pick up the papers and you start reading.

Question: And were you coding at this stage?

Silbey: Yes, we started making inductive codes, line-by-line coding, and then paragraph coding, generating words and themes. Coding an interview would take anywhere from two to four hours. I would do two or three a week. We'd have more than one reader on any transcript. So everything was overcoded. Then we would write a summary of the interview. What are the major stories they tell? What are some good quotes? Then we got a student to Xerox the transcript. Any page that had a code on it was copied as many times as there were different codes, including the page before and the page after so that we knew the context of what was being discussed. It took two, three years to do all that. Then we'd start reading within the coded folders.

Question: In addition to inductive coding, were you also looking for things highlighted in the existing literature?

Silbey: We used some a priori codes. That's where the other work on legal consciousness turned out to be problematic. We tried to use it and it didn't work. In the NSF proposal there were five to seven categories of legal consciousness that we were going to use: conformity, instrumental engagement, resistance, transcendence, and so forth. But we realized they didn't make sense. That was a struggle. There were just too many things falling in, falling out, and we realized that they weren't developed like variables. So let's say "conformity" – that was in the literature: conformity to law meant mobilization of law in a positive way. Well, you might go along with the law but not mobilize it, and they hadn't built that in. Or "instrumental engagement" meant you engaged it and used it, but maybe because it was an instrumental thing you wouldn't use it. So they never had the variation in the variable. I remember Patty and I were walking across the Wellesley campus and we were saying, "This doesn't work." It was literally "Oh my God. It's use and nonuse within a normative conception of law. We got it! That's it! That's what's wrong!" It's not that you have one norm when you use it and another norm when you don't use it.

Question: You say at one point that the analysis process was unusually exciting but you also seemed to hint that at the beginning it was quite daunting.

Ewick: It was and I don't think those things are unconnected. The sheer amount of information and the number of stories seemed to defy the possibility that it would ever fall into place. And, of course, it never does just "fall into place." By interpreting it, you're squeezing it into some kind of place. But once you get something, all of a sudden it makes sense. That's when the excitement comes.

Silbey: It's little steps at a time. You just have to discipline yourself all the time. You know you will get somewhere if you just take your time. How you handle the daunting part is to lower your expectations. Patty has a wonderful phrase. She says, "Whenever I don't know what to say I ask myself 'what would I tell my undergraduate class?'" What do you want them to understand about this and what do they need to know? Then you can keep layering it and adding to it.

Ewick: Actually, what we were most excited about were the dimensions of social action, the normativity, constraint, capacity, and time and space. We were really excited that we could use these to explain or to analyze and make sense of all kinds of action. Sometimes I think without those dimensions you can't really make sense of the three types – before the law, with the law, against the law – because they're really just variations, variables on those dimensions. But that's not what seems to inspire other people.

Question: The schema of "before," "with," and "against" the law certainly has been provocative and influential in the field. How did you come to those?

Silbey: We asked ourselves a big question. What do they imagine the law is? That was the first question. We started with the folder on law. Patty did that one first. She came one day to my office and said, "OK, this is what I think is there. It's about rules but there's also something about hierarchy." So we went to the folder on rules and we saw that rules both enable and constrain. People talked about the rules telling the judge what to do, or the rules telling them not to park there, or the rules telling the teacher to do X, Y, and Z. But people also said, "He could do that because the rule let him." So that's how we got the very important insight that rules constrain and rules enable.

Then we said, "OK, there's a literature about that. How are we going to connect the literature to it?" And then we came up with the story of "before the law." We wrote it as a conference paper. It didn't look like it does in the book. It didn't have those horizontals; it didn't have the normativity and constraint. We just had a story about objectivity and rules and the fact that it's not about ordinary life, it's a special sphere.

After that we said, "There's a lot more stuff here. Everybody said it's just a game. We've got to read about games." So we stopped for a couple of months and we started reading about games. I read Goffman on games. Then I found Arthur Leff's article "Law And."[1] So then I had all the tools by which to go read the files and the cases again. I had all the categories for a game. You go back into the files and you say, "OK, when it's a game what else are they talking about?" So we start to get the notion that it's playful, it's not special, it's just ordinary. We started to get some pieces – it's lawyers; lawyers play games and it's simultaneous with everyday life.

Now this is what's important about theorising. Once we had the "before" story and we started to have "the game" story, I said to Patty, "this can't just be idiosyncratic. It's not good sociology. There has to be a relationship between these two stories. These stories have to connect somehow." So I started reading. It was obviously not Weber. It wasn't Durkheim. So I got out all of Giddens' books and I spent the summer reading Giddens. I realized that you had to have basic concepts like constraint and agency, structure and agency. Then we started reading about narrative. It all just came together, that every story is about a struggle between structure and agency. We had that originally but we didn't see it and we didn't operationalize it in the same way.

So then we made the grid. In the first story, what's the normativity? It's objectivity. What's the constraint? The rule. What's the capacity or the agency? It's the rule. Time and space? (Time and space is what we got from Giddens.) Well, it's not here, its always someplace else in

[1] *Yale Law Journal*, 87(5): 989–1011 (April 1978).

space or time. And once we had that grid, we did the same with the "With" story. What's the norm? The norm is accessibility. The norm is selfishness. What's the capacity? It's resources, lawyers. Time and space? Simultaneous. But we had this big hole. What's the constraint? We did not see that without the reading on games. That literature gave us indeterminacy and closure. We got that from Goffman and from Leff. That's what games have. But you had to have the theory to know that games have to be indeterminate or you don't play them. But they also have to have closure. So that's how we were able to fill in that cell – by reading the theory of games. Once we had the theoretical category, we could go back to the interviews and see if there were indications that we had missed, and there were. But without the theoretical categories – indeterminacy and closure – we had not seen the significance of pieces of the transcripts.

And then once we had that, we came by the other story – "against the law" – by seeing the relationship between the two. They just play off each other. And then we realized that the first two were the hegemonic. This is from Alan Hunt. And the other is about counterhegemony.

So that's what I would call theoretically driven work that is inductive.

Question: Have you been happy with the book's reception?

Ewick: The book is used a lot more and has received a lot more attention than I ever thought it would. It's been much more generative. When I was writing it I was just hoping it would get published and I would get tenure. I never imagined that real people doing important work would even try to challenge it, or use it in their own research, that it was worthy of that.

Silbey: It's very, very flattering. I like it when somebody tells me they teach the book. But I think it's also misunderstood a lot. Some people think "before," "with," and "against" are types of people. They do not understand that this is not about people. People were the units of data collection, but the thing being analyzed is legal culture or consciousness. I wish we'd never used the term "consciousness." That was a product of our particular little research milieu in the Amherst seminar. It just begs for this error. I don't think it's helped the field. Some students recently asked me what the difference is between legal culture and legal consciousness. It's a very good question. These are terms we make up as tools and there should be no difference between them. But the way they have been deployed as research tools, culture has been adopted by the people who primarily count things. How much litigation? How many lawyers? How many rules? Consciousness has been adopted by scholars who are interested in the ways in which people use law or who interpret the part law has in their cultural apparatus. So it's just a tool – not the law, the concepts we use to analyze it. But the concept is like a hammer, doing good things, and hammers could do bad things, right? If you've got a hammer everything's a nail.

Ewick: Yes, some of the more nuanced parts of the arguments are brushed over. You can sometimes tell if someone's not read it very carefully. If it's in the boilerplate at the beginning of an argument it's the three kinds of law. That's frustrating. But we're so intimate with our own ideas in all of their complexity that I think that might be a problem for anyone who spent years writing something and then it gets reduced to four lines in a review or an article.

Question: This project was particularly long and involved. Did it make emotional demands on you as researchers?

Ewick: There were times when I felt very sad. Some of the longer stories at the beginning of the chapters I found to be very sad. You just get a glimpse of the people's lives that are disturbing. There are all kinds of ways of being disturbed – repulsed and threatened and saddened and so forth. You're interacting with human beings and yet you're assuming a very distinctive role in that relationship. You can't always respond to your own sense of endangerment or repulsion or even sympathy. You have to maintain that neutral role and that is difficult. Doing research with human beings is messy. There's also a fear that whatever you're doing is not going to turn out to be anything. Unless you're doing closed-ended interviews with very specific hypotheses, it's always open-ended, which means you don't know where it's going to go. I think collaboration, doing that with someone, makes it more enjoyable and much more reassuring, a second pair of eyes and ears.

Silbey: Patty also likes to tell people that she took her life in her hands driving with me on the New Jersey turnpike! She claims I made a U-turn on the New Jersey turnpike, but I don't think it was quite that. I think I just drove across a barrier. Maybe, in the best sense, our research did too.

CHAPTER 20

HAZEL GENN AND *PATHS TO JUSTICE**

A landmark sociolegal work in Britain, the Paths to Justice *project exemplifies very well the possibilities of large-scale social research on law. Well beyond what any junior scholar or student might undertake, the scale of the project may be uncommon among Law and Society scholars, yet it puts into sharper relief some important problems found in work on smaller scales. A project such as this involves many contributors, including professional interviewers to assist in the fieldwork, and the consequences of going into the field with a faulty research device (a survey or interview schedule) grow significantly. Although the researcher can largely control the content of a structured survey questionnaire, using research assistants or interviewers to conduct qualitative interviews means a loss of control and the danger of feeling distant from the material when it comes to analysis. In this conversation, Hazel Genn candidly reflects on the practices that most enabled her to manage these concerns during the project, while suggesting how no scholar can hope to avoid all mistakes and blind spots.*

Paths to Justice *may be an especially important example of sociolegal research for its relationship to activity in the policy-making process. The project began amid the reforming atmosphere of late-1990s Britain. The Master of the Rolls Harry Woolf (later Lord Chief Justice) proposed major revisions to the civil justice process, which were ultimately adopted as the Civil Procedure Rules of 1999. The new Rules aimed at improving access to justice by simplifying civil procedure and making legal proceedings more accessible and affordable. Much research undertaken by Law and Society scholars may be motivated by their interest in seeing change in society, but through a direct connection to political developments Genn begins by relating how active policy questions drew her into action.*

Methological Keywords: surveys, interviews, focus groups, multi-methods, qualitative methods

*Paths to Justice: What People Do and Think about Going to Law (Oxford: Hart Publishing, 1999).

Genn: I was concerned that the Woolf reforms to the civil justice system were being based on assertions about what the public thinks and does about law, without any solid information. In my inaugural lecture at University College London, in 1997, I reflected on why there was so little interest in researching civil justice issues and why it was important to understand how the system works if you are going to try to reform it.[1] My previous research projects had tended to involve hanging around the homes of people – for example interviewing people who had suffered accidental injury – or tramping around farms and factories talking about health and safety regulation. I had some sense of what people had to deal with when faced with legal problems, what they knew and what they didn't know, what troubled them and what didn't trouble them. I suppose I was frustrated that lots of arguments and assumptions were being made about the causes of the problems with the civil justice system and what the public thought about it, without much research evidence. I was worried about the fact that if you get the diagnosis wrong then your solutions may not work terribly well. I thought about it as policy making in the dark.

During early 1990s the Lord Chancellor's Department was becoming much more proactive about civil justice policy. They were starting to be strategic, yet they had little evidence about the system that they were trying to manage, or whether it was a "system" at all. They had no data themselves. People were complaining about the cost and length of civil cases but couldn't answer the most basic questions about what cases went to court, who was suing whom, how long cases took, or how much they cost. They were talking about the public being denied access to justice – but actually had no idea who was being denied access or what the real barriers were. Around the time that the Woolf report was published in 1996, I received an invitation from the Nuffield Foundation to attend a seminar to discuss creating a project on public knowledge of law. I remember sitting in the seminar feeling a bit irritated and eventually said, "This is completely ludicrous. If you ask what the public knows about the law, the answer is 'nothing' and why should they? If you are interested in issues to do with public access to justice and the experience of people with the legal system, those are not the questions

---

[1] The lecture was published as "Understanding Civil Justice," Chapter 6 in *Law and Opinion at the End of the Twentieth Century*, Michael Freeman, ed. (Oxford: Clarendon Press, 1997).

you should be asking." I was obviously quite boisterous about it. I got a letter afterwards saying, essentially, "If you're so clever, what is it you think we should be doing?" I wrote a proposal with the National Centre for Social Research, arguing that what we needed was information about what people do when they're faced with problems and disputes – issues for which the legal system could be used, even if people realize that or don't want to take legal action. What we were trying to get at was how and why the public engages or fails to engage the legal system. Those were the questions that I felt we didn't have any information about and that I thought were essential for policy aimed at improving access to justice.

Question: Taking on such a broad question – one that seeks to inform a whole area of recent national policy – what kinds of challenges did you confront in how to set up the research project?

Genn: A key difficulty for us was in conceptualising the kinds of problems we were going to focus on. Were we interested in everything in the world? No, we wanted to focus on problems that were "justiciable" and by that, we meant something for which a legal remedy theoretically existed, whether or not you used it or wanted it. The other three things that were very difficult at the design stage (and which I don't think we resolved perfectly), were, first, the distinction between criminal and civil problems. We were only focusing on civil matters, but often it is difficult to draw the line between civil and criminal. That was tricky. Second, we weren't going to include business disputes, but instead restricted the study to justiciable problems experienced by private citizens. That became very difficult when you were dealing with someone who was involved in a dispute as a sole trader. We really struggled with that. The last thing we struggled with was seriousness. Were we interested in everything that people could report or were we only interested in "serious" disputes? And if we were only interested in "serious stuff," what does that mean? How do you define that? We wrestled for a long time with those kinds of conceptual problems. In the end, we reached decisions by talking it through with our advisory committee.

Question: An advisory committee is not typical of most research projects. What was its role and was that a comfortable vehicle to have in your work?

Genn: The advisory committee was there as a sounding board. The Nuffield Foundation felt that for such a large project it would be useful to have an advisory board with policy makers, advice sector representatives, judges, etc. I was very happy to work with such a committee because I was sure that they would be able to help us to think through some of the difficult conceptual questions and also make sure we were covering all of the issues that needed to be covered. We chose people to sit on the advisory committee who would give us a broad spread. We had judicial input. We also had policy people from the Lord Chancellor's Department, people from the Scottish Office, the National Consumer Council, and academics. The idea was that we had a group of wise people who were not telling us what to do, but who could be asked questions like, "How can I do this?" and "Do you think this is right?" In the early stages, it was really very helpful. Aside from the intellectual contribution, having that sort of committee gives you fixed deadlines. A common problem with research is slippage. It always takes you longer than you think it will. You need to keep the momentum going and it's hard. If you've got advisory meetings set up, then that gives you dates by which you have absolutely got to get things done. You have to have done your thinking by then.

Researchers should be open to hear that there is another way of looking at things and thinking about their questions. We had some quite vigorous debates at advisory committee meetings and sometimes some disagreements, but I found that fantastically helpful. For me a real problem in doing empirical legal research has been isolation. You may be working with research assistants, but you can't necessarily expect to get help from them with the hard thinking that you need to do. Many people doing empirical research on law struggle with their projects on their own and don't necessarily have a critical mass of experienced researchers around to help them. For example, in this project it was really hard working out how the analysis ought to be structured. There were many different ways that we could have done it. The advisory board was quite helpful with that. I went to the advisory board with the first draft of the final report and they said, "No, we don't like the way this has been done." We talked it through and I made some quite major structural changes between the first draft and the final draft. So an advisory board can be fantastic. You choose the people because you know that they'll be helpful. Even if you reject what they say in the end, it forces you to think through your arguments.

Question: Though a significant contribution of your work was data that others could point to, your project design was quite pluralistic. What did the pairing of qualitative and quantitative approaches give you?

Genn: If you are asking "how many, or how much?" questions, then you have to collect quantitative data. But when you get to "Why do people do the things that they do?" or "What are the factors that influence choices?," although you can do that quantitatively, if you actually want to understand it, you have to do it qualitatively. What we did, and I think it was really very good, was a kind of "quant sandwich": we did qualitative work first – discussion groups – then the survey, and then qualitative interviews.

The initial qualitative work was fantastically helpful, just sitting, talking about the kind of aggravation that people have to deal with in their lives and how they sort these things out. Focus group transcripts are quite hard to analyze because you've often got people talking at the same time. But the important thing is that the focus group material was not used as a fundamental part of the analysis, it was used as a developmental tool. We were looking at the range of problems that were being mentioned, what people were saying about them, what kinds of paths people were pursuing to try and resolve problems. We never used the terminology of "legal problem" or "legal dispute" or anything like that. We didn't use the "law" word at all in the early stages. We talked not only to members of the public, but also to solicitors, Citizens' Advice Bureaus, and other kinds of advisers. We pulled all that together to be sure we had covered the range of everyday problems and disputes that were, in our term, "justiciable." So it gave us important clues about where we should be going with the research. Focus groups are not the answer to everything, but they are a useful way of getting a lot of information very quickly and of discovering where similarities in thought are.

What we weren't seeking to do with qualitative work was answer our research questions from that data. In focus groups you tend to hear from those who agree with each other, so they're very good for showing you areas of consensus. The weakness of focus groups is that you don't always get the differences in views, unless you've got very determined people. So you can't assume that you'll get the full range of views or experience from talking to people in a focus group, but it helped us work out whether we were covering the right kinds of problems, and whether we were using the right kind of language to describe problems and disputes. The focus groups were also good for throwing up things that we hadn't really thought about and for reinforcing some of the directions that we were going in. If you're going to do a large-scale survey, doing any kind of qualitative work first is terribly important. If you can't afford to do a focus group, you could just get out and talk to a few of the kinds of people that will be answering the questionnaires, just to help you think through the questions that you're going to put on the questionnaire.

Question: In terms of designing the primary survey, was there any other pretesting that you did? How did you gain a measure of confidence?

Genn: Oh, it was very complicated. The development stage of that questionnaire probably took a year. We spent ages on it. We did the qualitative groups. We then piloted the questionnaire. We then refined it and we then piloted it again. We needed to know not just whether the questions were working, but how many cases we were likely to pick up. The survey was in two stages – a screening questionnaire and then the full follow-up survey for people who had experienced a justiciable problem – so we needed to get a sense of how many respondents we would be likely to pick up. We were also very worried about the amount of time that we could spend asking questions. We needed to check whether we were taking too long, whether people would answer questions for that amount of time and whether we could afford to do it. My experience is that if you're talking to people about a subject that they're interested in you can keep people talking about that for a long time. The problem was the cost of having interviewers on the doorstep for that amount of time. It's very expensive getting interviewers to front doors. So we spent a year, maybe more, developing the questionnaire. A huge amount of the cost of the survey went into that developmental stage. But in the end that paid off because we felt we had a very good survey instrument and of course others have been able to adapt it and build on it to do similar studies.

Question: For all that investment, the response rate in the field is important but difficult to predict. Is there a sense of being at the mercy of the fates once you begin the fieldwork?

Genn: It's not out of your hands. How you devise your questionnaire, what you tell people about it, and how you try to recruit them will influence what the response rates are. We spent a lot of time thinking about that. It's also part of what you're looking at when you're piloting – What have we told them in advance? What kind of responses are we getting? What if they don't want to do it? Why are they saying that they don't want to do it? Is it because they're not interested? Is it because they think it's going to take too long? You do have some control over response rates. I think nowadays it's harder to keep response rates up because there seems to be "survey fatigue." You sometimes have to pay people to take part in a survey. We didn't do that. We tried to capture people's interest so that they would respond voluntarily. Certainly from the interviews that I did, I found that once you got your foot through the door there was no problem keeping people going. Often they were very interested in a particular problem and interested in talking about it.

Question: What was the role of the postsurvey qualitative interviews?

Genn: Well, once we had the quantitative data from the survey, we could see some of the issues that we hadn't been able to explore in depth during the survey interview. That was the purpose of the postsurvey qualitative interviews. They were really so that we could delve more deeply into certain kinds of cases and processes. We did about fifty in-depth interviews afterwards, which for qualitative work is quite a lot. We decided to pick certain categories of case, say, people who had had a problem and tried to deal with it themselves, or those who had done nothing. In qualitative interviews you can keep on asking questions: Why? What happened then? What did it mean for you? In what ways did it matter? How did it affect you? A lot of our information about views of the judiciary came from those interviews as well. We asked people about their perceptions of the legal system in general and about the judiciary. We got much more detailed information on perceptions out of those qualitative interviews than we actually got from the survey because we could go into much more depth. It helped me understand more about what the quantitative data were telling me. The qualitative interviews help you to understand a bit more of the "why." In a survey there's a limit to how many questions you can ask and it's very hard in a survey to ask people about things that they didn't do. So if someone didn't seek advice about something or if they didn't do anything about it, and you ask a survey question "Why not?", people say, "Oh I don't know, I just didn't." But in a qualitative interview you can actually explore that much more.

You can't use your qualitative data to say "twenty-five percent of people in the country think this." But it helps us to understand the sort of things that are lying behind the survey findings – a huge amount of color that you can't get from structured questionnaire responses. One of the major issues that the survey uncovered and which I wasn't really expecting was the phenomenon of problem "clusters." What we found was similar to what occurs in surveys of crime victims – that a large proportion of the reporting of criminal events is by a relatively small proportion of the population; that events are not evenly distributed within the population. So a number of our respondents mentioned having experienced several justiciable problems during the survey period. What you got from in-depth interviews was an understanding of how there is a "snowball" or "cascade effect" – the way that one problem may lead, almost inexorably, to a number of others. What it tells you in policy terms is that if you can break into the process at early stage you might be able to stop these other horrible things from happening. An example that sticks in my mind is of a man who was having unresolved employment problems which led to him being threatened with dismissal, which then led to depression, which then led to marital breakdown, and he ended up with the family breaking up and him living elsewhere on benefits. I don't think I would have understood these cascading problems in quite the same way without those qualitative interviews. This is really important for people who do quantitative work. If you're trying to understand your quantitative results, then the color that you can get from listening to people and from reading their stories helps you to understand it better. It's all much more real.

Question: Is there any sense of distance or frustration in reading a transcript when you haven't done the interview yourself?

Genn: Absolutely, because I'm a control freak! But you can't do everything yourself, and sometimes you have to depend on other people doing it for you. What I did was to sit in on some of the qualitative interviews and then listen to all of the interview tapes as quickly as I could after they had been done. I used to listen to the tapes as I was driving around and if I felt the emphasis was too much in one direction or the other I would phone up the interviewers and say, "Can we have a little bit less on this, and a bit more on that?" But it's inevitable that you lose control and you're stuck with the material that other people provide for you. But at least if you listen to the tapes, you can hear the voices in your head later on and it helps you in writing up. I think qualitative analysis is really hard and reading transcripts rather than doing the interviews is less interesting. For me listening to the tapes brings the thing alive. Having heard them I remembered stories. As I listened to the tapes I would think, "Oh, that's something that would be useful." Then I went through the transcript and would mark it up in different colors for different themes. I even sometimes cut the transcripts up and put bits of quotes in piles on the floor. (I don't use computer software for qualitative analysis.) But you've got those stories in your head and you remember the people. It's in listening to the tapes that you get a sense of the patterns that are coming up. You also get a sense of who has expressed something, who has captured something that is quite common but in a particularly articulate or interesting way. Of course, you've also got to be careful that you're not giving prominence to certain views because they've been particularly well expressed or because they fit in with what you are expecting. I do find dealing with qualitative stuff very time-consuming. It's interesting but it's hard to do.

Question: What would you say were the greatest limitations or risks in trying to do a large-scale survey about legal issues?

Genn: The biggest danger is the same danger that there is for any survey in my experience – that you don't get your thinking straight beforehand. The difference between doing a quantitative survey and doing qualitative work is that with quantitative work you have to get it right before you start your fieldwork. Once you have got your questionnaire fixed you are stuck with it. With every single survey I have ever done, there have always been questions that I wished I had asked. For example, one surprise with the *Paths to Justice* study was the very small proportion of people who had actually gone through any kind of court proceedings. We had a huge chunk of the questionnaire developed, designed, and tested for asking people about their court experiences. I thought that would be a really big part of it. But mostly those questions were left blank and I felt it had been a huge waste of time. We could have spent much more interviewing time on some of the earlier stages. There are other areas that I really wish I had asked more questions about. I wanted to explore attitudes to the legal system, but because we devoted so much time in the questionnaire to other things there was only one question on attitudes toward the judiciary and one on courts. If I'd asked more questions about that it could have been helpful in explaining some other things. It would also have provided some useful information, because aside from attitudinal material on the criminal justice system, there's very little research on attitudes to the justice system or the judiciary or courts. That's still quite a big research black hole.

I hope and I believe that as I've gone through my career it has become less likely that I will fail to ask critical questions. What you need to be doing in designing a survey is, in a sense, frontloading your thinking. That's why the qualitative work and the piloting work is absolutely essential. It is not just about what information you want to collect in the survey; it's about how you are going to analyze the data. It's only through thinking about the kinds of analysis that you want to do that you know which questions are going to be critical. If you have one critical thing that's missing, it might muck up your analysis.

Question: What was the most challenging aspect of the project?

Genn: The hardest thing was working out how to do the analysis. It was very, very complex because people do take so many different paths in dealing with justiciable problems. So as you go through the questionnaire you're filtering people off into lots of different subgroups. For the analysis I needed to put the groups back together again so that it was possible to say, for example, "X number of people did this and then got to there." It was unbelievably difficult to check that we'd got the right number of people who'd made it to a certain stage in resolving their problem – self-helpers, people who had had advice, people who abandoned the issue, people who kept going, people who settled, people who issued legal proceedings. That made the analysis, the number crunching, fantastically difficult. It also made the analytical distinction between a person and a problem difficult. A person could have more than one problem. So it was constantly necessary to decide whether one was going to talk about problems or people. That was harder in the analysis than I'd anticipated.

Also, projects always take longer than you think they're going to. One of the dangers of working in teams is that as you get toward the end of the project people may start to disappear because their contracts are coming to an end and they want to take up other jobs. My experience with almost every project that I've managed is that by the end, the only person holding the baby at three o'clock in the morning was me. And it can be really hard getting projects in on time. You have to be prepared for the fact that at the end of the day you're the person carrying the can. You have got to finish it and you have got to be capable of doing that.

Question: Is there anything in hindsight that you would change about the project?

Genn: If I was doing it again I would do much more qualitative work about people's decision processes at the early stages of dealing with justiciable problems. I don't think that I really got enough of that from the quantitative questions we asked about people's decisions to do or not to do things. I know the strengths and the limitations of quantitative research. In the end, for some questions, you have to get out and talk to enough people in a probing way using much more open-ended interviewing techniques to get a better understanding of those processes.

On a lighter note, if I ever run a focus group north of the Scottish border I won't give them alcohol again! The standard procedure for our focus groups was that we invited people to come along, paid them twenty pounds, and gave them peanuts, crisps, and some wine so that they were relaxed. I do this with all sorts of people, including judges (not including the twenty pounds!) and generally it goes off fairly well. Of course, we had groups with different... let's say that the social makeup of the groups varied. With one particular group in Edinburgh, the wine disappeared virtually before we'd sat down at the table and there were a couple of people who started to get a bit belligerent with each other. Eventually one guy just jumped up, picked up a bottle, smashed the bottle and was about to have a go at another person in the focus group. You can hear it on the tape, and there's me saying, "Oh no! Oh no!" There were three of us running the focus group and we were completely hopeless. The only reason that it didn't end up in total chaos was because there was one guy at the table who seemed to be the Scottish equivalent of a mafia godfather. He just stood up, and said to the bottle-wielder, "Put it down," and that seemed to sort the men out. If he hadn't been there I don't know what would have happened. So one of the things I've learned is to be careful with alcohol. Since then people have said to me, "How could you have been so crazy to have wine in a focus group?!"

Question: Did you have any anxieties about criticism or review?

Genn: The thing I always fear, and every quantitative researcher fears, is getting the numbers wrong. I agonized over the numbers. It was really,

really hard putting groups back together again. It was unbelievably difficult to be sure that I'd reconstituted the groups so that I could say, for example, what proportion of "self-helpers" went to get legal advice or subsequently proceeded to court. I remember that Michael Zander was doing the Hamlyn lectures[2] and he asked me for a copy of the page proofs of the book. It hadn't yet been published. I had lunch with him at the LSE and at the end he said, "I think you've got some of those numbers wrong." He told me which ones they were, but I couldn't check because I didn't have the draft with me. I remember walking from the LSE back to UCL in a horrified daze and was nearly run over crossing the road. In fact the numbers were fine but it was a bad couple of hours. Any quantitative researcher has got to care passionately about the integrity of what they're doing because readers cannot check what you are asking them to believe and what you are telling them about the results. And you have to be absolutely honest in your interpretation. You know, I even agonize when I'm going to round up: when I've got .5, do I round up or down?

Question: *Paths to Justice* focused on England and Wales. But you almost immediately did an identical study in Scotland with Alan Paterson.[3] What was that like, to replicate your project in a new setting?

Genn: I have to say I would never do that again because I found writing it the second time really hard. It was good that I was writing it with Alan because I don't think it would ever have been finished if I had been doing it on my own. I just thought, "Oh my God, not again!" I don't think I would ever repeat the same thing unless there was a very good reason for doing it.

Question: How do you feel about the way the work has been received and interpreted?

Genn: I'm staggered, frankly. At the time I just thought it was a really interesting piece of work to do. But its publication coincided with the Access to Justice Act 1999 and big changes to legal aid. The Lord Chancellor's Department was trying to persuade everybody that the community legal service was the answer to access to justice problems and the study helped with what they were doing. So they picked it up and ran with it. I have had people in the LCD say that it did change

---

[2] Published as Michael Zander, *The State of Justice* (London: Sweet & Maxwell, 2000).
[3] *Paths to Justice Scotland* (Oxford: Hart Publishing, 2001).

the way that they thought about what they were doing. They said it helped with a shift to what they called a "customer focus." Now I don't know whether it did or it didn't. It may be that that was a change that was occurring in any case. But it certainly supported that change and gave policy people some solid evidence when they were talking about what the public wants from the justice system. It also gave the developing community legal service a better understanding of what kinds of things people needed, in particular the idea of dealing with problem clusters. So I think it was a piece of work that was done at a time when policy thinking was beginning to shift. It helped with that and perhaps reinforced it.

CHAPTER 21

JOHN BRAITHWAITE AND PETER DRAHOS AND *GLOBAL BUSINESS REGULATION**

Perhaps the greatest frontier for the study of law in society is the global. The production and maintenance of "law" in its global dimensions has generated new forms of interaction, interdependence, and international institution building. Students and scholars seeking fodder for exciting new projects are drawn to a topic as ripe and intriguing as globalization. History reminds us, however, that excursions into frontiers are frequently difficult and dangerous. Here the challenges are not of life and limb, of course, but of resources and intellectual energy. Are you able to locate all of the pieces of the puzzle that contribute to the "global" pattern? Can you find the time and money necessary to get you where you need to go? Then, can you bring theoretical meaning or order out of an evolving and complicated mess of interaction?

While studying even a single field or institution poses challenges enough (see, respectively, Dezalay and Garth, Chapter 18, and John Hagan, Chapter 22), what must empirically minded scholars do to capture a portrait of globalization processes across many substantive areas? Some of the answer provided by John Braithwaite and Peter Drahos in their monumental volume, Global Business Regulation, *deserves a mixture of respect, appreciation, and trepidation: ten years, over five hundred interviews, and a final text 629 pages in length. Yet, in other respects, their experience provides some reassurances. English was nearly universal, for example, and much of the story of globalization remained concentrated in relatively few places – the power centers of the United States and Europe. As they explore in this interview, the perpetual issue of access may have been made easier by their world travel. Even more important, finding the global comes down to what happens in the local: the skill and art of getting past the secretary, leading a good interview, and finding a way to squeeze meaning out of the data.*

Methodological Keywords: interviews, multiple interviewers, snowballing, note taking, documentary research including primary materials, participant observation

* *Global Business Regulation* (Cambridge: Cambridge University Press, 2000).

Question: How did your collaboration come together? Were you looking for a particular mix of disciplinary background, skills, and experience?

Drahos: The collaboration was serendipitous, like a lot of good things. It began, as I recall, over a barbecue and some drinks. I think the mix of disciplines that we had between us – anthropology, criminology, law, philosophy, and sociology – turned out to be useful.

Braithwaite: The other thing that was important was that I started on my own and then Peter joined the project fairly early on. One of the reasons for that was that I quickly came to the realization that the intellectual property regime was the one where the most dramatic things were happening in terms of globalization. The history of the subsequent decade proved that to be correct and I found that technically very difficult. I really would have been in trouble if Peter hadn't come on board with that substantive competence as well.

Question: When you began in 1990, were there any assumptions or hypotheses helping you to frame the initial project?

Braithwaite: We went into it with the standard set of globalizing hypotheses, about the decline of the nation state, which turned out in a significant way not to be true. The most significant actor across the largest number of domains was the United States. It was not so much a decline of the clout of states as the rise of many different dimensions of influence, a rise of the regulatory state, and the rise of regulatory capitalism, where there are many different kinds of actors, but where the state control of resources was very important. We were assuming that some domains would be globalizing more than others and we were interested to find out why.

Drahos: Yes, we were actually very open to where the fieldwork led us. We had ideas about aspects of what we were looking at, such as Jon Elster's idea of mechanisms, that perhaps one couldn't explain all of globalization with some giant general theory but one could explain aspects of it, using, for example, this idea of mechanisms.[1] So we had theoretical ideas rather than a lot of hypotheses.

Question: What strategy did you have for entering the field and collecting the empirical data?

[1] Jon Elster, *Nuts and Bolts for the Social Sciences* (Cambridge, U.K.: Cambridge University Press, 1989).

Braithwaite: I guess we had a kind of an action orientation – find the actors and follow the networks through which those actors worked, starting with some middling actors. I had initially thought that it would be a matter of starting with the lead players in the Australian regulatory regime, sort of middling players in global regimes, and then move up from them. But that's not really how we did it. Preliminary reading and early conversations quickly generated a list of key targets to talk to. Then we would ask them who would be even more important people than themselves. In the case of the intellectual property regime, that very quickly led to the discovery of these legal entrepreneurs and policy entrepreneurs operating out of small offices in Washington. They had come up with the idea of the regime and sold it to a couple of CEOs who then sold it to a bigger set of CEOs who then sold it to the President of the United States. So it was quickly cutting to the chase. We really didn't have much idea of where to start when we started but a few good names very quickly led to better and better names. We were also able to maintain the momentum just because it was so much fun. The people who we were interviewing were really interesting, clever people, people who had the imagination to be actors who would craft regimes – bold people. They were interesting to talk to.

Drahos: We did some interviews in Australia on the intellectual property issue and rapidly discovered that the Australian players were, essentially, irrelevant. They were simply not players. So we realized that we ultimately had to go to the United States and Europe. I think one of the geographical findings of the book is that there are only a few cities in the world out of which globalized regulation happens. Although we did quite a lot of follow-up work in developing countries – following the trails that led from core cities out to the periphery – we kept on going back to Brussels, to Washington, to Geneva, and London occasionally for some things like marine regulation. It was just a few key cities where these networks of individuals or key actors congregated.

Question: If the project aims at understanding some aspect of the global system, there would seem to be a tension for creating an efficient research strategy. One may expect to learn the most in a few places but it would be difficult to defend a project that didn't go out to other countries.

Drahos: One year I did quite a lot of follow-up work in newly industrializing countries, so I went to Taiwan and South Korea to look at competition regulation, financial regulation, and intellectual property regulation. The purpose was really ultimately to check hypotheses and information that we'd gotten out of Washington or Brussels. It was enough for just one person to go and do this kind of checking.

Braithwaite: The interviews we were doing together were mostly the most important ones and we were really planning to do them together. The solo ones tended to be more serendipitous. I represented Australia at an ISO standards-setting conference in Tunisia. There was no particular reason for targeting Tunisia to interview trade bureaucrats and others, but I did. There's an efficiency in being able to get stuff done if globalization is your topic. What would be the most interesting kind of people to talk to about our project in Tunisia?

Drahos: What was interesting about those interviews was they profoundly corroborated the story that we were getting from Europe and the United States. Although a lot of our fieldwork was focused out of necessity around these key cities, we did follow the trails that led from those cities out to the periphery and the semiperiphery because that was one of the initial assumptions that we made – that there would be the core states, the states on the semiperiphery, and the peripheral states, a sort of general systems theory.

Question: The people you interviewed were elites – unquestionably, very important people. How difficult was it to get them to give you some of their time?

Braithwaite: Well, I think we had an advantage in coming from afar. In those days, perhaps a bit more than today, people might think, "These guys really want to come all the way across the world to talk to me?!" We'd often have patched into the letter a few little sentences about why in particular we wanted to talk to them. We got very few outright rejections, though we did get a lot of nothing coming back. Then I think it's the skill of how you get on the phone and talk in a way that makes you and the project seem interesting to the PA. It's mostly about persuading Personal Assistants. That's the part that takes most skill: that assertive phone call follow-up when they're just not interested enough to do anything about it.

The other thing that I think which is quite a good tip is to say, for example, "We'll be in New York for all of such-and-such a week. We can see you at any time, but can we propose 11 AM on Tuesday morning?" We would do this six weeks in advance so that it was easy for them to say, "Oh well, they're coming from the other side of the world and that's a long way in the future. I'll block that off and agree to it." If it had been a week before they'd probably say they were too busy. Once we were locked into traveling a long way to come and see them, I think the politeness carries you a fair way.

Drahos: We followed a basic pattern in which we would describe the project, indicate some of the issues that we'd like to talk about, and then send the letter by fax to the CEO of the particular corporation or the head of the particular department or whoever it happened to be. That produced a remarkably high positive response rate. So, for example, we wrote to Bill Gates. We did not get to interview Bill Gates but it was a very effective way of getting access to the people that really mattered in Microsoft – those who understood the IP issues, who understood what Microsoft's position on the patentability of computer software was and how it differed, for example, from IBM's position, and so on.

Braithwaite: That's right. The right method is to write the letter that says, "Dear Mr. Gates, we realize that you're an extraordinarily busy person. If you could refer us to the right person in your office . . . " And the easy thing for Bill Gates' PA to do then is not to bother him with it but to pass it down two or three levels in the organization to someone who really has control of what's going on in that issue. And if a suggestion comes down from Mr. Gates' office to take care of the query, you get the interview.

Drahos: I also think that simple technique of sending a fax is even more important today because people are flooded by e-mails, so much so that they may well just forget to reply. We would only ask for forty or forty-five minutes of people's time, yet often we would end up being given a couple of hours. People were very generous in their time. They were very interested in the project.

Braithwaite: Yes, especially the ones who really had played a big role in shaping regimes. Their accomplishment was one that was quite an obscure one to their mums and dads. To be able to tell the story to someone who really appreciated its significance and was going to write about its significance was important. I think that's why a lot of our informants would give us hours and were open to us coming back and follow-up telephone conversations to clarify. They would tell these interesting stories that brought to life the way they operated.

Drahos: A good example of a very powerful person who wanted to tell his story is Jack Valenti. At that time he was the single most powerful lobbyist in Washington. He was the Head of the American Motion Picture Association. Even now that association is described as the "little State Department." They hold enormous power in American politics. Valenti wanted to talk about the kind of influence he had brought to bear in the intellectual property area – not just at the multinational level but at the bilateral level. He wanted to say, "Look, this is the kind of thing that I'm doing behind the scenes."

Question: Did you use the same approach for seeking access to actors in developing countries?

Braithwaite: No, although the developing country work in the end is easier, I think, once you've learned how to do it. You arrive at the capital and you set yourself up in a reputable hotel. You are seen to be inviting some important people to dinner in the public space. Then other people want to find out what you're doing. And over time, once you get on a roll, it's easier, so long as you don't really put a foot wrong and come to be regarded as dangerous – or some terrible story goes around about you, which can happen through no fault of your own.

Question: How did you prepare for the interviews?

Drahos: There was generally a lot of preparation. The reading was important, particularly for technical areas like banking regulation. Part of getting good responses from your interviewees is the ability to project credibility. I remember one interviewee who clearly didn't want to see us. At the time he was the assistant to Mickey Kantor the then United States Trade Representative, so a very senior person in the United States trade office. He was extremely busy as you can imagine and impatient when we went into his office. But then John launched into an introduction about the study in which he was able to project a tremendous amount of credibility about the project. I could see our interviewee thinking, "Gee, these guys really do know something about this area. They're not fools."

Braithwaite: He also had a better analysis. He was a very clever man. And so he wanted to tell us his analysis: "What you say is interesting but you missed this and you missed that . . . "

Drahos: If you're dealing with smart players you have to be able to project that credibility in the interview. So we would discuss the interview questions beforehand, what kind of hypotheses we were going to test in this particular interview, and so on.

Braithwaite: Often the conversations between us were in the taxi on the way to the interview. You've got to be efficient in the way you structure these things. There were lots of discussions over breakfast as to who we'd be interviewing that day and what the priorities were to focus on. But there were also interviews where we weren't well enough prepared. It happens a lot when you're busy. That's why the logistics are important. There are always points where you fall behind, where you haven't done the reading that you should have done, or where you set up the appointment and you just go ahead with it. We certainly did interviews that were almost a complete waste of time because we made idiots of ourselves. They could see we didn't know what we were talking about and they would send us packing fairly quickly. You learn from those.

Drahos: Yes, I remember one interview we did in the U.S. Internal Revenue Service. But really we should have been at the U.S. Treasury because we wanted to know all about international tax harmonization. Much of that policy comes out of Treasury. We were in the wrong place, but we soldiered on. So some of the interviews were not very productive. When it happened the first few times I expressed disappointment but John said, "Well, that's life as a fieldworker." So there were highs and lows.

Braithwaite: There's a lot of virtue in picking a project where if some people don't cooperate or some interviews don't work out you can always move on to someone else. If it's a study of Ministers, for example, and the Minister won't talk to you, you're in difficulties.

Question: You talked there about the importance of projecting credibility. Were there other strategies or techniques for making interviews with elites successful?

Drahos: The other thing we tried to do was to put the person in a state of reflective equilibrium about what it was they were doing. There's no recipe for doing this but one of the things I noticed was that a lot of interviewees quite liked the opportunity to sit back and reflect on what they had done. By the end of an interview, because by then people had relaxed into the process, you would get good reflections. One way to do that would be to try for some sort of simple summary hypothesis of what was happening: "What do you think of that as a hypothesis that explains this particular area?" People in these busy positions don't necessarily engage in that kind of self-reflection.

Braithwaite: Humor is important for getting people relaxed too. One of the simple strategies there is to retell a funny story already told to you by another interviewee. Interviewees will generally reciprocate with a like tale of their own. The other thing that's important is to make them feel important and fairly quickly get to a point where you can ask a question about what their role was in a particular issue. When they are a real player they will sometimes really get off in telling you exactly what they did – that's the thing, of course, that they're most knowledgeable about. So it's sort of moving backward and forward between their action and the abstraction.

Question: Did you encounter any interview situations that were especially difficult?

Drahos: I think there is a real challenge for any fieldworker having to deal with a group interview. They're much harder to conduct, a lot tougher. In that group situation the people are sort of checking each other. I don't think you get as much honest reflection and as much casual talk as you would in a one-on-one situation. I always thought that when we encountered those group interview situations, they weren't as successful. That's a difficult one for fieldworkers to handle because from the organization's perspective it's efficient for them to bring five or six people around a table together. Somehow you have to find ways of engaging with all of those people around the table, find out what their position is in the organization. But of course while you're talking to one person the other people can drift off. It's really difficult I think.

Question: Was it an advantage having two of you doing the interviewing?

Braithwaite: Yes, one of the difficulties of taking notes when you're on your own is getting the judgment right between maintaining eye contact to keep the flow going and taking good notes. But with the two interviewers you alternate – one is working hard at maintaining the rapport and smiling and nodding and looking at them while the other is working hard at the writing.

There are also some moments when a bit of arguing with each other makes interviewees more comfortable. You've got this problem with elite interviews of the person being a bit of a politician and sticking to the traditional party line, or a senior bureaucrat just saying what their Minister would want them to say. If one of you tries being provocative and says, "Well, we spoke to people at such-and-such a department who had a completely different analysis," then the other might make the interviewee feel more comfortable by disagreeing or partially disagreeing. So the other might respond, "But you know those guys in that department, they were trying to take the mickey out of you, weren't they?" Your interviewee might then say, "No, what he says is right." It has broken open the shell and created a kind of comfort. Again, I don't think you can cookbook how to do that but it's having a natural sense of openness and enquiry yourselves. That's what I mean by the importance of having these sort of "disagreements" with each other and creating a comfort all round so they're not seeing you as, maybe, leftwing academics or anti-American.

Question: Did you record your interviews?

Braithwaite: No, we took notes and wrote the notes up that evening and talked about it over dinner. I tend not to tape interviews. It's a practical reason for me. I'm a fairly sleepy sort of person. If the interview gets boring I figure it's generally my fault. You need to work hard at setting a new direction that will not be boring and irrelevant. If you've got the tape recorder running, it's easy to just drift and let them be in charge. You might think that you've done a great job and got a lot of data, but unfortunately they may not be as relevant than if you were testing the interview against the quality of what you're writing in the notes as it unfolds.

I use the method of handwriting the notes with lots of spaces. When there's a juicy quote, I try and get the keywords with gaps between the words so you can get the verbatim quotes. It might be embarrassing to the interviewee for you to put your head down and scribble this rather confronting, politically sensitive quote. So you just get those odd keywords down and keep them going. You can let the interview wander on to something that's of great interest to them but not of great interest to you, building up their rapport. And while they're talking about this thing, you're furiously writing. They think you're writing what they're saying at that point but you're really going back and getting that juicy quote down in detail. That's an important part of the skill.

While you're writing the notes you're also writing in key theoretical words. Then over dinner that night you're arguing over the interpretation of that bit of the text. In fact, the interpretive bits of the notes are much more important than the juicy best quotes, at least in this kind of research.

Drahos: There is something about the note-taking method that makes you a more active participant in the process. It also forces you to re-engage with the interview that night. You have to do that because you know that there are gaps in the notes, that you've left spaces deliberately for you to do that.

Braithwaite: It's also cost-effective because you get back home with all the notes that you need done. You're not spending weeks getting things transcribed or transcribing them yourself where what's transcribed is not what you actually want. If you've got the whole transcript with every word that was uttered, then it becomes a very big ask to be reading all the way through again and again.

Question: Even so, the volume of data you must have had when you finished the fieldwork must have been very imposing. How did you begin analyzing it?

Drahos: We were constantly thinking and having conversations about the data along the way. So over time certain categories of analysis would begin to emerge. The book has an explanation of globalization in terms of these basic categories of principles, actors, and the mechanisms of globalization. It's a simple structure, but those categories of analysis provided a way of beginning to organize the data. It was sort of actor-led, so a natural structure really evolved out of the material. That then allowed us to write up the empirical chapters.

Braithwaite: I use a fairly crude method compared to a lot of people – physical piles of material. For this project I had a very inefficient method of photocopying bits of fieldwork notes and dropping them in different piles. So let's say I was doing air transport regulation. There are all sorts of interesting theoretical insights, both in the interviews that connect to that regime and in the books and articles that connect to that regime. They're all in this big pile together. And of course when we were writing up there was an "actors" subpile, then a "mechanism" subpile, a "principles" subpile. It's a bit like the taping I guess. If you put them into End Note they go into a hole and they get forgotten.

You need a sort of a crude redundancy about your engagement with the materials and I think piles and a messy office does that for you.

Question: Is there anything in retrospect that you feel didn't work well or anything that you might do differently?

Braithwaite: I think we wasted some time trying to get to see bigshots. For example, I put a fair bit of energy into getting an interview with Bob Hawke, who was the Australian Prime Minister for ten years during this period. A lot of research time went into setting it up. In the end it was very lacking in focus. A lot of these guys are more about being front stage, winning the election. He didn't really have an understanding of the things I was trying to interview him about. I think we put a bit too much energy in trying to track down people in important positions who weren't that important.

Drahos: Yes, I think the politicians were disappointing. But that in itself is an important finding in a way – probably one that doesn't really come through in the book. Ultimately it is these clever technocrats behind the political figures that really understand the system. If you want to know about the evolution of the system, those are the people you have to talk to, not the politician who in a sense is a transient figure in all of this.

Question: You conducted over five hundred interviews, around the world. Is there any less resource-intensive way of doing the data collection?

Drahos: I'm a great believer in doing the fieldwork myself. If you're interested in building theories and you do so on the basis of data collection it should be you that goes out and collects that data. It's just going to be hard for junior people to be able to gather the data and order it and interpret it and do that on the spot in the way that you can.

Braithwaite: If you're sufficiently clear about what you want to ask – that you feel those precise questions would work – then perhaps you should send a questionnaire off and have standardized answer formats. But if you're trying to discover and interpret an unfolding story with a history where you can't predict its twists and turns in advance, then you've got to be there. Or, to put it another way, if a research assistant is so good that he or she can handle the most important part of the research process without you, then they probably should be the senior author.

Question: Is the scale and ambition of a global, multisector project such that it would be too difficult for junior scholars to undertake?

Drahos: I think it's only because John had the confidence that the project could be done that we undertook it. It took someone who has a lot of experience and a sense of confidence about the outcome. It was a very long-haul project. There's no guarantee that you are going to come out at the end of the day with anything that will make people sit up and take notice. What junior academic could go to a dean and say, "I'm going to embark on a major paradigm-changing piece of scholarship, it'll take ten years to produce, and nothing will be produced along the way. Do I have your OK to do that?"

Braithwaite: You've got to have self-belief to do a project like that, because nothing was published out of that project in the first seven years. Our attitude was, "Don't be distracted by doing pieces along the way. Push on so you will get to the conclusion of the two big books at the end." There are very few academics who have been as privileged as I have to have my time freed up for research over a large number of years. I think the obligation with that is to take on the projects that you could only take on if you're in that position. It's a matter of gradual confidence-building. My career has been about taking on bigger and bigger projects and being more focused on the long haul and longer term.

Question: What are your feelings about how the book's been interpreted and used in literature?

Braithwaite: I think people have been fairly kind to it. It's not been savaged much, but it's never been used as much either. There's something a bit terrifying about a book that big. It's daunting I think. And yes, we get a lot of doorstop jokes about it!

CHAPTER 22

JOHN HAGAN AND *JUSTICE IN THE BALKANS**

Having reached a certain degree of maturity as a field, Law and Society may not appear to offer much "low-hanging fruit" – topics ripe for examination and easily within reach. Whereas Stuart Macaulay, as recorded in the first interview in this collection, made an enduring contribution by asking local companies about their understanding and use of "contracts," after a half-century of work, seemingly no field of law can be said to be truly bereft of critical, social scientific examination. New advances in the field, by this accounting, must stand on the shoulders of others: filling in ever-smaller gaps in the field, employing creative reinterpretations, or deploying innovative project designs. The student or young scholar today, wondering where to "make one's mark," may look with a hint of jealousy on the prior generation of scholars who had so much new ground to plow.

Yet the last interview in this book shows the preceding account to be too dour. Setting aside the question of whether scholars have even fully mined the potential in the local aspect, since the 1970s, John Hagan for one, saw the vast potential in giving Law and Society global horizons. As Dezalay and Garth (Chapter 18) and Braithwaite and Drahos (Chapter 21) likewise appreciated, a changing society reshapes "the law," from its identities to its institutions. A globalizing world gives scholars today an even more significant opportunity to be present at the creation of a whole new genus of legal developments. With Justice in the Balkans, global developments finally caught up with Hagan's latent interest in the international dimensions of criminal justice. In his reflections on the project, Hagan describes the steps necessary to access and understand the workings of the International Criminal Tribunals. The challenges are familiar, as are many of the solutions, which, ironically, include harnessing local connections. Plus change . . .

Methodological Keywords: surveys, interviews, observation

---

*Justice in the Balkans: Prosecuting War Crimes in the Hague Tribunal (Chicago: University of Chicago Press, 2003).

Question: Can you say a little about the background to this project? How did you come to it?

Hagan: I started out in graduate school being interested in crime and law. My dissertation research was on the treatment of First Nations people in the courts of Alberta, Canada. But I was always interested in criminal justice in a much broader way. I wasn't interested in just doing localised kinds of studies. I'd always wanted to do a study of criminal justice in an international context. But when I began doing this work in Canada it was in the middle of the 1970s. There really was no international criminal justice. We'd had Nuremberg in the postwar period but then nothing happened institutionally in a major way until the 1990s.

In the course of having a position at the law school at the University of Toronto I became aware of the work of Louise Arbour, the second prosecutor at the Hague Tribunal. She is Canadian and periodically would come to speak at the law school at the University of Toronto. I began to realize that I knew someone and so could get access to begin this study of international criminal law and justice that I had always wanted to do. In that tribunal we had ideas about international criminal law that had been evolving theoretically in an abstract way ever since Nuremberg but without a concrete institutional home and application. But with the effort to find various ways of responding to the conflict in the former Yugoslavia we had the beginning of a new important international criminal venue. I could see it was starting from scratch. People were literally acquiring the space, doing a sort of lead-up study to justify the Security Council's establishment of the tribunal. They were beginning to hire the first people; beginning to write the rules and procedures that would govern the court; developing a prosecutor's office, a judiciary, and an administration. It was already building when Louise Arbour became the second chief prosecutor, but it was still on its way. The people who had done the initial building were still very much around and accessible. So I began to do a social and institutional history of the birth and growth of an important institution.

Question: Given that it was a completely new institution, did you have any kind of a model or inspiration for how to undertake such a project? What did you take as the inspiration or model for what you wanted to do?

Hagan: Well, I didn't have a template for the study. I had a set of ideas I wanted to explore – particularly the idea of legal actors as having careers, as having a life course both individually and as part of an institution. I had in mind the idea of focusing on the prosecutor's office. In my prior research in criminal justice decision making I'd reached the conclusion that the prosecutors were where the action was. They make the most important and foundational decisions for individuals and the institution. I had this idea of studying the people in the prosecutor's office, trying to understand their careers and how they linked into the institutional setting that was evolving around them.

Question: What kind of theory was influencing you in the development phase?

Hagan: What was most in my mind was that, in looking at the prosecutor's office, I could see there had already been one prosecutor, and then a second, and soon there was to be a third. This represented a very important instance of having an agent and a structure and an interaction between the two – how the agent helps to shape the structure and how the structure shapes the agent. I was thinking about that in the kind of terms that William Sewell, Jr., has talked about in a classic article where he sets out how basic ideas and an institutional structure are reciprocally embedded and evolve into something.[1] I was conscious of the fact that the tribunal had to make a series of strategic decisions about who it was going to indict and for what. Then it was going to have to bring these individuals into detention and mobilise trials that would not only assign individual criminal responsibility to the individuals but also begin to build a history of the conflict and the response to it by this new institution.

Bryant Garth and Yves Dezalay were probably my biggest influences – their drawing on Bourdieu and this notion of understanding careers within institutional structures and competition among legal elites. More and more I began to see the tribunal that way. Garth and Dezalay were very important to me all the way through, from research method through ideas and undertaking the project.

However, it was very much a "grounded theory" project: ideas were coming out of the individual interviews that I was conducting over time in that setting. I was also reading the transcripts of the cases that were beginning to develop and various reports that were around. All that was a grounding for working with these loose theoretical ideas.

[1] "A Theory of Structure: Duality, Agency and Transformation," *American Journal of Sociology*, 98:1–29 (1992).

I became persuaded in the course of studying this particular institution that there had to be more of a role of agency in it than sociologists typically have recognized. I became taken with the idea that what this meant – this connection between the agency and structure – was the creation of a kind of collective charisma around this particular person who was most central to the story, Louise Arbour.

Question: How did you get from listening to Louise Arbour's lecture in the University of Toronto to entering the field and collecting data?

Hagan: Well, that is also a story of agency and structure. I had to persuade someone in a position of influence in the tribunal to allow me in to do interviewing and begin to create this social history of the place. There are always issues of secrecy and security in a prosecutor's office, of course, but these are really intense in this particular office because it's just getting off the ground and it's dealing with global politics. It was dealing with a violent conflict in Europe. It's located in Europe and so there was a tremendous amount of concern about the security of the people involved. So I knew it wasn't just going to be a matter of walking in the front door and having open access.

I had to begin to build a trust relationship with Louise Arbour – getting to know her, persuading her of the value of the study. She was transitioning out as prosecutor and a new prosecutor was coming in. I had to have my relationships and the research setting with others who would sustain me. I had to find a way of introducing myself to the people in the prosecutor's office and getting them to talk to me, to trust me, and respond to me. It may seem backward to portray it this way, but the survey that I did with the people in the tribunal became my calling card. After first establishing some rapport with the higher level people in the tribunal and establishing some ground rules, I got them to agree to me doing the survey, both as a way of collecting information on the lives of these individuals before, during, and hopefully as they went along in this institution, and as a way of introducing myself to them.

The deputy prosecutor told them what I was doing and encouraged them to talk to me. At the end of the instrument I asked whether I could meet them for an interview. I then followed up to make those appointments and did the interviews. As this unfolded I was able to talk to more and more people. Even the people who wouldn't take the time to answer the instrument, they knew about me and could see me around. I could keep pestering them in the hallways and then I would get them to sit down and talk with me. They'd see me in court, be interested that I was watching what they were doing and that sort of thing. So that's how I built the methodology. Ultimately the project became a mixture of what survey researchers would see as a panel study and what Michael Burawoy calls "rolling ethnography." The latter ultimately overtook the former and there was an interesting sense of remixing the methods as the project evolved.

Question: Sometimes the advice about gaining access is not to go in at the top because, if you get the answer "no," you're stuck. Did you consider trying to informally gain the support of those lower down the hierarchy of the tribunal before seeking access at the top?

Hagan: No, the security barriers at the tribunal and the suspicion about people coming in were so intense that it was impossible. In any event, outside of the tribunal people are very reluctant to talk about what's going on inside the tribunal. So I really had to get authorization from the chief prosecutor and then the deputy prosecutor. But I approached them at a time when they were beginning to realize how important the tribunal was becoming in terms of, for example, the indictment against Milosevic and the trials getting under way. They began to see a value in someone creating a social history of this institution and their places in it. So that was what I was trying to build on. And then I needed a routine and a bureaucratic way of making it seem normal and natural that I was doing this. That was what the survey instrument was about. I'd say to the deputy prosecutor, "We have these kinds of instruments and we want to have individuals answer them and then, of course, we'd want to follow up and learn more about their answers from the interviews." That was the context in which it was possible to make them feel like it was normal and appropriate that I was going to be there and that I would keep coming back. Some people would say, "Why is he here? He's always here. He keeps coming back." So I'd tell them there were multiple waves of the interview, that I needed to interview everybody, not just a few. So those were the ways in which I built the rapport and used the method as a mechanism to make it possible to do the research.

Then as that evolved, as it became normal and natural from their perspective that I would be doing this as a social scientist, they became less concerned about setting up ground rules. Ultimately I remember there was only one key phrase that the prosecutor laid out. He said, "Of course, you won't be discussing immediately relevant operational details of the cases." That was it. We didn't go into a further discussion of what that meant and I didn't regard it as binding in any restrictive way other than I didn't ask very specific questions about which witness they would be calling in the next short time, or which questions they were going to ask the next day, and so on. Beyond that I didn't feel any real restraints on what I was asking.

Question: The survey does not seem to be used much in the book. Was its importance more as a device for getting you in the door and less as way of collecting data?

Hagan: I like to think that the survey results are embedded in the narrative in more of a way than is initially apparent. I say things that I could only know from the survey – for example, the nationalities of the employees of the prosecutor's office, and the proportion which were American, Canadian, New Zealanders, and so forth. I also found the instrument very important in preparing for interviews. It gave me enough background knowledge about the person and a little bit of their attitudes and views and experiences that I could draw on for the interviews. That was an important function of the instrument as well.

Question: How was the survey instrument structured? What kind of data were you seeking?

Hagan: I tried to parallel the kinds of information which I collected in other studies and which I was seeing in other people's studies. In particular, it tried to get a sense of the person's personal and professional biography. I was also looking for something of a life history calendar – when they were having children, when they were in school, where they went to school and the steps in their careers, and so on. I was also interested in their emotional well-being. Their work was challenging, particularly the investigators who were out in the field in exhumation pits. Taking testimony and preparing witnesses to testify, especially the work on rape, was stressful. They were coming back and forth, in and out of their family lives. I always remember one of the persons saying, "You come back from two weeks in the field where your co-workers are your best friends and you're back in your own family who can have no idea of what you've been doing and perhaps shouldn't. It's not like you come back from your vacation with your pictures." So there was this give and take with families and co-workers and the subject matter. The survey instrument asked a number of questions about mood and feelings and tried to get some of that.

257

Question: The interviews in fact ranged across a very diverse set of officials, with diverse backgrounds. Did you adopt different approaches for different subjects?

Hagan: I had at least three different game plans going into the interviews. It seemed to me that there was clearly a relationship between the status of the person in the organization and their willingness to talk openly about what they were doing – the larger strategies and tactics of the office and the tribunal. So when I would talk to the lead prosecutors, the prosecutors' advisors, and the deputy prosecutor, I would spend some time on their backgrounds and career histories, but tried to preserve the majority of the interview for talking about the bigger issues of the big cases and prosecutorial strategies. At the middle levels I would begin with career questions – biography and personal experiences – but then ask them to describe how they worked with the people above and below them and what the nature of those sort of patterns were. Then I would try to get them to talk more specifically about actual cases and actual areas of prosecutorial initiative. Often they would have the greatest insights. Sometimes people at the top are too far removed. It's those midlevel people that can tell you an awful lot about what's going on. Then with the people at the lower levels who had more technical skills and clerical and administrative responsibilities, I tried to get them to talk about the tasks they had. I was trying to make it comfortable for them because they were most aware of warnings they would hear about talking about their cases. By asking them more specific and technical questions about their work I thought I was able to get the most out of them.

Question: Despite the sensitivities of the institution, you recorded all of the interviews.

Hagan: Yes, and all of the interviews were transcribed. That proved to be extremely important. I have become totally convinced of this, particularly when researching a legal institution that's developing itself and developing new law. There was a lot of new stuff that was coming up all the time. They were talking about it and there was no way as the interviewer I could hear it all as they said it. You don't recognize it all because you don't know quite what they're talking about and how it fits together. But later on down the road you do see the larger picture and you go back and you read those transcripts and you see how it fits together. What you didn't hear then you read on the transcribed page. So I found that an extremely important part of the process. The development of that qualitative data was the core challenge of the project.

Question: You also observed tribunal proceedings. Were you concerned about your presence having any effect on the officials?

Hagan: No, I was able to be more in the background. I was familiar. I think of it as like the early research on riding in police cars, developing observational data on police encounters with suspects and complainants and so on. Everyone who's done that kind of work says that after a while they don't notice you're sitting in the backseat. I think that was in the nature of my presence there. I was familiar enough that they didn't respond apprehensively to me. They weren't paying a lot of attention to me.

Question: During fieldwork, as opposed to blending into the background, did you ever sense that you were breaking down the barriers with your subjects, or that you might have learned something different by becoming closer to their community?

Hagan: I was conscious of not wanting to socialise with them and become a part of that outside community. I just thought it would interfere in all sorts of ways and would be totally unnatural. I thought it would take over my life and not allow me to do the project properly. There was at least one instance where it seemed to be clear that there was a big conflict going on and the different parties were trying to get their stories in place. I had to think about the competing stories and try faithfully to articulate what I thought was theoretically significant about what was going on. That didn't happen until right at the end of the research. I don't know if that was because it took until then for people to recognize me well enough to try to manipulate me. I could feel the pressures coming to bear on me more at the very end. People wanted to get their own version of events on record.

Question: How did you move from interviews and observations to the process of writing this into a book?

Hagan: I wanted to connect the project to the field of criminology. Nuremberg had connections into the study of law and crime so I started with that. I began by trying to do archival work on Nuremberg to try to understand that connection. I was able to work on that while I was writing the research proposal and getting in the door. I made a conscious effort to get an early interview with Richard Goldstone, the first chief prosecutor of this new International Criminal Tribunal. My colleague, John Comaroff, was a friend of Goldstone. That was helpful in getting the interview.

Then I started to talk to the people like the deputy prosecutor, Graham Blewitt, who were there from the very outset. We talked about how they worked with Goldstone and how they began to build it. So I did approach it chronologically initially. I then got interested in the teams that were working on different cases within the institution. I began to get an idea of the people who had come and gone from these teams and I tried to get a sense of how they had evolved. Then the big cases started to happen, the big rape case, Srebrenica, the big genocide case, and the Milosevic case. In some ways it was pulling everything together but I began to be afraid that it would be unending. I decided I had to bring the book to a conclusion before that case was going to finish.

Question: Did you feel any pressure to write up your findings and publish quite quickly, given the particular timeliness of the material?

Hagan: Yes, there was that thing that everyone talks about in qualitative research, that after a certain number of interviews you feel like you've heard it all and it's repeating. You've got the story and that's the time to write it. If you don't, you eventually begin to forget the story. I also thought it was important that it be out there. I felt I would lose the feeling of the emergence of the institution if I just sat back and played with it for a longer time.

Question: Your voice comes through clearly in the book. Indeed, perhaps uncommonly for the distant prose of the social sciences, you put yourself into the story in the first person in a couple of spots. Can you say a little about why you did that?

Hagan: Well, it was dramatic and I felt like I was in the middle of it, less as a participant and more as an observer, but with the element of something like being a spy. There were people in positions of power who really did want someone to write a social history. But they didn't feel they could just say that and tell me that I could reveal things and talk about things. So I was discovering them as I was going along. I wanted to give that feeling of the research as it unfolds, that this is how it can happen in a research setting like this.

But there are other really strong voices in this story, particularly in the Foca rape case. Anyone who was around that institution realised that Louise Arbour, the Chief Prosecutor, had a unique capacity to frame the story in ways that would advance the institution-building. She came to realize her gift for that as she was doing it. A big part of the story was her active agency and the building of a social structure. So I wanted to preserve a lot of her words and her ways of characterizing things. I made a good bit of use of her voice and I was pleased with that part.

Question: What were the most challenging aspects of the project?

Hagan: The real challenge I encountered was with the third prosecutor, Chief Prosecutor Carla del Ponte. She was universally recognized by the press as being more prickly and difficult than those who came before and after. She is a challenging person. I talk about that in the book. When she came I was very concerned that she was going to shut the project down. I was maybe two-thirds of the way through it but the biggest third was still there to do. I was getting the most gains out of the rapport I had with people and cases were moving along into their higher levels. So the challenge was to make sure that neither she nor the people around her shut it down.

Question: How did you do that?

Hagan: Well, I knew that she had to be a part of the study. I made it late in the process. On several occasions I made appointments to see her which she broke. I had to spend a lot of time waiting and just being available. Her secretaries would tell me, "Oh, we think we might be able to get her to you. We may be able to help you and channel her in your direction." In a sense, the secretaries became my allies and assistants in completing the project. Finally, one day while I was waiting and she was about to leave for Rwanda, she appeared right before me. She just materialized suddenly. I was seated at a desk, probably half asleep, waiting. She glared down at me: "What are you doing here?" And so my worst fears were all manifesting themselves. I don't remember what I answered but I was able to initiate a conversation and begin to get her to move. She had recently been in Bosnia with the survivors of Srebrenica. It was a very emotional experience for her and I think she wanted to talk about it. So I was able to do a useful interview with her. In some ways that was the most interesting interview. People felt it difficult to make that connection with her. The conversation seemed to reassure her about my presence.

Question: With the benefit of hindsight, is there anything about the project that you would do differently?

Hagan: I can imagine doing it differently. One part of the story, the Srebrenica case, had so many components to it – the intercept evidence, the exhumations, the military command structure. It had an organizational structure that was unique to the case. And the lead prosecutor was a very energetic French-speaking investigator who was often hard to follow. He went in a lot of directions at once. That team operated somewhat on their own with very distinct personalities involved. If I had known French and had more time and earlier access, I could have done a better job with that lead character. The Srebrenica case is very important and I did a lot with it, but I can imagine a different way of doing more.

I also would have liked to have gone with the teams into the field. I wanted to see how the various actors worked together outside the tribunal. At first they weren't comfortable with that idea at all. There were liability issues. I eventually got to a place where they were agreeable but it just didn't happen for one reason or another. That bothered me. I wanted to be out there, wanted to get a sense of what it was like being with these teams in the field.

Question: To what extent was your ability to access the field and conduct this research due to your seniority as a scholar? Could an enterprising graduate student have achieved the same?

Hagan: I don't think someone in the early stages of their career as a graduate student could have done quite what I was able to do in terms of talking to so many people and getting them to fill out survey instruments. It seemed important that I was connected with a law school. I had some sense of being someone like them or having some background connected to them. Louse Arbour's connections to my law school made me seem more normal. The other thing I found useful in doing this is that at the time I was making the transition from the University of Toronto to Northwestern University and the American Bar Foundation. The director of the Bar Foundation, Bryant Garth, took the view that lawyers know what they can say and what they can't say. They are responsible actors who don't require the normal sort of protections that other human subjects do. I very much took that approach and felt it worked well. I also really needed a senior administrative research assistant to help keep everything organized and to manage the survey instruments and the multiwave data collection involved in that.

Question: You approached this subject as a scholar of Law and Society, but was there any sense in which you felt you were writing a history and analysis for a wider audience?

Hagan: It was definitely a Law and Society story. There's a big central part about primary and secondary law enforcement and the role of the team in developing that work. But it became more and more apparent to me that, because this was a new and unique institution, there had to be a social history of it involving human rights activists and journalists as well. In a surprisingly large part it became to me a social history of an institution. Because it's an institution, it has got its own chronology and its own unfolding nature. Someone had to tell that story or it was going to be lost. And I was right in the middle of it. I had this access. So I felt like that was what I should be doing as much as the Law and Society of it. It was a unique opportunity to be there when international criminal law was renewing itself and making its most important advances. I felt good about recording how that happened.

CHAPTER 23

CONCLUSION: "RESEARCH IS A MESSY BUSINESS" – AN ARCHEOLOGY OF THE CRAFT OF SOCIOLEGAL RESEARCH

Herbert M. Kritzer

A common experience among those of us who talk to lawyers about their work is to hear the lawyers recite their war stories. In contrast, when you talk to an experienced social scientist about his or her work, you tend to get something of a sanitized version of the research process much like the "methods" section of a research article. However, if you start to dig, as the creators of this volume have done, you often start to see a much messier business, as Keith Hawkins ("Research is a messy business") and Stewart Macaulay ("[W]hen people write about research methods – it's all so neat and pretty. The messiness of much of it just doesn't come through in the books") so honestly tells us. The more vigorously you dig, the messier things often get. If, in addition to the wonderful interviews that compose this book, the editors had looked at early documents from the research projects – memos, research designs, grant applications, and the like – they would have often discovered that many of the authors started from very different points than the authors themselves now recall (I by no means exclude myself from this phenomenon, although I have not gone back to my own early research materials).[1]

The ability to produce high-quality and influential social science research products is a craft that is acquired through a combination of

---

[1] This is what I discovered in the course of my own archeology of research projects. See "Interpretation and Validity Assessment in Qualitative Research: The Case of H. W. Perry's *Deciding to Decide*," *Law and Social Inquiry*, 19:687–724 (1994); and "'Data, Data, Data, Drowning in Data': Crafting *The Hollow Core*," *Law and Social Inquiry*, 21:761–804 (1996).

instruction from those who have previously mastered the craft and one's own practice doing that research.[2] Dealing with the unexpected and being able to cope with messiness is a common feature of "craftwork."[3] The nature of the messiness depends on the specific craft involved. The interviews in this book show how skilled sociolegal scholars have confronted the dilemmas that have arisen in the course of their work. In this concluding essay, I highlight several themes that I found cutting across the interviews: problems in figuring out the right question to be asking and how this relates to designing research, the joys and complexities of original data collection, the challenge of analyzing data – whether qualitative or quantitative, the centrality of writing to the analysis process, and the challenges of working collaboratively. I also discuss two current and possibly growing problems for Law and Society researchers: problems in conducting surveys and the "problems" of increasing demands from Institutional Review Boards charged with protecting human subjects.

TYPE III ERROR

Anyone who has taken a course in statistics has heard about Type I and Type II errors. The former refers to "rejecting a null hypothesis that is in fact true" and the latter refers to "failing to reject a null hypothesis that is in fact false." More generally, one can describe these as "thinking you see something that is in fact not there" (a false positive) and "failing to see something that is in fact there" (a false negative). In their brief monograph, *Reliability and Validity in Qualitative Research*, Jerome Kirk and Marc Miller describe a third error ("Type III error"): asking the wrong question.[4] Although they describe this in the context of qualitative research, it is equally true of quantitative research.

I can identify a number of my own experiences where I discovered early in the data-collection or data-analysis process that I had asked the wrong question. For example, in the early 1980s I went to Toronto to spend a month interviewing large-firm lawyers and officers of the lawyers' corporate clients about how the availability of fee reviews by a court official affected concerns about rising legal costs. Before I had

---

[2] Kritzer, "Toward a Theorization of Craft," *Social and Legal Studies*, 16:321–40 (2007), esp. pp. 326–7.
[3] Ibid., p. 328.
[4] Beverly Hills, CA: Sage Publications, 1986, pp. 29–30.

completed even a half-dozen interviews, I realized that this was an irrel-evant question, and the interesting question was that of understanding the broader structure of lawyer–client relations at this level.[5]

In the interviews you see many indications of this kind of evolution of research questions:

- Michael McCann (Chapter 16): "We tell ourselves that we have a research question and a set of hypotheses but in the process of developing [the] book, the questions were changing all the time."
- David Engel (Chapter 8): "The "Oven Bird's Song" article was not one that I had anticipated as a product of the research when starting it."
- Sally Merry (Chapter 12): "[T]his was a book where the hypothe-ses I began with were all collapsing around me."
- Doreen McBarnet (Chapter 14): "I think the breakthroughs come from coming up with the things that you wouldn't have thought about . . . until you actually start doing the research."
- William Felstiner (Chapter 17): "[I]f you could dig up the appli-cation we made to NSF I doubt if you would see very much other than, 'here is the paper we wrote and now we want to try to see if these dispute transformations actually happen as we predict'."[6]

All of the projects just referenced were primarily qualitative in nature. One might ask whether things are different for quantitative projects. If one looks at the interviews with Hazel Genn, with Tom Tyler, and with John Heinz and Edward Laumann, you see very different images of how research evolves. Genn captures this well when she observes that "[t]he difference between doing a quantitative survey and doing qualitative work is that with quantitative work you have to get it right before you start your fieldwork. Once you have got your questionnaire fixed you

[5] See Kritzer, "The Dimensions of Lawyer–Client Relations: Notes Toward a Theory and a Field Study," *American Bar Foundation Research Journal*, 1984:409–28.
[6] Felstiner is referring to the well-known "Naming, Claiming, and Blaming" paper that he and Sarat coauthored with Richard Abel. W. L. F. Felstiner, R. L. Abel, and A. Sarat, "The Emergence and Transformation of Disputes: Naming, Blam-ing, Claiming," *Law & Society Review*, 15:631–54 (1980–1981). Another of my archaeology of research endeavors was a study of Sarat and Felstiner's divorce lawyer project; I have looked at the original grant application, and Felstiner is correct in stating that the original project proposal focused on dispute transformation, a topic that you cannot even find in the index of their book, *Divorce Lawyers and Their Clients*.

are stuck with it. With every single survey I have ever done, there have always been questions that I wished I had asked" (Chapter 20). She goes on to describe a second problem that one frequently encounters in survey research: including questions that you later discover are not of much use; in the case of the study she describes, this involved asking detailed questions about court experiences only to discover that too few respondents had such experience to allow for any meaningful analysis.[7]

In a sense the difference between qualitative and quantitative research is reflected in the ability to obtain data. If one is doing a survey or a series of social psychological experiments, the data you have in hand constrain your analysis, and the data-collection process often limits your ability to make adjustments. Moreover, in a lot of survey work, you do not know what you missed until you have finished collecting the data. For example, John Heinz and Edward Laumann describe how client type turned out to be a central dimension, but that their questions about specialization had not taken that into account; this limited the analysis they were able to do with the 1975 data, which they sought to correct when the study was replicated in 1995. In the context of experimental work, it may be the case that individual experiments are limited, but through a series of experiments you can hone in on something that is very different than what you originally set out to look at. The classic example of this is the working condition experiments done in the 1920s at a Western Electric's Hawthorne Works in Cicero, Illinois; many of the apparent effects of modifying working conditions reflected not the impact of the conditions but the impact of the workers being singled out in a positive way – what is now known as the Hawthorne effect.[8]

Even in survey-based studies, it is not uncommon to discover that the main effects one is looking for are not the central story in the data. Early studies of voter behavior in American presidential elections had an image of how the voter made his or her choices at election time; what the researchers found was a very different kind of

---

[7] Genn's experience mirrors my own experience with the data collected for the Civil Litigation Research Project (CLRP). We designed quite elaborate questionnaires to get at lawyer and litigant experiences in litigation. We discovered that for the vast majority of cases, we could have used a much simpler survey instrument.

[8] H. M. Parsons, "What Happened at Hawthorne? New Evidence Suggests the Hawthorne Effect Resulted from Operant Reinforcement Contingencies," *Science*, 183:922–32 (1974).

process.[9] The researchers designed subsequent election studies to try to get at the kinds of things the first studies uncovered.[10] The differences between qualitative and quantitative research in this regard do not reflect that quantitative research is designed more carefully than qualitative research. Rather, it reflects the fact that, in quantitative research, particularly survey-based quantitative research, analysis does not start until data collection is completed. In contrast, in qualitative research, whether it is based on observation or interviews, much or all of the data are usually collected directly by the primary researcher(s), and the initial analysis of those data starts simultaneously with the data collection.[11]

Sometimes the question changes not because the researcher posed the wrong question to start with but because of changes that occurred that during the research or data-collection process. When I taught graduate research methods I would routinely recount the following mythical tale.

> Some years ago, a political science Ph.D. student arrived in a foreign country to undertake her field research on some aspect of how the country's democratic system was operating. The day after she arrived there was a military coup, and her research plan was out the window. She sent a cable back to her advisor describing what had happened and pleading for advice about what to do. Her advisor sent back a two-word response: "Take notes."

A college classmate of mine went directly to graduate school in political science. In 1971 or 1972 he began work on his doctoral dissertation focusing on the presidency, and by early 1973 he was largely finished. However, his work was overcome by events – the Watergate burglary by Republican operatives, the subsequent investigations, Supreme Court cases, and President Richard Nixon's resignation in 1974 – and in the

---

[9] Paul Lazarsfeld, Bernard R. Berelson, and Hazel Gaudet, *The People's Choice: How the Voter Makes Up His Mind in a Presidential Campaign* (New York: Columbia University Press, 1948).

[10] Bernard R. Berelson, Paul F. Lazarsfeld, and William N. McPhee, *Voting: A Study of Opinion Formation in a Presidential Campaign* (Chicago: University of Chicago Press, 1954); Angus Campbell, Philip E. Converse, Warren E. Miller, and Donald E. Stokes, *The American Voter* (New York: John Wiley, 1960). A recent book finds that the patterns in *The American Voter* largely continue to describe contemporary voting behavior. See Michael S. Lewis-Beck, William G. Jacoby, Helmut Norpoth, and Herbert F. Weisberg, *The American Voter Revisited* (Ann Arbor: University of Michigan Press, 2008).

[11] See Kritzer (1994), pp. 696–8.

end he abandoned both his dissertation and graduate school. His topic: executive privilege.

Of course change need not be this dramatic, and it may clearly create an opportunity (see interview with Robert Kagan, Chapter 3) rather than undermine a planned or ongoing research project. In 2000 I had a survey in the field at the time of the U.S. Supreme Court's decision effectively making George Bush the President-Elect. While my original research had nothing to do with the public's view of the Supreme Court, I knew that one of the stock questions on the survey was a measure of confidence in the Court. I was able to swap out one of my original questions and substitute a question about agreement or disagreement with the decision.[12]

The fact that researchers often encounter Type III errors raises the question of whether one should engage in the work of preparing a research design. Yves Dezalay describes his project with Bryant Garth as not having started with a design or plan of any clear sort ("There was no plan"; Chapter 18). Similarly, Doreen McBarnet comments, "I don't know that I had a plan as such. You have to make it up as you go along because you have to take the opportunities that you either create or that come your way" (Chapter 14). Although some readers might interpret this as Dezalay and McBarnet having begun their research with nothing more than an idea that it might be interesting to investigate their broad subjects, there clearly was some thought about what kinds of questions to ask and how to go about doing the research, with a more detailed plan evolving in the early stages of the research. Undoubtedly, some very good research is done without an initial plan, but having a plan provides a starting point to enter the field and it is easier to rethink a research project if you have something to rethink from. Michael McCann says this extremely well: "It is important to develop a good formal research design, while at the same time recognizing that, once you go out into the field, you have to be very willing to adjust, reconstruct, adapt, or maybe even throw it out. But you need to come in with an organisational framework of understanding and analysis and expectations" (Chapter 16).

When I counsel students or colleagues who are designing an empirical research project, whether the project is qualitative or quantitative in nature, one of the first things I tell them is to ask themselves how the

---

[12] Kritzer, "Into the Electoral Waters: The Impact of *Bush v. Gore* on Public Perceptions and Knowledge of the Supreme Court," *Judicature*, 85:32–8 (2001).

material they plan to collect will help them answer the question they are posing. It is very easy to ask questions or to collect *some* data, but frequently we fail to explicitly ask ourselves what we might find in the responses or in the data that will help us answer our own question. Hazel Genn captures this well from the quantitative perspective when she talks about "frontloading" your thinking (Chapter 20), by which she means thinking very explicitly and systematically about the analysis you will do as you design the data collection.

THE MESSIEST MESS IN THE RESEARCH PROCESS: COLLECTING ORIGINAL DATA

One of the features of all of the projects described in the interviews is that they involve original data collection. Although several of the interviewees mention both the time-intensive nature of their data collection and the large quantity of materials that they found themselves with, what is less clear is how messy data often (usually?) turn out to be. Imagine that you want to study something about trials in federal court. You could turn to the statistical reports published by the Administrative Office (AO) of the U.S. Courts and extract information from the Reports' well-digested tables. Or, you could obtain from the Interuniversity Consortium for Political and Social Research (ICPSR) the case-level data reported to the AO and deposited with the ICPSR (these data form the basis for the published tables); you could then process these data to create whatever summaries you need. Or, if you have adequate resources, you could access the raw case files through the federal court's Public Access to Court Electronic Records (PACER) system; you would then extract and code the information you want from the raw case records.[13] Clearly, the work involved increases as you move from the reports through the archived case-level data to the raw case file data. However, you will also discover that things are a lot messier, and you have to make a lot of decisions and judgment calls as you move away from the predigested information in the reports, or away from the preprocessed and precleaned data stored at ICPSR.

---

[13]PACER provides access to materials in the federal courts' Case Management/Electronic Case Filing (CM/ECF) system. Before Pacer, collecting data from the case records required going to individual courthouses, something that is still necessary for many state courts (and probably most courts outside the United States, assuming that you can even get access to such records in other countries).

Consider a comparison to a decision to have fried chicken for dinner. One option is to go to your nearest fried chicken emporium (e.g., Kentucky Fried) or a neighborhood grocery store that sells prepared foods, buy the ready-to-eat chicken, go home, and enjoy your dinner. That's comparable to going to the published reports and pulling together some information. A second option is to go to the grocery store's meat department and purchase raw chicken, take that chicken home, cut it up if you saved money by buying a whole chicken, fry it, and then sit down to dinner; anyone who has ever fried chicken knows that this is not only more work than buying ready-to-eat chicken but also a lot messier (grease splatters, grease to dispose of, greasy pots to wash).[14] This is comparable to getting the data from ICPSR in a relatively ready-to-use form. A third possibility is to go out to a farm and buy a live chicken (or, perhaps there is a market not far away that sells live poultry). You take the chicken home, chop off its head, watch it dance around your yard for a while (imagine your neighbors observing this scene), pluck it, gut it, cut it up, fry it, and eat it – much, much messier than going to the store and buying a chicken that is ready to cook.

The messiness of data shows up even in what would seem to be a straightforward context. For example, for a current research project I am compiling data on state supreme court elections back to 1946. One thing I want to look at is winning margins. How do I treat elections where candidates do not run for specific seats but the top candidates win (i.e., if there are three seats, the top three vote-getters win). How do I compute the margin of victory for each of the three seats? Or, in a partisan election where there are two seats up for election and there are two candidates from one party but only one from the other, should I designate one of the candidates as unopposed? Or, what should I do when the official county-by-county totals do not sum to the state-level total reported? Or, how should I handle counties where the official reported vote shows that no one voted, or that one candidate got all the votes, or that one candidate's name was left off the ballot?[15]

[14] As someone who has done this many times, I will also note that it is more dangerous. You risk burns from hot grease and cuts from the slip of the knife while you are cutting the chicken if you bought it whole.

[15] Another element of "messiness" here is locating the data. I have been compiling county-level election returns for state supreme court general elections (partisan and nonpartisan) and primaries back to 1946. For some states, all the information I need is in published reports or online. For other states, the materials have to be requested from a state archive. For still others, the only way to get the information appears to

Another issue regarding data collection is *how* you collect the data. Of course the biggest divide here is between qualitative and quantitative data. I have found that usually you are better off combining qualitative and quantitative data when possible because you learn different things from different types of data. An observation from Sally Merry (Chapter 12) reflects a somewhat traditional view on this: "It seemed clear to me from that study that the best approach was to do an ethnographic observation first so you know what the categories are and you know what people think about. Then you do the survey so that your survey includes their categories, not yours"; that is, use qualitative work in a kind of exploratory way and then use quantitative data for confirmation or generalization.[16] Hazel Genn (Chapter 20) describes a different way of thinking about combining qualitative and quantitative work, the "quant sandwich," which she describes as doing "qualitative work first – discussion groups – then the survey, and then qualitative interviews." This is closer to how I see the combination of qualitative and quantitative work. In particular, I find that doing qualitative work after I have quantitative results in hand helps me understand the mechanisms underlying the quantitative patterns.

A separate issue arises in doing qualitative work, and that is the choice between data collected through interviews and data collected through observation. Several of the interviews touch on this point:

- Malcolm Feeley (Chapter 4): "Psychologists tell us all the time that our map of what we do is colored by the more problematic things that make it rather than the boring, ordinary routine. At any rate, as I hung around the courthouse, I became suspicious about the abstract things people would say. That's why I liked to hang around the court and to ask people to comment on things they were doing or had just done – explain particular actions."
- Stewart Macaulay (Chapter 2): "One of the problems of these interviews is that people like to entertain you. So what gets presented as the way things are is really the best story that they've got."

be to have someone go to the archive. Interestingly, for one state I have not been able to find anyone who has information on the specific terms served by justices (information is available on start and end dates of service, but not when justices were subject to a potential election to retain their position).

[16] Merry is not entirely convinced of this because she goes on to say, "But how valuable that survey data is, I'm not really persuaded on it."

- Sally Merry (Chapter 12): "I believe that observation is the best way because then you can actually see what's happening. If you rely on interviewing people about events and experiences you clearly have to get multiple perspectives on what happened and triangulate them as much as possible."

Sally Merry makes another statement that captures some of this issue very nicely: "Fieldwork is a process where you become the research instrument" (Chapter 12). Of course many kinds of situations exist where observation is not possible (e.g., trying to reconstruct past events). Still, in understanding processes, the richness that you obtain from observation cannot be readily matched from semistructured interviews.[17] Ways exist of getting better and worse information from interviews, and one of the best ways is to focus as much as possible on concrete situations the selection of which is in some way controlled by the interviewer. For example, instead of asking a respondent to describe a recent case, which will typically result in the respondent choosing something interesting and nontypical, you can ask the respondent to describe the *most recent* case defined by some characteristic (opened, concluded, etc.); this provides something akin to random selection.[18]

DATA ANALYSIS

Several of the interviews described the respondents' process of analyzing qualitative materials. Often this involved extracting or copying quotes from interviews or sections from field notes, and engaging in some sorting process. Hazel Genn describes this kind of process well: "I went through the transcript and would mark it up in different colors for different themes. I even sometimes cut the transcripts up and put bits of quotes in piles on the floor" (Chapter 20). Doreen McBarnet describes a similar process (Chapter 14): "Going through the notes, annotating with numbers and categories, marking a quote as interesting for raising

---

[17] See Robert Dingwall, "Accounts, Interviews and Observations" in *Context & Method in Qualitative Research*, Gale Miller and Dingwall, ed. (London: Sage Publications, 1997); Herbert H. Kritzer, "Stories from the Field: Collecting Data Outside Over There" in *Practicing Ethnography in Law: New Dialogues, Enduring Methods*, June Starr and Mark Goodale, ed. (New York: Palgrave Macmillan, 2002).

[18] While there are many books available on how to do interviews, the best I have found for the kind of interviewing I have done is James Spradley's *The Ethnographic Interview* (New York: Holt, Rinehart and Winston, 1979).

some point in my mind" (see also Silbey and Ewick, Chapter 19).[19] This kind of sorting and categorizing involves lots of judgment calls because language is often very ambiguous. One can develop "coding rules" or "sorting rules," but inevitably there will be lots of things that do not fit. We see this often in some category that is reported as "other"; seldom do we get a good sense of what is in "other" or what might have been in "other" but a coder or sorter judged was "close enough" to go into a named category.

I have written elsewhere about the role of interpretation in the analysis of both quantitative and qualitative data.[20] Simply put, that process is not well understood. It draws on a combination of the data themselves, side information possessed by the analyst, and the creativity of the analyst. One often hears something akin to, "What do the data say?" or "This is what the data tell me." These kinds of questions and statements assume that data speak, and the analyst just has to listen to what the data say. Lawrence Friedman (Chapter 5) suggests that when he observes, "Somehow you look at the data, you see what you have, and somehow a plan forms in your mind about how to write it up and you just do it. There was a great political scientist who once said that you gather your data, you look at it and you say, 'Speak to me!' And somehow, it speaks to you and says, 'This is how we should organize it.' Somehow an organization suggests itself."

Data do speak, *but only when asked*. What Friedman does not say is that having the data speak involves looking at the data, whether that involves reading qualitative materials or producing statistical summaries, through some set of expectations. Sometimes those expectations are confirmed in whole or in part, but often they are not confirmed. One does not look at a set of data with the mind in a *tabula rasa* mode. What the data say depends on what they are asked, and how well the

---

[19] Central to this sorting process is grasping the content of the data. Keith Hawkins (Chapter 9) describes his process as follows: "The data analysis was a fairly banal thing. There was nothing romantic or adventurous or intriguing about it. It's just very banal reading the data so that you are utterly familiar with it, so that the patterns and regularities become really very clear. I knew of no other way except a constant reading and re-reading of the stuff." Although he does not describe this as a sorting process, it is a mental sorting process, and I suspect that in practice he did some physical sorting as well.

[20] Kritzer (1994); Kritzer, "Data, Data, Data" (1996); Kritzer, "The Data Puzzle: The Nature of Interpretation in Quantitative Research," *American Journal of Political Science*, 40:1–32 (1996).

asker listens to the data. You can see this quite clearly in the Heinz and Laumann interview. John Heinz (Chapter 6) speaks of "a lot of staring at the numbers and saying 'what are these numbers telling us?'" Yet, Heinz and Laumann went into their analysis with a specific interest in networks and interrelationships among lawyers, and the analyses they did (i.e., the "numbers" they generated in the analysis) focused heavily around their questions about these kinds of relationships.

Just as in human conversation one must be attentive not just to what is said, but also to what is not said and the nonverbal forms of communication that come along with the verbal.[21] The analyst interrogating her data must be mindful of what is not to be found and for indications that might be analogous to nonverbal communication. Just as the ability to interpret conversation comes with experience, the ability to interpret the results of data analysis draws heavily on experience. We can teach particular techniques of analysis; we can teach the formal meaning of things like regression coefficients; and we can teach the need to look beyond the simple results. Still, drawing conclusions often requires thinking beyond the explicit materials in hand.

Analyzing data, whether they be qualitative or quantitative, is directed toward arriving at conclusions. The path from data to conclusions is often a difficult and tortuous one. Central to finding one's way down that path is the process of writing and showing to your audience how you get from the data to the conclusions. The centrality of the writing process, and the view that writing is essentially analysis, comes up in several of the essays:

- Michael McCann (Chapter 16): "[Writing is] really about organizing, about trying to put it all together."
- David Engel (Chapter 8): "The first draft would be almost unrecognizable now because I added layer after layer as I understood my own materials better and better. This little article took a long time to write, probably over two years."
- Carol Greenhouse (Chapter 10): "[T]hat's when the thesis began to emerge – very much in the midst of writing."
- Sally Merry (Chaper 12): "When I wrote this book I had a lot of data from a lot of different programs. I see the problem as a kaleidoscope where you try different ways of foregrounding something

---

[21] P. E. Converse, "Nonattitudes and American Public Opinion: Comment: The Status of Nonattitudes," *American Political Science Review*, 68:650–60 (1974), p. 650.

and backgrounding something else, deciding what's your core problem and what's the framework within which you think about that core problem. It's a matter of experimenting to see which one works."

Although it may sound specific to qualitative research, it is also very true of quantitative research. When I sit down and start writing a paper based on quantitative analysis, I will have produced the statistical results that I think I will need to report in the piece. Very frequently, perhaps even most of the time, as I write I discover questions or issues that take me back to the data for additional analyses. Sometimes these additional analyses lead the writing in directions I did not originally anticipate.

WORKING COLLABORATIVELY

Several of the studies covered by the interviews reflect very successful collaborations. Collaboration can be wonderful when it works! To use a clichéd idea, a good collaboration is a bit like a marriage, although perhaps we should replace "until death do us part" with "until publication do us part." Hazel Genn (Chapter 20) provides one cautionary note: "One of the dangers of working in teams is that as you get toward the end of the project people may start to disappear because their contracts are coming to an end and they want to take up other jobs. My experience with almost every project that I've managed is that, by the end, the only person holding the baby at three o'clock in the morning was me." Another problem, changing priorities or demands, is alluded to by William Felstiner (Chapter 17) when he mentions Austin Sarat's decision to enter law school rather than spending the coming year in Oxford writing (for which they had obtained a second NSF grant). Priorities can and do change among collaborators; fortunately for Law and Society scholarship, the result of Austin Sarat's change in priorities (and William Felstiner's appointment as director of the American Bar Foundation) was a delay and not the demise of a project.

Crucial to successful collaboration are a balance of skills and an understanding about how those skills play out in the course of the project and the overall work involved in the project. One person may have stronger theoretical skills and the other may have experience and skills related to data collection and analysis; these points are briefly mentioned in the interviews with William Felstiner and Austin Sarat (Chapter 17) and with Bryant Garth and Yves Dezalay (Chapter 18).

276

This can work if the balance across the project involves both sets of skills. The collaboration can break down if it turns out that the project is very heavily tied to one of the skills and less to the other. For example, in one very large project I was involved in, the demands of the data analysis phase were much greater than anyone anticipated, and the majority of the collaborators either lacked the requisite skills or found other things to do that were more interesting to them. The collaboration disintegrated, the individuals involved went their separate ways, and only one continued to work with the data that were collected. My own experience is that collaboration has worked best when, rather than taking on specialized tasks, all of the collaborators were able to work on the various aspects of the project. This is not to say that who took the lead on various tasks was not related to skills, but simply that no collaborator felt that he or she was left "holding the bag" at any one point.

THINKING ABOUT THE FUTURE

In reading these interviews two issues loomed out as issues for the future of Law and Society scholarship, at least in the immediate future: increasing problems with conducting surveys and institutional review boards (IRBs). Hazel Genn makes explicit reference to the problem of "survey fatigue" (Chapter 20): "I think nowadays it's harder to keep response rates up because there is a kind of survey fatigue going on." This fatigue arises from a variety of sources: the use of "fake" surveys that are in fact either sales calls or efforts to influence voters ("push polls"); the explosion of the customer satisfaction surveys that one seems to receive after just about any purchase of $100 or more; and the development of Internet surveys or automated telephone response systems (often used in the customer satisfaction surveys), which cost relatively little compared to traditional telephone surveys or mail surveys. Survey fatigue decreases response rates as does another issue: the increasing proportion of the population who have only cell phones.[22] In the United States, where cell phone users typically pay for incoming

[22] See S. Keeter, C. Kennedy, A. Clark, T. Tompson, and M. Mokrzycki, "What's Missing from National Landline RDD Surveys?: The Impact of the Growing Cell-Only Population," *Public Opinion Quarterly*, 71:772–92 (2007); P. J. Lavrakas, C. D. Shuttles, C. Steeh, and H. Fienberg, "The State of Surveying Cell Phone Numbers in the United States: 2007 and Beyond," *Public Opinion Quarterly*, 71:840–54 (2007).

calls, most survey organizations now offer to pay respondents contacted via a cell phone, but this is only one of many issues raised by contacting respondents via cell phone.[23] These problems threaten the ability of legitimate researchers to use surveys, either of the general population or targeted individuals, as a data collection tool. In fact, the last survey-based study I tried to do was an utter failure. That study, which focused on a particular group of lawyers, sought to use email as a contact method and a web-based survey tool as the data collection method. Between the time the study was designed and the survey was fielded email spam went from a minor annoyance to a major problem requiring heavy filtering of incoming email, resulting in an abysmal response rate even though I sent the contact email out through an organization to which most of the lawyers belonged. I concluded that there was no way I could even begin to argue that the responses were representative, and I ended up abandoning the study even though substantial money had been invested in it.

General public opinion survey operations and market research firms are beginning to rely increasingly on Internet surveys, but they do this by forming panels of potential respondents who agree to participate in such surveys, often providing incentives of some sort. For example, the day before I wrote this paragraph, I received an email from Northwest Airlines inviting me to become part of a consumer panel; Northwest offered me frequent flyer miles as an incentive to participate (I deleted the email). The enduring concern about Internet-based surveys is representativeness.[24] Moreover, the panel model is not a solution if the population of interest is a very specific group that is a relatively small portion of the population or is a group with some very specific

---

[23] According to Scott Keeter of the Pew Organization (email of September 25, 2008), most polling organizations follow the recommendation of the American Association for Public Opinion Research and offer to pay respondents contacted by cell phone ten dollars to offset any costs of the call. Regarding the range of problems associated with contacting survey respondents by cell phone, see the AAPOR Cell Phone Task Force Report (April 2008) http://www.aapor.org/uploads/Final_AAPOR_Cell_Phone_TF_report_041208.pdf (last visited September 25, 2008).

[24] R. P. Berrens, A. K. Bohara, H. Jenkins-Smith, C. Silva, and D. L. Weimer, "The Advent of Internet Surveys for Political Research: A Comparison of Telephone and Internet Samples," *Political Analysis*, 11:1–22 (2003). Response rates tend to be low in Internet surveys, typically varying between five and twelve percent; see S. R. Porter and M. E. Whitcomb, "Mixed-Mode Contacts in Web Surveys: Paper Is Not Necessarily Better," *Public Opinion Quarterly*, 71:635–48 (2007), p. 637.

experience. Still, it does suggest that finding ways of motivating participation in surveys will be a key to solving the problem. Motivation can
be created through compensation or through framing of the purpose
of a survey to make it look appealing to the target population, which
might involve sponsorship.

This does not get around the problem of establishing initial contact. I
suspect that for targeted surveys traditional mail may prove to be better
than either telephone or Internet methods.[25] The RAND Corporation's
Institute for Civil Justice did a mail survey of members of the American
Association for Justice (AAJ – formerly ATLA, the Association of
Trial Lawyers of America) and obtained a reasonable response rate
(about twenty-five percent); the mailing of the survey included an
endorsement letter from the then president of the AAJ. The survey
process involved two mailings of the complete package plus telephone
follow-ups (up to five attempts to make contact) to nonrespondents
for whom telephone numbers could be located.[26] What this experience
suggests is that researchers planning targeted surveys need to factor in
significant costs in terms of both time and money if they want to obtain
a useful level of response.

The second issue concerns IRBs and the increasing intrusiveness
of the process originally intended to protect human subjects from the
risk of substantial harm.[27] It is virtually unimaginable today that Robert
Kagan could have done his study of the price control bureaucracy in the

[25] However, one study of an Internet survey found that adding a mail contact did not
increase the response rate (Porter and Whitcomb, 2007).

[26] It is worth noting that the researchers gave the potential respondents the option
of completing the questionnaire online using a web-based survey; the web alternative was utilized by only 20 of the 965 respondents (Steven Garber, Michael
Greenberg, Hilary Rhodes, Xiaohui Zhua, and John Adams, "Do Non-Economic
Damages Caps and Attorney Fee Limits Reduce Access to Justice for Victims
of Medical Negligence?" Working Paper, Rand Institute for Civil Justice (2008),
6n14).

[27] The intrusiveness of the IRB process has been a subject of much discussion in
recent years. Malcolm Feeley devoted his Law and Society Association presidential
address to the issue. R. Dingwall, "Turn Off the Oxygen..." *Law & Society Review*,
41:787–96 (2007); and M. M. Feeley, "Legality, Social Research, and the Challenge
of Institutional Review Boards," *Law & Society Review*, 41:757–76 (2007); see also
J. Katz, "Toward a Natural History of Ethical Censorship," *Law & Society Review*,
41:797–810 (2007); and L. Stark, "Victims in Our Own Minds? IRBs in Myth and
Practice," *Law & Society Review*, 41:777–86 (2007). One of the publications of
the American Political Science Association, *PS: Political Science & Politics*, had a
symposium on the IRB process in its July 2008 issue.

early 1970s. He seized upon an opportunity that came up unexpectedly and that required immediate action. As I write this (mid-September 2008), the financial crisis is in full swing. I could imagine a variety of research projects that one might want to launch immediately if access were possible and the researcher's time were available. However, under current regulations it would take three to six months to get the requisite approvals from an IRB.

Carol Greenhouse describes how it was not until she got into the field that her focus became the church community; as discussed earlier, it is very common to discover that, once one has started a project, the focus changes. Under current regulations, Greenhouse would have been expected to go back to her IRB and have the revised project approved. Under these circumstances, a field researcher is confronted with the choice of observing the expectations of the IRB, which means bringing the research process to a grinding halt while the revised project is reviewed, or proceeding with the research without informing the IRB of the changes that have occurred. This is only one of many problems raised by the IRB process as it is applied to the kind of field research that is common among Law and Society scholars.[28]

Law and Society research can raise significant human subjects issues. A good example is in Sarat and Felstiner's *Divorce Lawyers and Their Clients* and the issue of attorney–client privilege raised by their observations.[29] Specifically, the presence of an observer technically waives attorney–client privilege. To deal with this, Sarat and Felstiner had planned to ask the lawyers to go to the lawyer on the opposing side and ask those opposing lawyers to sign a waiver of the waiver of privilege. As it turned out, the lawyers did not want to do this and expressed the view that none of the local judges, who had approved or endorsed the project, would treat the observers' presence as having waived attorney–client privilege. Imagine how this would be treated by an IRB. If the

---

[28] See D. Yanow and P. Schwart-Shea, "Reforming Institutional Review Board Policy: Issues in Implementation and Field Research," *PS: Political Science & Politics*, 41:483–94 (2008). The problem of changing research on the fly is not necessarily limited to fieldwork situations. Some IRBs have required that survey instruments be reviewed and approved as part of their process. Presumably, they would also insist that any changes to a survey instrument be reviewed. Under these circumstances, it would not have been possible for me to change the survey instrument I was using at the time of *Bush v. Gore*.

[29] See D. L. Chambers, "25 Divorce Attorneys and 40 Clients in Two Not So Big but Not So Small Cities in Massachusetts and California: An Appreciation," *Law & Social Inquiry*, 22:209–30 (1997), p. 217.

IRB had required a signed waiver of the waiver, what would they have said when the researchers came back and told them that the lawyers would not agree to such a process?[30]

In a number of the projects covered in this book, respondents and contacts were identified through a snowball process. I recently learned that at least some IRBs will not generally allow a researcher to use a snowball sample.[31] The rationale is that a snowball sample puts pressure on the respondents to participate because they were recommended by someone who knows them. If one takes this to its logical conclusion, I could have never done either of my research projects involving observing in law firms because the only way I could gain access to some of the settings was through referrals by people I knew who in turn knew relevant people in the law firms. It also raises the question of whether one could use "letters of introduction" in interview projects more generally. For example, when I did interviewing of corporate lawyers and corporate officers in Toronto,[32] I relied very heavily on a letter of introduction from a person in the community who was known by most of the people I wanted to interview. This letter of introduction was crucial to my ability to get the interviews I was seeking.

Institutional review boards have been moving to procedures that try to ease some concerns that have been expressed by social scientists, creating different modalities for "exempt" research, research that can receive an "expedited review," and research that needs a "full review." Undoubtedly this tracking has helped, but it does not go far enough. The process is built around a model that sees "subjects" as possessing little or no power and researchers as possessing significant power. Certainly this is true for some groups of subjects (e.g., prisoners) or for some researchers (e.g., medical providers who can control access to treatment). However, in a lot of research done by sociolegal scholars, the power relationship is reversed: it is the subject/respondent who sits in the position of power. The review process needs to consider where the power lies in the researcher–subject relationship and whether a group of subjects/respondents is in a position to make a considered judgment about their participation without being confronted with a formal consent form.

---

[30] In my own working observing in lawyers' practices I have dealt with the attorney–client privilege issue by assuming the role of a paralegal in the firm.

[31] Elizabeth Heger Boyle, "Human Subjects and Institutional Review Boards," presentation at Midwest Law & Society Retreat, Madison, Wisconsin, September 19–20, 2008.

[32] Kritzer (1984).

Often IRBs insist that subjects be told that their participation is voluntary, and in some situations there may be some element of coercion. However, in other situations, such as many (most?) types of interviews and telephone interviews in particular, the participation is by its very nature voluntary because the respondent can terminate participation at any time and the researcher has no power over the respondent. When I was arranging interviews with lawyers, I was told that I had to tell the lawyers that their participation was voluntary; nothing I said to the IRB would convince them that including such a statement was superfluous and made the letter I was sending as my initial contact sound stupid (fortunately, the IRB did not insist that I have the lawyers sign a consent form – probably something I could not get away with from many institutions' IRBs). Eventually I was able to convince the IRB to let me say something along the lines of "I would like to ask you to volunteer an hour of your time . . . ," rather than the more legalistic, "Your participation in this interview is voluntary."

The issues do not end with the question of power and consent. As suggested by the Kagan example, there should be procedures to allow projects to get quickly into the field when some unique situation arises. There should be a category of "exempt-exempt" research that does not require any submission or review by an IRB (e.g., routine surveys that do not touch on a predefined list of subjects such as criminal behavior or sexual behavior, or research within a governmental agency that does not involve access to confidential case files of the type that would be protected under the Freedom of Information Act).[33]

Unfortunately, I am not overly optimistic that these kinds of changes will occur. The IRBs have become increasingly institutionalized. There are now what amount to professionals in the IRB process. Most important, however, is that institutions' big fears here relate to the loss of large amounts of research funding. The research funding involved is not Law and Society–related, nor is it social science more broadly. The

---

[33] The web page of the University of Minnesota IRB does list several types of research that "do not need IRB review," and among these are "Interviews of individuals where questions focus on things not people (e.g., questions about policies)," http://www.research.umn.edu/irb/applying/whichstudies.cfm (last visited September 25, 2008). I suspect that in practice the IRB still insists on reviewing projects involving interviews "about policies" because any such interview will almost always include some information about the respondent's views or participation in the policy process or implementation.

big bucks are in the biomedical arena; social science is the tail and Law and Society is the very tip of the tail, if even that.

CONCLUSIONS: WHAT DOES THIS MEAN FOR TRAINING AND FOR CONDUCTING RESEARCH

What broad lessons can we draw about the research process from these interviews that might inform how we train the next generation of Law and Society scholars? During my thirty-year tenure in the political science department at the University of Wisconsin we had many debates about how to train our graduate students in methods. In the early 1990s we adopted a program that offered students the option of a research design course focused on quantitative approaches or a design course focused on qualitative approaches. I would argue that our best-trained students took both courses. Too many scholars see themselves as doing either quantitative research *or* qualitative research. Too often scholars on one side of this divide attack research on the other side. Research design needs to fit the question, and researchers should be able to choose questions based on their theoretical or practical importance rather than based on a researcher's limited methodological repertoire. This does not mean that every researcher should be able to do the most sophisticated statistical analysis, nor does it mean that every researcher should be trained in conversation analysis.

The challenge in training students how to do research is that it is not something that can be learned by just sitting in a classroom. As suggested at the very beginning of this essay, I see research as a "craft"; the skills of a craft are acquired by practice, by doing. Research projects, particularly projects involving the collection of original data, do not fit nicely into the semester (to say nothing of the quarter) framework. Students' participation as research assistants is one important way of integrating research practice with research instruction. Designing curriculum to allow students to work on multisemester projects is another way to provide the opportunity for realistic research experiences, although there is the ever-present problem of students putting off working on something until a due date looms on the horizon (not necessarily a problem limited just to students!). One of the lessons of the interviews in this book is the need to be able to adjust when the unexpected happens, and if that unexpected problem does not happen until the week before a project is due because the student has put off working on the project, making an adjustment or refocusing the work is not really possible. The design of research requirements needs to include ways to force students to get started early and to plan (and hold to) a realistic work schedule.

Finally, what might these interviews tell us about how we should describe our methods in our own reporting of our research? In *Tales of the Field*, John Van Maanen describes three genres of ethnographic writing: realist, confessional, and impressionistic.[34] One of the central elements distinguished among these genres is how the research process itself is treated in the presentation. In the confessional genre the research process is central. We see reviews of the output of individual scholars, sometimes in award citations, sometimes in festschrifts, sometimes as part of field histories;[35] however, these tend to focus on the intellectual contributions. It would be interesting to have what might be called "research biographies" (or autobiographies) in which accomplished scholars are asked to think back over *how* they carried out research over their careers. Many of the scholars interviewed for this book would be great candidates for such a biography. The problem is whether any publisher would see a market for such biographies. One could imagine a professional association taking on such a project, possibly as a kind of oral history of the research careers of major scholars. Rather than producing traditional books, the oral histories or biographies or autobiographies could be made available electronically. A possible place to start on such a project would be with recipients of the Law and Society Association's Harry Kalven Prize, which is given for a body of work that has contributed to the advancement of research in Law and Society.

But what about our reporting of our research results? One of the challenges is that journal editors are typically under pressure to limit the length of articles. Detailed descriptions of how a project evolved take up space that could go to other articles. Even so, it would be interesting if articles regularly included a paragraph or two about where the project started and how the project ended up with the particular focus of the article. Books often include a methodological appendix, but often those appendices do not trace the evolution of a research

---

[34] *Tales of the Field: On Writing Ethnography* (Chicago: University of Chicago Press, 1988).

[35] See, e.g., Nancy Maveety, ed., *The Pioneers of Judicial Behavior* (Ann Arbor: University of Michigan Press, 2003).

project. Why not include a project biography as an appendix? A good example of such an appendix is in the late Elliot Liebow's *Tell Them Who I Am: The Lives of Homeless Women.*[36] Liebow describes how the project came to be, how it evolved, and how he dealt with writing the book. Alternatively, perhaps we could ask some of the key editors at major university presses to include as appendices to books something similar to the interviews in this volume. Regardless of whether a project biography is written by the author or is in the form of an interview, students, other scholars, and "lay" readers would all have a better grasp of the research process if such material were readily available.

In his book on Supreme Court advocates, Kevin McGuire describes how the "regulars" of the Supreme Court Bar will frequently go watch oral arguments both to see what might be currently motivating the justices and to see other top advocates practicing their craft.[37] Our craft is producing research products. It is generally not possible for us to watch others practicing that craft. The interviews in this book provide our community with a view of how the masters of our craft confront the struggles and apply the techniques of social science research in the legal arena.

[36] New York: Macmillan, 1993.
[37] Kevin McGuire, *The Supreme Court Bar: Legal Elites in the Washington Community* (Charlottesville: University of Virginia Press, 1993), p. 185.

INDEX

Abel, Richard, 120, 188
advisory committee, use of, 64, 85, 229, 230
American Bar Foundation, 8, 60, 64, 65, 70, 84, 85, 144, 195, 199, 206, 262, 266, 276
Amherst Seminar, 138, 216, 225
analysis
  categories, 137, 222, 249
  coding, 41, 64, 222, 274
  conversational analysis, 119, 125
  headnotes and fieldnotes, 136–137
  organization of, 68, 90, 103, 126, 195, 230, 236, 273
  quantitative analysis, 41, 42, 47, 59, 97
  role analysis, 80–81
anonymity
  of research subjects, 48
archives, 50–53, 106

Baum, Larry, 171
Black, Donald, 27, 97
Bourdieu, Pierre, 204, 205, 208, 212, 254
Burawoy, Michael, 256

case studies
  selection of, 167, 176, 177, 207
cause lawyers, 172
Centre for Socio-Legal Studies, Oxford University, 8, 9, 74, 76, 79, 119, 195
Chambliss, Bill, 215, 216
collaboration
  effective, 52, 59, 194–195, 276–277
  emergence of, 91, 117, 201, 216
  friendship, 62
  shared interests, 241
conferences
  presentation of work at, 171, 175, 243
  to develop links, 156
confidentiality, 48, 66, 77, 80, 207
content analysis, 169

criminology, 94–97, 145–147, 259
Critical Legal Studies, 138, 175, 184

Dahl, Robert, 166
Dezalay, Yves, 254, 269, 276
disputing, dispute framework, 17, 18, 22, 32, 83, 85, 87, 92, 110, 114, 117, 120, 132–133, 136, 138, 188, 196, 201, 203, 208, 229, 231, 232
dissertations
  converting into publications, 32, 35–36, 105, 166–169, 175–176
  topic selection, 27, 110, 164
  writing of, 34, 138
documents. *See also* archives
  coding, 21, 35, 63, 222
  collecting, 21
  court records, 52, 54, 55, 89, 90, 130
Durkheim, Emile, 224

emotions of researcher
  anxiety, 89
  depressed, 29, 165, 184
  disappointment, 2, 177, 206, 246, 250
  excitement, 33, 53, 70, 106, 113, 196, 223
  exhausted, tired, 11, 36, 183, 206, 211
  fun, 55, 86, 186, 192, 196, 242
  nervousness, 5, 79
Engel, David, 115, 266, 275
Epstein, Lee, 171
ethics, 161. *See also* IRB
ethnography, 65, 84, 91, 96, 105, 107, 118, 131–137, 207, 256
  distance, 84, 88, 131
  legal anthropology, 106, 113, 120
Ewick, Patricia, 139

Feeley, Malcolm, 188, 272
Felstiner, William, 120, 266, 276, 280
fieldnotes, 31–33, 102, 137, 273

Continued from page iii

Constituting Democracy:
Law, Globalism and South Africa's Political Reconstruction
Heinz Klug

The Ritual of Rights in Japan:
Law, Society, and Health Policy
Eric A. Feldman

The Invention of the Passport:
Surveillance, Citizenship and the State
John Torpey

Governing Morals:
A Social History of Moral Regulation
Alan Hunt

The Colonies of Law:
Colonialism, Zionism and Law in Early Mandate Palestine
Ronen Shamir

Law and Nature
David Delaney

Social Citizenship and Workfare in the United States and Western Europe:
The Paradox of Inclusion
Joel F. Handler

Law, Anthropology and the Constitution of the Social:
Making Persons and Things
Edited by Alain Pottage and Martha Mundy

Judicial Review and Bureaucratic Impact:
International and Interdisciplinary Perspectives
Edited by Marc Hertogh and Simon Halliday

Immigrants at the Margins:
Law, Race, and Exclusion in Southern Europe
Kitty Calavita

Lawyers and Regulation:
The Politics of the Administrative Process
Patrick Schmidt

Law and Globalization from Below:
Toward a Cosmopolitan Legality
Edited by Boaventura de Sousa Santos and Cesar A. Rodriguez-Garavito

Public Accountability:
Designs, Dilemmas and Experiences
Edited by Michael W. Dowdle

Law, Violence and Sovereignty among West Bank Palestinians
Tobias Kelly

Legal Reform and Administrative Detention Powers in China
Sarah Biddulph

The Practice of Human Rights:
Tracking Law Between the Global and the Local
Edited by Mark Goodale and Sally Engle Merry

Judges Beyond Politics in Democracy and Dictatorship:
Lessons from Chile
Lisa Hilbink

Paths to International Justice:
Social and Legal Perspectives
Edited by Marie-Bénédicte Dembour and Tobias Kelly

Law and Society in Vietnam:
The Transition from Socialism in Comparative Perspective
Mark Sidel

Constitutionalizing Economic Globalization:
Investment Rules and Democracy's Promise
David Schneiderman

The New World Trade Organization Agreements:
Globalizing Law Through Intellectual Property and Services, 2nd Edition
Christopher Arup

Justice and Reconciliation in Post-Apartheid South Africa
Edited by François du Bois and Antje du Bois-Pedain

Militarization and Violence against Women in Conflict Zones
in the Middle East:
A Palestinian Case-Study
Nadera Shalhoub-Kevorkian

Child Pornography and Sexual Grooming:
Legal and Societal Responses
Suzanne Ost

Darfur and the Crime of Genocide
John Hagan and Wenona Rymond-Richmond

Planted Flags:
Trees, Land, and Law in Israel/Palestine
Irus Braverman

Fictions of Justice:
The International Criminal Court and the Challenge of Legal Pluralism in
Sub-Saharan Africa
Kamari Maxine Clarke

Conducting Law and Society Research:
Reflections on Methods and Practices
Simon Halliday and Patrick Schmidt

After Abu Ghraib:
Exploring Human Rights in America and the Middle East
Shadi Mokhtari

39709320R00171

Made in the USA
Middletown, DE
23 January 2017